# MURDER
## of a
# MAFIA DAUGHTER

# MURDER
## of a
# MAFIA DAUGHTER

The Life and Tragic Death
of Susan Berman

# CATHY SCOTT

BARRICADE
BOOKS

Published by Barricade Books Inc.
2037 Lemoine Avenue
Fort Lee, NJ 07024

Reprint Edition 2015
Copyright © 2002 by Cathy Scott
All Rights Reserved

No part of this book may be reproduced, stored in a retrieval system, or transmitted in any form, by any means, including mechanical, electronic, photocopying, recording, or otherwise, without the prior written permission of the publisher, except by a reviewer who wishes to quote brief passages in connection with a review written for inclusion in a magazine, newspaper, or broadcast.

Library of Congress Cataloging-in-Publication Data
Scott, Cathy.
        Murder of a Mafia Daughter: The Life and Tragic Death
    of Susan Berman / Cathy Scott.
        p.cm.
    Includes bibliographical references.
    ISBN: 1-56980-238-6 (hardcover)
    ISBN: 978-0-934878-49-4 (paperback)
    1. Berman, Susan, 1945-2000. 2. Murder victims --Nevada--
    Biography. I. Title

 HV6533.N215 S38 2002
 364.15'23'092--dc21
 [B]
                                                                2002026063


10 9 8 7 6 5 4 3

Manufactured in the United States

# CONTENTS

# ALSO BY CATHY SCOTT

# DEDICATION

*For Susan*

# ACKNOWLEDGMENTS

THERE ARE MANY to thank.

First, agent Frank Weimann with The Literary Group and publisher Carole Stuart with Barricade Books, who each took on Susan's murder story and biography in 2002 when others chose not to because it was an unsolved case. My thanks as well to Carmela Cohen, Barricade Books' art and production director, for her expert touches in preparing the manuscript for publication. My thanks to them all for getting Susan's story out in the public eye.

This book would not have been complete but for those who generously agreed to be interviewed so that their friend's story could be told. My warm gratitude to Susan's friends, former co-workers, associates on projects, and schoolmates: Stephen M. Silverman, Ruthie Bartnof, the late Ed Bayley, Danny Goldberg, Patrick Bailey, Kevin and Don Norte, Elizabeth Mehren, Guy Rocha, Lou DeCosta, Harvey Myman, Marcy Bachmann, Juline Beier, Anita Pinchev Dash, the late Dick Odessky, Michael Greene, Deke Castleman, the late Hal Rothman, David Millman, former Governor Bob Miller, mob-attorney-turned Las Vegas Mayor Oscar Goodman, Rilo

Weisner, Kevin McPherson, Gilberte Najamy, Morgan King, and the late Mickey Freiberg for their insightful recollections of the real Susan; to her cousins Dave "Davy" Berman, Rosalie Bruce, Tom Padden Jr., Tom Padden III, and Shirley Ward for their family memories of Susan.

To the men and women in uniform of the Los Angeles and Galveston police departments, in particular LAPD Lieutenant Clay Farrell and Tom Thompson, detectives Paul Coulter and Jerry Stephens; and detectives with the San Francisco and Eureka, California, police departments, and the L.A. and Westchester county prosecutors' offices, especially former DA Jeanine Pirro, for their help in pointing me in the right direction; the Clark County Library; and the Special Collections office at the University of Nevada, Las Vegas.

In addition to those who helped me indirectly, I salute my colleagues in the press whose articles provided background information, in particular the *New York Times*, *Los Angeles Times*, *New York Post*, *Galveston County Daily News*, *Texas Monthly*, and *New York* magazine. I should also mention the television specials, including those that appeared on Fox's "America's Most Wanted," "ABC News," "Prime Time Live," as well as Court TV, MSNBC, the HBO documentary series *The Jinx: The Life and Deaths of Robert Durst*. I also thank producers at Dateline NBC, CNN, MSNBC, the Today Show, Fox News, and Connie Martinson Talks Books for putting me on camera to talk about Susan's investigation.

To my family, as always, for believing in me, especially: My twin sister Cordelia Mendoza and her husband Bob; my big brother Dr. J. Michael Scott and his wife Sharon; my son Raymond Somers Jr. and daughter-in-law Karen; and my grandkids Claire and Jake. I don't know what I'd do without them.

Thanks also to my late mother, Eileen Rose Busby (who forever encouraged me to write, write, write), and to my late father, James Melvin Scott (who proudly published his memoir *The Missouri Kid*), for their erstwhile encouragement before their deaths. Did I thank them enough while they were here? Probably not. If they are listening, I thank them now, with all my heart.

—*Cathy Scott*

# PROLOGUE

*Murder of a Mafia Daughter* is a story about a path to murder that begins in old Las Vegas with gangsters and the boys from the Jewish Mob. It moves to San Francisco with the movers and shakers, to New York City with its literati, and ends in Beverly Hills with the glitterati.

The slaying of Susan Berman in the winter of 2000 had all the earmarks of a professional hit aimed at a person born into the Mafia. Or was that just what the killer intended everyone to think, to lead investigators to the assumption that it was a mob hit when it was not? Or was it her best friend Robert Durst who wanted her dead? If it was not a Mafia hit, then who else could have done it? And why? These are the questions I've pursued in the many years I've covered Susan Berman's murder, looking for evidence, clues, and the who, what, and whys of the case. The book also looks into who had motive, means, and opportunity. It invariably comes back to one person: Susan's old friend Robert Durst.

In my research, I got to know Susan, an author and screenwriter. I drove the route from her Las Vegas childhood home to her final house in Benedict Canyon. I visited the restaurants and bistros she frequented in the Beverly Hills town she loved and called home during the final seventeen years of her life. I walked through the Las Vegas house on South Sixth Street where she lived with her parents during her first twelve years. It was a bright, cheerful house. I imagined her as a child, running down the long hallway into the welcoming arms of the father she adored.

I went to the University of California, Berkeley campus where Susan got her master's degree in journalism and where protests against the war in Vietnam were rampant. Susan made lifelong friends while attending Berkeley – many in the writing world who later tossed work her way.

I went to her home in Benedict Canyon where she was murdered. I stood in front of her house on the same path her killer walked before ending her life.

And, finally, I visited the Home of Peace cemetery in East Los Angeles where Susan's body is entombed in a marble wall alongside her mother, father, and uncle. A recent visitor had left flowers in bud vases, one on either side of Susan's shiny-brass headstone. It is where family and friends waited patiently for Robert Durst to arrive, but he didn't show for the funeral of his old friend.

Susan's murder was one of three Durst was accused of committing since 1982. At the LAPD's Robbery-Homicide Division, her murder was a cold case. But it was hardly over. Police began closing in on Robert Durst.

It came to a head on an early spring evening when a visitor to New Orleans casually enjoyed a meal at Chef Emeril Lagasse's NOLA restaurant on St. Louis Street.

But this was no ordinary tourist. It was multi-millionaire Robert Durst, heir to a New York City real estate fortune, seemingly on the run in anticipation of being arrested for the murder of his one-time confidant and best friend, Susan Berman. Susan was no ordinary person either. She was a mob princess and the daughter of notorious Jewish mobster Davie Berman, a bootlegger running rackets in the Midwest before he was tapped to run the skim at Las Vegas casinos. When they met in college, Susan and Durst were instant soul mates. Outside the New Orleans restaurant, throngs of pedestrians celebrated St. Patrick's Day and St. Joseph's Day. As Durst left, he was anonymous amidst the crowd and no doubt felt confident that he was just one step away from leaving the country and being out of reach of U.S. authorities.

Thin, gray, and a much older-looking man than the public had previously seen, Durst, wearing a button-down shirt and jacket, entered the lobby at the Canal Street Marriott mumbling to himself, a habit he'd taken up in recent years. To his surprise, there to greet him were two FBI agents with a first-degree murder warrant signed by a Los Angeles County judge for Susan's death. The G-men approached him and asked for an ID. He told them it was in his hotel room. They accompanied Durst to room 2303, verified his identify, and put him under arrest.

During a search by the Feds, along with New Orleans police, they discovered a loaded .38 Smith & Wesson revolver with four live rounds and one spent shell casing in his jacket pocket. In his room they found a fake Texas ID used for checking into his hotel, a new cell phone, more than $42,000 in cash stuffed in small envelopes, his birth certificate, a passport, a map of Florida and Cuba, a flesh-colored latex mask to cover his face and neck, complete with salt-and-pepper hair attached, and five ounces of marijuana. Authorities also found a UPS tracking number that led them to a package with $117,000 cash inside.

Durst was taken to the New Orleans rough-and-tumble city jail on South Broad Street, where he was booked and charged with murder based on the Los Angeles County arrest warrant. He was also held on Louisiana state charges of illegal possession of a weapon by a convicted felon and possession of a firearm in the presence of a controlled substance—felonies that carry a maximum penalty of 10 and 20 years for first-time offenders. Durst was in deep trouble.

Upon learning of his arrest, Durst's family, long estranged from him because of his often bizarre behavior—he was court-ordered to stay away from his family's homes because of stalking allegations—issued a statement that read, in part, "We hope he will finally be held accountable for all he has done." In 2006, the multi-billion dollar Durst Organization paid out a settlement of $65 million to Robert Durst in exchange for no contact ever again with the family or the Durst Organization. At the time of Durst's 2015 arrest for Susan's murder, law enforcement put his worth at $100 million.

The thwarted attempt to flee justice in New Orleans wasn't the first time Robert Durst had attempted to avoid arrest. He'd once been on the lam after he skipped bail and went to live in Texas as a cross-dressing mute woman. And then Durst was accused of the murder of his former neighbor, Morris Black, whose dismembered floating remains were discovered in Galveston Bay by a 12-year-old boy fishing with his father after Durst chopped up the remains and dumped them in the bay. Durst, 71 at the time of his 2015 arrest—the same age as Black when Durst killed him—now faced extradition from Louisiana to California and a second murder trial, this one in a California courtroom. But first he faced extradition from Louisiana.

In early appearances in a New Orleans criminal court facing the new charges there, at Durst's side was high-priced defense attorney Dick DeGuerin, who'd represented Durst during the Galveston trial for killing Morris Black. Even though Durst admitted to fatally shooting Black, DeGuerin successfully argued it was done in self-defense after Black pulled a gun on Durst, the two scuffled, and the gun went off, accidentally killing Black. The jury bought it and acquitted Durst. He was sent to prison for three years after pleading guilty to separate felonies of skipping bail and running away from justice in the midst of a multi-state manhunt. After his 2006 release, Durst lived as a free man until his March 2015 arrest. Durst's high-priced attorneys, including Dick DeGuerin, quickly filed a motion to set bail, which was denied because the court said Durst was a flight risk. Then DeGuerin, a mild-mannered Texas rancher who carries a Stetson and wears leather cowboy boots to court, filed another motion in Orleans Parish Magistrate Court claiming his client was being held illegally without probable cause. It too was denied. DeGuerin also said his client had recently undergone neurosurgery.

Three days after Durst's arrest, authorities transferred him to a state hospital designated for inmates with acute medical conditions. Durst's attorneys fought the transfer, calling their client competent and suffering only from Asperger's syndrome, a mild form of autism that Durst was diagnosed with as a child. "He does not have an acute medical or mental condition," DeGuerin told the court, noting that his client's competency was not in question.

Former Judge and Westchester County District Attorney Jeanine Pirro, whose office once investigated Durst in the disappearance of his first wife and who in 2000 reopened the investigation into the Kathleen Durst missing person's case, agreed with DeGuerin that Durst was a sane man. "I believe that Robert Durst is an intelligent man who knows how to get away with murder," Pirro, who later became host of FOX News Channel's "Justice with Judge Jeanine," said in a telephone interview after Durst's 2015 arrest. "He premeditates and decides how he's going to kill them, and he kills. That's not mental illness. It's just pure evil."

During an impromptu news conference with reporters on the courthouse steps, DeGuerin proclaimed his client's innocence: "Bob Durst did not kill Susan Berman. He doesn't know who did."

Meanwhile, court watchers have opined that Durst might very well beat the rap, especially since he armed himself with the best defense that money can buy. But this time around, should Durst be acquitted once again, the felony charges in Louisiana would be tough to walk away from, since Durst was caught red-handed in possession of a handgun and marijuana, both of which are illegal in the state of Louisiana.

Meanwhile, with Susan's murder investigation, Los Angeles police had known that Durst was on the move, but they lost him in Houston after he turned off his cell phone and headed out of town in a car registered under another man's name. Then Durst checked his voice mail. It was the ping detectives had needed, and it led them to the plush J.W. Marriott Hotel in New Orleans.

This latest probe into Durst's activities began in 2012 when northern California detectives, looking into a missing teen's murder and Durst's possible association with the girl before she vanished, tipped off Los Angeles police. It wasn't, as had been widely reported, because of the HBO documentary "The Jinx: The Life and Deaths of Robert Durst," which began airing in February 2015, finishing six weeks later.

But the series did speed up Durst's arrest on suspicion of killing Berman. Durst had approached filmmaker Andrew Jarecki about producing a documentary about him, and Jarecki agreed. Part five in the series aired the night before

Durst's New Orleans arrest, because, as the LAPD later told the media, the episode focused on Susan's relationship with Durst, and because of Durst's history of fleeing police when he sensed the authorities were closing in, the FBI took Durst into custody to prevent him from running. In the sixth and final episode of "The Jinx," which aired after Durst was in custody, Durst made shocking statements while alone in a bathroom in an unguarded moment. "What the hell did I do?" he asked himself. "Killed them all, of course."

Those words were caught on a live microphone Durst still wore after filmmaker Jarecki, on camera, confronted Durst with handwriting that was eerily similar to what has become known as the "cadaver note." It was postmarked and mailed to the Beverly Hills Police Department before Susan's body was discovered. In "The Jinx," Susan's stepson, Sareb Kaufman, discovers another letter, this one in a box of Susan's possessions and written on Durst's letterhead that he sent to Susan, misspelling "Beverley," as did the cadaver letter. Police have said only the killer could have sent the cadaver note, because it was mailed the day before Susan's body was found when no one except the killer knew about it. Police have also said they are not depending on the documentary film for evidence. "We based our actions on the investigation and the evidence," LAPD Deputy Chief Albanese told reporters.

In the course of the LAPD's re-investigation of Durst's involvement in Susan's death, detectives learned through financial records that Durst had been in the Los Angeles area at the time of Susan's murder, which, according to forensics gathered during her autopsy, placed her death 24 to 36 hours before her body was discovered on December 24, 2000. Police now had not only motive, but also opportunity and the means.

The widely believed motive is that Susan knew too much about the 1982 disappearance of Durst's first wife, Kathleen McCormack Durst, a medical student who had planned to leave Durst. Susan acted as Durst's spokeswoman for media and police inquiries. Then, years later, in late 2000, when it leaked to the media that New York police sought to interview Susan in a re-investigation of the Kathleen Durst disappearance, authorities said that Durst worried that Susan would talk. A couple of weeks after news broke about the re-investigation, Susan was murdered. By 2015, Kathleen's case had not been solved, at least not officially. In recent years, even more names had been added to the growing list of missing-persons cases police began investigating because of Robert Durst's connection.

I interviewed then-LAPD Lieutenant Tom Thompson, who oversaw the Susan Berman investigation in 2012. He told me in a telephone interview that investigators with San Francisco and Eureka police, in whose jurisdiction a teenage girl's murder had occurred, reached out to LAPD's Homicide-Robbery bureau to share with them what they'd discovered through Durst's financial records. The revelation was stunning and caused the LAPD to re-open its then-cold-case investigation into Berman's murder. "San Francisco police contacted us when Durst resurfaced there," Thompson, now retired, told me in the telephone interview. "They said they could put Durst in Los Angeles at the time of the murder."

Armed with that 2012 revelation, the LAPD, along with federal agents and other jurisdictions where Durst had lived or visited, formed a task force to investigate Durst in not only Susan's murder, but in 16-year-old Karen Marie Mitchell's 1997 disappearance from Eureka, California, as well as missing San Francisco-area teenager Kristen Modafferi five months after Mitchell turned up missing. As now-retired Eureka Detective John Bradley told me in a phone interview, "We have a hunch that all of these cases are interrelated." In addition, Vermont authorities are looking into Durst in connection with the 1971 disappearance of Lynn Schulze, a college student who'd shopped at Durst's Vermont health-food store, which he owned at the time, and stood at a bus stop across the street, where she was last seen.

The question that begs to be addressed and is covered in *Murder of a Mafia Daughter*, is how could Susan have trusted someone she knew may have had something to do with his wife's disappearance? The answer is complicated. Susan kept people around her who were influential in one way or another, often in the film and literary worlds. Susan wanted so much to be recognized for her work, and she counted on friends to help her succeed. She also leaned on Durst for friendship, for status, and, occasionally, for money.

Today, after her death, Susan's work has become well known and has left its mark on Las Vegas history on its own merit. Susan's name and books have been the subject of scores of news reports. There are long waiting lists at public libraries to check out her writings. Her books sell for high prices, in the hundred range, on Internet auction sites. Had she lived to see it, Susan would have been pleased. She no doubt would have chuckled at the irony of it all.

Susan would have pondered the intrigue of her own murder investigation as it unfolded. It was her forte, titillating clues pursued vigorously. All evidence points to Susan being cut down by someone she not only knew, but who was a trusted and beloved friend. That irony, too, however tragic, would have piqued Susan's interest, especially since she was a loyal supporter of Robert Durst, whom she called, until the bitter end, "The brother I never had."

This is the story of Susan's life as the only child of a wealthy mobster and heir to his casino financial interests, with Robert Durst intertwined at every twist and turn, and her undying loyalty to the man she called "Bobby."

# CHAPTER 1

# MURDER OF A MOB PRINCESS

*Time it was, and what a time it was, it was*
*A time of innocence, a time of confidences*
*Long ago, it must be, I have a photograph*
*Preserve your memories, they're all that's left you*
—Simon and Garfunkel

THE DRIVER OF a shiny new Mercedes-Benz pulled onto campus and into a parking space next to a beat-up Volkswagen bug. The two cars, in stark contrast with the other, juxtaposed against each other. The environment of the day at the University of California, Berkeley was tense. Hippies and activists had arrived that school day for an anti-war rally. Planted nearby, National Guard personnel were on duty in case it turned from passive to violent.

Students typically drove VW vans and beetles, brightly decaled with peace symbols and flowers, not luxury cars. Susan Berman, however, proudly stepped out of her bright, white, shiny sedan and onto the university grounds to attend classes, seemingly oblivious to her surroundings and out of sync with the troubled times. In so many ways, she had come from a different era, a different place. It was the age of innocence, the 1960s, and a time of Vietnam anti-war activism on campus. But Susan Berman was in her own world, in her private age of innocence. She was a creature of her past, a product of the glitter and glamour of Las Vegas royalty. Her feet appeared to be firmly planted in the past.

Fast forward to the Saturday before Christmas 2000. It began with a rude awakening.

On the morning of December 23rd and the last weekend before the holiday, nonstop barking of dogs made sleeping late impossible for Marvin Karp. Irritated, he glanced at the clock as he walked to his kitchen sink and looked out the window to see what all the ruckus was about. *It's not even 7:30 yet. So much noise from two small dogs,* he said to himself.

All seemed to be normal, from what he could see—other than the two loose dogs.

It's not unusual to hear the sound of barking in that upscale Benedict Canyon neighborhood. But this was different. The barking was excited and so prolonged that residents besides Marvin also noticed the commotion. A leash dragging behind one of the dogs raised a red flag in Marvin's mind.

He recognized the dogs as belonging to his next-door neighbor, Susan Berman. She mothered those canines as if they were her children, perhaps as a projection of her own unusual childhood, treating them in a protective manner just as her father, until his death, had treated her. So it was more than surprising that Susan's beloved dogs were outside unattended.

2

*That's it,* Karp thought to himself as he peered out the window at the noisy canines. "Those dogs were *always* barking," he said as he stood outside his house months later. "I was ready to go over there and ask her, 'Hey, why are your dogs loose?' I didn't know her very well, so I didn't." Still, the dogs were never outside without Susan, and that worried him.

His next-door neighbor was often away. "She wasn't home much," Marvin Karp said. "I'd occasionally see her in the backyard with her dogs. She kept very much to herself."

But something must be very wrong, he thought, for the dogs she adored to be alone and wandering the street at that early hour. He'd heard them bark the night before. He thought Susan must have had a visitor.

He was right. Susan had received a killer of a visitor. Thirty hours after first seeing Susan's dogs running, Karp would learn the real reason her canines were outside.

The neighbors on the other side of Susan also thought it odd when her third dog, Lulu, ran to their house. It was unusual—unthinkable even—for Susan's dogs to be outside on their own on a busy road, especially since Susan was in a lease dispute, in part, because of her noisy canines. Still, the neighbors didn't do anything. They didn't want to intrude.

By the next morning, however, on Sunday, December 24, when the dogs were still outside running around the neighborhood and at risk of being hit by cars, Marvin Karp decided to investigate. He glanced toward Susan's house. He didn't see any activity. He walked up to her house and knocked on the door. No one answered. Then he walked down her driveway, past Susan's house, to the neighbors on the other side to ask if they knew why her dogs were loose. The neighbors told Marvin they looked into Susan's yard and discovered that her side gate was open and her back door ajar. They were alarmed.

"Nobody wanted to go inside that house," Marvin said. "It looked suspicious." They called the Los Angeles Police Department.

Christmas Eve 2000 marked the day the lifeless body of Susan Berman, born to a Las Vegas mobster in 1945, was found in her modest home in a wooded neighborhood. Her three precious wire-haired fox terriers had been running in and out of her house, barking frantically. If the dogs—Lulu, Romeo, and Golda were trying to tell someone something bad had happened, it worked.

The dogs were the only witnesses to the murder.

The neighbors soon learned that the dogs' owner, Susan Jane Berman, fifty-five years old, had been cut down with a single gunshot blast at close range to the back of her head, Chicago mob-style. At home in her canyon cottage, Susan spent much of her time at her computer. She was a writer.

But she was no ordinary writer.

She was the daughter of a big-time gangster—a mob boss—from Las Vegas's heyday, and she enjoyed, and received notice, for writing about those days.

About the same time the neighbors began to take notice, some of Susan's friends were alarmed as well when Susan failed to attend a holiday get-together after telling her friends she'd be there. Susan was excited about the dinner and seeing her old friend Susie Harmon from their Chadwick school days. For that circle of friends, the days before Christmas were a happy time, as they all anticipated their annual party. But instead of gathering with friends for the holidays, as Susan had done every year before, patrol officers, detectives, and crime-scene analysts began swarming her modest bungalow in Benedict Canyon just above the city of Beverly Hills. Susan had also scheduled a dinner that Saturday night with her cousin Deni Marcus. She talked to Deni the day before. "I cannot wait for you to come to my house tomorrow night," Deni told her. "We're going to tell my son all the stories of our big, loud, crazy family."

When she didn't attend either event, Deni and Susan's friends knew something was amiss; it wasn't like Susan not to show up. That Sunday afternoon, Deni called Susan to ask what happened, why she didn't show up the night before. Instead of Susan picking up the phone, a cop answered. He told Deni the awful news that Susan had been fatally shot.

Word of her tragic fate spread quickly to Susan's inner circle of friends and family. One by one, they gathered at Susan's house, which had been transformed into a crime scene.

As a child, Susan had been protected by her father, Davie. Susan's bedroom was at the back of their house, down a long hallway. Her father had the windows heightened to thwart an abduction or drive-by shooting. Davie even whisked his daughter away from Las Vegas's mob unrest for Los Angeles getaways. Susan later referred to those L.A. trips as "flights to freedom." This time, however, her father was not there to protect his precious daughter. Instead, Susan Berman died all alone, except for her dogs by her side.

The wooded Benedict Canyon, home over the decades to untold numbers of Hollywood stars, has a storied past. The site of a handful of high-profile tragedies, Susan Berman's murder became one more on the growing list.

Not far from Susan's home was the horrific scene of actress Sharon Tate's murder at the hands of the Manson Family. That grisly slaying happened in the summer of 1969 in Tate's rented house on Cielo Drive was less than a half mile from where Susan Berman had moved to nearly three decades later. Tate, wife of director Roman Polanski, and her unborn child were brutally murdered by deranged disciples of Charles Manson.

Also, George Reeves, best known for his role as TV's "Superman" in the 1950s, had shot himself in the upstairs bedroom at 1579 Benedict Canyon Drive, across the street and just a couple of houses from Susan's. For years, some have claimed that Reeves' house was haunted and swore they'd seen a ghost in the front yard wearing a Superman cape.

In 1838, a Spanish land grant was assigned to El Rancho Rodeo de las Aguas (which, translated, means The Ranch of the Gathering Waters), named for the streams that emptied into the area from the canyons above, including Canada de los Encinos, or Glen of the Green Oaks, now known as Benedict Canyon. After oil exploration in the area in 1906 failed to pan out, Burton E. Green formed the firm Rodeo Land and Water Company to develop the parcel. The next year, Green opened luxurious, curving, tree-lined streets in the subdivision of Beverly Hills, so named in honor of President Taft's Massachusetts vacation hideaway. In 1911, Beverly Gardens Park was established, with fourteen lavishly planted neighborhood blocks back dropped by canyons slicing into the Santa Monica Mountains above. Then, in 1914, P.E. Benedict allowed holdings in Benedict, Franklin, and Higgins canyons to be included as part of the community.

The Ranch of the Gathering Waters was incorporated and the city of Beverly Hills 90210 was born. Benedict Canyon Drive, not far from downtown Beverly Hills, intersects with the famous Sunset Strip and the landmark Beverly Hills Hotel. Celebrities' homes dot the winding, narrow canyon road. Home to the elite, it is a small town for the wealthy with luxury homes and shops within just six square miles where mostly the more fortunate live in comfort. Its first mayor was rope-twirling actor Will Rogers. The city has no billboards or industry. There is no hospital or cemetery to remind residents of their eventual mortality. Because of that, it has been said that "no one is born or dies in Beverly Hills."

Susan enjoyed the prestige of living among the upper crust, especially in Benedict Canyon. She looked at it as her birthright. She felt safer there than anywhere else she had lived after having resided, at one time or another, on both coasts. It was no mistake that Susan chose to live in a town that's considered the diamond of Los Angeles.

Even so, she lived her life with caution, almost as a recluse, in her rundown Beverly Hills home, surrounded by wealth, something she had been born into more than five decades earlier. Throughout her life, her wealth came and went. She was either up or she was down, without a lot in between. Susan wrote about it in her 1981 memoir titled *Easy Street: The True Story of a Mob Family*:

"There are scars within me that will probably never heal; I have uncontrollable anxiety attacks that occur without warning; I am never secure and live with a dread that apocalyptic events could happen at any moment. I am never settled but prefer instead to live a rather nomadic existence without much furniture or possessions. Death and love seem linked forever in my fantasies, and the *Kaddish* will ring always in my ears."

Easy Street may have been where Susan grew up. Toward the end of her life, it was anything but easy.

Susan's rustic, wood-shingled rented bungalow sat on the edge of a busy canyon road in contrast to the fashionable and popular district, where directors, musicians, and stars choose to live. The wooded area on the bank behind her home was long overgrown. Even worse, Susan's house was in dire disrepair. She blamed her landlady.

Susan had very few belongings—mostly mementos from her early years with her parents. "She had lovely jewelry that were her mother's things," Susan's friend Ruth Bartnof said. "She had a gold bag and a diamond watch."

Susan Berman also had the prized, lengthy, gold key chain presented to her father by Denver gangster and gambler Raymond Ryan, who, nearly two decades later, died during a car-bomb explosion. Ryan's inscription to Davie read, "DB from Ray Ryan, 1949."

Susan used the key chain until her death.

She didn't own real property. Her most expensive possessions were a used SUV and a desktop computer, which her friends described as her "precious computer"; it was her lifeline to freelance work. The few pieces of furniture she owned were in bad shape. Most of her friends shuttled her to and from veterinary and doctor appointments, the movies, restaurants, the supermarket, and the occasional meeting with an editor or producer. She enjoyed the company, preferring not to drive herself. Her car was out of commission most of the time anyway. And Susan was paranoid about driving, especially over anything remotely resembling a bridge.

Susan's home was on a busy road. She'd lived in the Beverly Hills house, at 1527 Benedict Canyon Drive, years earlier in better times. Her friend Ruth Bartnof could not understand why Susan stayed, especially at $1,500 a month for a house that was falling apart.

When a bullet exploded in that same house, no one but the shooter—and Susan's dogs—heard it. The killer walked out of her home and into the night undetected. But could the killer be traced?

Even though Susan Berman was Jewish, each year she'd

spend Christmas day with Susie Amateau Harmon, a close friend ever since they boarded together at the preparatory Chadwick School in Los Angeles. Susie Harmon lived in Arizona, but Susan joined her at Harmon's mother's Los Angeles home for the holidays. Just like every year before, the Amateau family expected Susan for Christmas dinner. She told them that Nyle Brenner, her friend and personal manager, would be going with her.

Susan no longer had immediate family of her own, aside from her cousins and step-children. Her closest friends had become family to her, and she depended on them for moral support. More times than not over the years, Susan also leaned on them for financial backing. She made a point of surrounding herself with successful people, those with clout in the entertainment, music, and literary worlds, people she could count on.

That Friday night, December 22, Susan had an unexpected late-night guest. Police believed it was a friend who appeared unannounced, one who ended up killing her. Susan had been working on her computer at home. Earlier in the day, she'd made her usual lengthy phone calls to friends. Nothing she said to any had alarmed them. And she didn't mention she was expecting company that weekend.

It was a typical winter day in the Los Angeles basin. No rain, mostly clear, with a few scattered clouds and the temperature reaching 63 degrees—a pleasant December day in southern California.

On that second day of winter, Susan had scheduled a script-editing session at her home with an aspiring screenwriter she was helping, between 1 and 3 p.m. But the writer called ahead of time to cancel. Earlier that evening, Susan went to dinner and then to a movie with friend and comedy writer Rich Markey. Using their Writers Guild passes at a theater on Santa Monica's Third Street Promenade, they watched *Best in Show*, a comedy about dog competitions. Susan was upbeat and her usual talkative self. They discussed over dinner her latest TV pilot idea and an agent's interest in representing her with a book idea.

Markey did not detect anything that pointed to Susan being fearful for her life.

"Was there something, some clue, lying there unrecognized for what it was? I can't think of one," Markey later said.

She didn't mention to Markey that she was expecting anyone.

After she arrived home at about 9 p.m. Susan Berman changed clothes. Because the temperature had dropped that evening and there was a chill in her aging bungalow, she put on her favorite kick-around purple-colored sweat pants and a white T-shirt with a Hula Girls Cigar emblem stenciled on the front. She checked her phone messages to see if she'd missed any calls.

She always screened her calls, letting the recorder pick up, and, when she needed or wanted to, she returned the calls. That's how paranoid she was, her friends said. But on this night, Susan appeared to trust whoever it was who knocked on her door. From the evidence, it appeared Susan knew the intruder and freely let him or her into her home.

Police surmised that Susan's killer had arrived not long after she returned home that Friday night, with the cover of darkness protecting the visitor from being seen.

It wasn't until a day and a half later that Susan's neighbors became alarmed, on December 24, when her three dogs were still running loose a day after they were first spotted outdoors.

When the neighbors picked up the phone and called 911,

it was just before 12:30 in the afternoon. A dispatch operator radioed it out as a "possible 459"—which, translated, means a possible burglary call.

Responding patrol officers arrived a few minutes later at Susan's home. A uniformed officer knocked on her door, but no one answered. He tried the handle on the front door. It was unlocked. He opened it and called out, "Hello? Anybody home?" No response. The house was quiet.

A second officer walked to the side gate, next to the attached single-car garage, and into the backyard. There, he saw that Susan's back door was wide open. Both officers, with their sidearms drawn, slowly went inside the house. They found Susan's body lying on the hardwood floor of her spare-room. The body was face up and a pool of blood was next to her head.

The officers immediately radioed for paramedics and a crime-scene team. "This is a one-eighty-seven," a homicide, an officer radioed to dispatch.

They secured the home and then walked outside, standing in front of the house while they waited for back-up.

Drivers, usually in a hurry speeding along the country-like meandering road, slowed to a crawl to see what was going on.

Within minutes, an ambulance and fire truck arrived. Susan's body lay face up on the spare-room floor. Paramedics checked her body for a pulse. There was none. Her head and hair were covered in dried blood. There was no need to take her to a hospital. She had expired between one to two days earlier. She was ice cold to the touch. Paramedics pronounced her dead at 1:20 p.m., about forty minutes after neighbors dialed 911, death from a gangland-style shot to the head.

Two of Susan's dogs darted back and forth in the room

as paramedics worked. An LAPD officer, one of the first on the scene, caught the small dogs and put them in his patrol car. The third dog, Lulu, had stayed outside, wandering to a next-door neighbor, who took the dog in.

A few minutes later, the first member of the investigative team arrived, then the second. They were detectives Brad Roberts and Ronald Phillips, on call and dispatched to the house that holiday afternoon. A decision was made to have the station detectives investigate the crime themselves and not dispatch a Homicide Special Unit to the scene. It was a decision that, a few weeks later, would prove to be a fatal flaw in the probe.

The detectives were briefed by the uniformed officers who arrived first on the scene. The two patrol officers stepped aside and let the detectives take the lead, per investigative protocol.

At first glance, detectives had little to go on. The screens on the windows looked untouched. It didn't appear to be a burglary gone wrong. Susan's wallet remained on the kitchen counter with credit cards and a small amount of cash still inside. Nothing seemed out of place or disheveled.

The phone rang while detectives were still at the house investigating the scene of the crime. A detective answered. On the other end of the line was Deni Marcus, Susan's cousin. She told police that Susan always peeked out a window before opening her front door to anyone. Police surmised that Susan must have known her killer, recognized the person through the window, and let him in.

As for the open back door, it was unlike the careful and cautious Susan to leave her house unlocked, let alone leave a door ajar. Police quickly determined that Susan may have been surprised by an assailant or, most probably, had known and trusted her killer. By the time police were alerted to the scene, Susan had been dead at least a day.

The bullet wound at the back of Susan's head was from a small-caliber handgun, a 9-millimeter pistol, which is a common handgun. The slug fragmented on contact. A spent bullet casing was found near Susan's body. Later, former Las Vegas mob attorney Oscar Goodman would refer to the murder as "a Chicago mob-style hit." But that did not mean it was executed by the Mafia, he pointed out. Investigators felt it looked staged, as if the killer had wanted it to appear as if the mob had done it to steer police away from the real killer.

Officers followed bloody paw prints left by Susan's dogs to the spare bedroom, where Susan's body lay on the cold, hardwood floor. Near her body was a lock of her long, dark hair next to a pool of dried blood. Her friends often teased her that she'd kept, since her girlhood days, the same dated style, always with bangs and very much a 1960s' hairdo. It had a Cleopatra look to it: long, straight, near-black hair with flat, perfectly cut bangs. Like her mother, she had kept it long, shiny, and black. Throughout her college years, Susan's hair was waist-length.

Later in the day, as a few stunned friends made their way to Susan's home, the sight of the grisly but spartan murder scene left them numb. There was nothing valuable in her house, nothing to be stolen. Lieutenant Clay Farrell, the lead early on in LAPD's Robbery-Homicide investigation into the Berman case, commented, "Her house was sad. It was barren. Let me put it this way, you wouldn't want to live there."

In a corner of the kitchen, where Susan ate, was a plastic fold-up card table. The windows throughout the house were covered with old blankets. The floor of her bedroom was bare wood, as if the carpet had been pulled up and not replaced.

Ruth Bartnof, who was a close friend and referred to by Susan as "Ruthie," said Susan's home was yet another side of the complicated Susan. "I don't know why she chose to live such a spartan life," Bartnof said. "It was always like that." At least during the majority of her years in Los Angeles. In that town, luck had not always been on her side. A lack of money appeared to be the driving force in the way she lived.

It was shocking to officers that Susan had gone from living such a rich and lavish childhood only to die a pauper, with nothing of value in her name except copyrights to her out-of-print books and a used car. She had no other assets. In fact, she had owed money to many of her friends at one time or another. At the same time, over the years she had owned a bowling alley and part ownership in an apartment complex in Las Vegas, bought a Victorian three-story house in San Francisco, a pricey apartment on New York's upper eastside, and a house in Los Angeles's tony Brentwood neighborhood. But she lost them all.

When she died, even though Susan had very little of value, she had documented it all in a will, as if she were hopeful that eventually it would be more.

Julie Smith, a mystery writer and a close friend to Susan, was executor of her will.

"Susan had three wills," said Julie, who met Susan when they each were staff writers at the *San Francisco Examiner* in the early 1970s. "The last one was the one in force."

Ainslie Pryor, a children's book author and a close friend to Susan, said in a telephone interview, "She had made certain provisions in her will, including a home for her fox terriers."

Police, Pryor said, had taken two of her dogs—Romeo and Golda (named after former Israel Prime Minister Golda Meir when Susan adopted Golda and her two puppies, Lulu and Romeo)—to the local humane society. The main issue with Susan's dogs, said a friend who met Susan in San

Francisco and later moved to L.A., was that Susan "drove her dogs insane." When Susan took the dogs out in public, two at a time, they wore muzzles to prevent them from not only biting people, but each other too.

"Lulu went to Susan's next-door neighbors," she said. "The other two eventually went to a sanctuary, living on a ranch for fox terriers." Ainslie visited Romeo and Golda at the sanctuary and told Susan's friends she had never seen them happier.

Susan also included her college friend Bobby Durst in her will. To him, a man described in his younger years as both brilliant and eccentric, Susan bequeathed her prized silver medallion that was once her father's, given to him by Davie's sister Lillian. Susan's modest Writers Guild insurance policy went to her surrogate son Sareb Kaufman. After probate ended, about a year after Susan's death, her cousin Deni Marcus went to the West Hollywood Police Department with Sareb and presented Susan's death certificate to clear hundreds of dollars worth of parking tickets Susan had amassed over the several months she'd had the car, so that the cloudy title could be cleared. Tom Padden, Jr., Susan's mother's first cousin, was given the car. He and his son, Tom, had helped Susan over the years, and it was decided that Tom Jr. would get Susan's SUV.

Other than the used SUV, Susan Berman had nothing else of value and very little cash. Her book royalties had either ended or trickled down to barely nothing as her titles, one by one, went out of print.

Not long after Susan's death, Sareb told a reporter, "Susan loved mysteries. She even wrote a few. She would have loved this one."

Sareb and Susan's closest friends pointed out that she would have been mystified at the circumstances surrounding her own death. She would have loved to stick around to find out the ending. Susan's life—and even her death—was colorful. It was always that way, starting from birth. Her life was one drama after another. Her death was no different.

# CHAPTER 2

# WHO LET THE DOGS OUT?

*I am never secure and live with a dread
that apocalyptic events could happen at any
moment. . . . Death and love seem linked
forever in my fantasies, and the Kaddish will
ring always in my ears.*

Susan Berman
from *Easy Street*

WEST LOS ANGELES Community Police Station
patrol officers responded to a radio call at 12:30 on the
afternoon of December 24th, 2000. The call came is as "an
open door in the 1500 block of Benedict Canyon Drive" in
the Beverly Hills area of Los Angeles. The officers entered
the location and discovered a deceased victim in a bedroom
of the residence. It was Susan Berman's house, and her body
was inside.

Susan became the LAPD's Case No. 000825485 and one
of 548 homicides committed that year within the LAPD's
jurisdiction, up from 432 the year before, for a 27-percent

increase. By the time LAPD's Robbery-Homicide unit got the case, it became their unit's first assignment of the year. The detectives who caught the case are part of an elite unit that handles just the high-profile investigations—the movie-star murders, organized crime killings, and serial murders. Still, they couldn't seem to solve Susan's murder.

Early on in the Berman investigation, a lead detective commented that if they learned who let Susan's dogs out of her house, they'd learn who her killer was. Yet thirteen years after Susan Berman's body was found, no arrests had been made.

The day Susan's body was discovered, detectives Brad Roberts and Ronald Phillips, partners in the detective unit at the West Los Angeles Community Police Station at 1663 Butler Avenue, were assigned the Berman murder. They were dispatched to the scene. It was a Sunday afternoon and a holiday when they were dispatched from home just after 12:30 p.m. They were told a female body was found in a Benedict Canyon house and that the woman had been shot to death.

It didn't take the cops on the scene too long to figure out that the dead woman was the daughter of a casino operator and member of the Jewish mob, a notorious gangster who was once wanted by both the FBI and Chicago Police.

The detectives learned a piece of Chicago history soon after arriving at the scene. Hanging prominently—and proudly—on a wall in the front room was a police "Wanted" poster for Susan's father. It read, "Reward $8,000. Wanted for hold-up and post office burglary."

Below a photo of the suspect were the words, "Dave Berman—Alias 'Dave the Jew.'" It was a Chicago Police Department mural for her father when he'd been wanted by authorities decades earlier in the 1920s.

"The poster in her living room can tell you a lot about Susan," said Las Vegas historian Michael Green. "It's to make herself look important, and it's a conversation starter." For the first detectives on the scene, they looked at the "Wanted" poster as a clue to who killed Susan. That was the first mistake that led them for a short time in the wrong direction.

Crime scenes tell a forensics story. In this case, however, police initially assumed that Susan had been whacked by the mob. Had detectives from the LAPD's Robbery-Homicide Unit been dispatched to the scene instead of the detective from the local precinct, it very well might have been another story. But the unit was not called. Robbery-Homicide investigators would not be on the scene for nearly three weeks.

By that time, precious evidence had been trampled over unknowingly by Susan's friends, who filed into the house, one by one, after learning of her death. Allowing Susan's friends onto the property, into the unsealed, unsecured scene of the crime, inside the house, turned out to be an early mistake in the investigation. The crime scene was corrupted. The scene had also been innocently mopped up. A friend and a relative did it. "One of her friends and I cleaned up the blood at her house," said Susan's relative, who asked not to be identified. "I couldn't stand there and watch, so I helped." "I got why her friend was doing it," the relative continued. "That was the last contact with her good friend, and I felt the same way."

A key move that often determines whether a murder is solved or unsolved is properly and thoroughly processing the crime scene, which is considered by experts to be the most important step in a murder investigation. This does not appear to have been done in Susan's case.

"It was not taped off as a crime scene," said Susan's close

friend Kim Lankford, who went to the house after Susan's body was found. "I moved freely through the house. I put my fingerprints all over the house."

Retired Sergeant David Rivers, who worked for the Metro-Dade Police Department, once said, "The three most important aspects of any death investigation are crime scene, crime scene, crime scene."

What police were able to determine was that Susan's home had not been ransacked, and she had not been robbed. Chanukah gifts remained unopened in her living room. There were no signs of a struggle—at least, according to early assessments—and no unusual sounds coming from inside the house to alert neighbors or passers-by. The lights were off in the house. And there were no eyewitness descriptions of a suspect. Holiday greeting cards were taped to the walls. Also, uncharacteristically for Susan, her mail from the day before had been left unopened, pointing to her being killed the night before, on Friday. Susan never missed the mail and obsessed about it to her friends as she did with most everything. Her mail and her answering machine were her lifelines to the outside world and writing assignments.

Also in the living room, in the center of the room, was Susan's computer, placed next to the printer on a table with white chipped paint. Investigators confiscated the hard drive to her personal computer. It was full of clues, and crime scene investigators bagged it and carried it away. Susan's Rolodex with more than a thousand telephone numbers in it was also taken as evidence and later pored over by detectives. On the table next to her computer was a piano-shaped Liberace ashtray with butts in it. Susan never smoked. In fact, her friends said, she was allergic to smoke. The butts were in the ashtray nearly three weeks after Susan's death and could have been put there by crime scene analysts, investigators, and even friends who'd visited Susan's home after her body was removed from the house. One thing is sure, Susan would not have been pleased that people had been smoking in her home, let alone that they'd extinguished their cigarettes in her prized Liberace ashtray, where she'd usually kept paper clips. It isn't known whether the cigarettes were processed for DNA. Former LAPD Detective Tom Lange said investigators and crime scene analysts are not allowed to smoke at scenes they're investigating. And it isn't likely that Susan's friends would have smoked, because they knew how much she disliked it. The cigarette butts were another mystery.

The crime scene pointed to the killer choosing the victim, choosing the weapon, and carrying out the crime.

As a result, Susan had died like a character in one of her own books. Only this time, her friends later said, Susan was not there to solve it.

The irony of Susan's death was not lost on investigators nor on her friends, nor would it have been lost on her, had it happened to someone else. Susan Berman had gone from being a rich mob daughter to a respected journalist and screenwriter, only to end up a struggling, penniless writer, shot to death gangland style like one of her father's mob associates. Susan knew better than most the truth about Las Vegas history. She'd reconstructed her father's past in her writings, only to die like the main character in a movie-land mystery. But she did not have any recent or new information that would have caused wiseguys to want her dead. And she had not been writing about anything that would irritate today's underworld associates.

Susan was far removed from the mob and its activities. That Susan was shot once in the back of the head led to wide speculation early in the investigation that her work may have prompted her slaying. Police, months into the investigation,

21

said they had not ruled out that scenario. In hindsight, it appeared to be a copy-cat crime by someone trying to make it *look* like a gangland killing. Because Susan died living one step away from homelessness was another strong indication that she did not have close relationships with anyone tied to the mob. If she had, she would have been rich instead of poor, because mobsters would have made sure her financial needs were met.

Detectives Roberts and Phillips began their investigation at the scene of the crime, starting in the bedroom and the room's entranceway where the body was found.

The odd thing about the scene of the crime was the way Susan's body was found. Her body was lying on its back with her arms at her side. According to investigators at the scene, it was not physically possible for a gunshot to hit the back of Susan's head and cause her to fall backward. The force instead would have sent her body to fall face down.

No gun was located on the premises. At the scene, however, investigators did find a casing next to Susan's body from a spent bullet used in a small-caliber weapon. It was the best evidence they had. If a gun were later found, ballistics tests could be done to match the pistol with the bullet casing. During the crime, a single round was fired, hitting the killer's target squarely on the back of the head. Susan didn't see it coming, since there were no apparent signs of a struggle. It appeared she didn't know what hit her.

A crime-scene team dusted Susan's house for fingerprints, leaving black soot behind.

The area was relatively quiet—besides the loose dogs and passing cars—when Susan's neighbor Marvin Karp, a physician, left Benedict Canyon for Los Angeles International Airport to pick up his daughter. He left for the airport just before 12:30 p.m., shortly after the neighbors on the other side of Susan's house told him they were going to call police about the barking dogs.

When Marvin arrived home, two squad cars were blocking his driveway. He found a spot on the street next to the curb, parked his car, and walked toward his house. Sitting on the back seat inside a squad car were two of the dogs he'd seen roaming the neighborhood for more than 24 hours. They barked at him through the car window.

Karp approached a uniformed officer who stood near the patrol car.

"What's going on?" he asked.

"The lady in that house was murdered," the cop said, beckoning toward Susan's home. "We're taking her dogs to the shelter."

"It was a big shock to me," Marvin said afterward.

Karp, shaken by the news, walked next door, to Susan's front yard. A detective in a business suit asked him a few questions. Marvin did not recall whether it was Detective Roberts or Phillips.

"The most curious thing was that her dogs were in my yard," Marvin told the detective. "My first clue that something was wrong was the dogs running around outside. They were barking. But they really were very friendly. I saw one of them make a beeline across the street. It was the little one that went across the street first. Then the big one went across. Then they ran back to the house, like they were going home. They could have been hit by a car."

Police said Susan had been dead from one to two days when her body was found. Her neighbors insisted she was killed late Friday night, more than a day and a half before her body was found. The dogs were a big clue for them.

Marvin Karp agreed. From his vantage point, the murder occurred on Friday night, December 22, "because the dogs were outside early Saturday morning. And they barked all night."

That was evidence enough for him.

"I probably was home when it happened," he said. "I didn't hear anything, except the dogs. He [the gunman] must have used a silencer."

The other next-door neighbor, who didn't want to use her name, said she and her husband had gone to see a movie on Friday night. "We didn't hear or see anything," she said, then added, "Thank goodness." She didn't notice a car in Susan's driveway. She told police she and her husband wanted to keep Susan's dog Lulu. The dog was Susan's favorite. Susan's other precious dog, Oomi, who was said to be better behaved, had passed away years earlier.

Had the intruder pulled into Susan's driveway, one of her neighbors would have seen the person. Plus, a car would have alerted Susan, because of the headlights and the sound of the engine. To arrive undetective, the gunman would have had to park down the street and walk to Susan's house. There was no sidewalk. The area between Susan's front yard and the street was covered in grass, thick foliage, and trees.

A year and a half after Susan's murder, Marvin Karp said the short conversations he'd had with police back in December 2000 were his only interviews. There was no follow up. "I haven't seen police or anyone for a while," he said. "Nobody."

Neither neighbor could fathom how such a horror could happen there, right under their noses, without them hearing a commotion.

"The police questioned us—a lot," said the next-door neighbors, a husband and wife, who lived on the other side of Susan's house.

Marvin Karp, as he said, was interviewed just once, on

the day Susan's body was found after he returned from the airport. It was as if, Marvin said, police thought she'd been snuffed out during a mob hit and that the case was not worth pursuing further.

"They thought it was mob-related," he said.

Chip Lewis, one of Robert Durst's attorneys, said Berman's death was a clear and simple mob hit. "The fact of the matter is Susan Berman had cried out soon before her murder that she was about to expose the mob in a tell-all book about what she knew," Lewis told "48 Hours." "It was a hit-style murder."

When detectives at the West L.A. police station found no connection to Susan's murder and her underworld past, they moved on.

But by the time investigators began looking at people who might have had disputes with Susan, the case had gone cold. When they hit a dead end two weeks later, West Los Angeles detectives forwarded the case on to the LAPD's elite Robbery-Homicide Unit, where, many say, the investigation should have been from the start.

The list of people Susan had had recent disagreements with was short. It included three people—Susan's landlady Dee Schiffer, manager Nyle Brenner, and best friend Bobby Durst.

The first dispute police were told about was a bitter one with Berman's landlady, Delia "Dee" Baskin Schiffer, an elderly woman in her seventies. She and Susan had been in a lengthy and acrimonious battle over both back rent and Susan's barking dogs. Schiffer had taken Berman to court twice to evict her. But, in court, Susan successfully had argued to a judge that she was not going to pay rent until repairs were made. The judge's favorable ruling bought Susan more time. Susan's cousin Dave Berman noticed when he visited a few months before her death that her house needed repairs. "When I saw her at her canyon home, there were a lot of little things that needed to be done. Her doorbell didn't work and the electrical plugs needed to be rewired. I offered to fix them, but she said it was okay." Dave also wanted to buy Susan a new computer. "Somebody had given her a computer," he said. "It was junk. I put a menu program on it—that was before they had Windows—so she could access her word processor. I told her I would get her a new computer. She said no, she was going to be okay." Susan had gotten a reprieve in the form of a check from Bobby that allowed her to buy a new computer and a used car.

Susan had to pay up and appease Dee Schiffer by giving her the thousands of dollars owed in back rent, as well as future rent paid through March 2001, thanks to the $50,000 gift of cash, in two payments, from Bobby Durst. In exchange, Schiffer agreed to let Susan stay in the Benedict Canyon house until June 2001 to give her time to find another place to live. Police, during their investigation, learned that Schiffer had told Susan she owned a gun and had threatened Susan and her dogs. But in an unusual twist, investigators also learned that when the landlady was in the hospital after being injured in a car accident the year before, Susan, in an attempt to mend fences, had taken Dee flowers and also had sent her a holiday greeting card. Still, Susan had told her surrogate son Sareb, "If I ever turn up dead, it was her." Dee Schiffer told police she had never threatened to harm Susan or her three.

Detectives attempted to interview Dee Schiffer. Reached by telephone, she told an investigator she was hesitant to talk with police without an attorney present. At the house, police found copies of letters Susan had sent to her landlady.

One said, "Please don't ever threaten me again, saying that if I don't pay the rent, 'something bad is going to happen to you and your dogs,' or that you'll come up here and 'throw my ass on Benedict Canyon.' I take such threats seriously." In a second letter Susan had written, she quoted Schiffer as saying, "Something bad is going to happen to you and your (boyfriend's) daughter." Despite the threats, Schiffer, to investigators, seemed an unlikely suspect, and they moved on.

The second person police were interested in was Nyle Brenner, Susan's sometime manager and one of the few people she'd invite into her home. She had met Nyle a few years earlier while walking her dogs on Sunset Boulevard, near her apartment at the Park Wellington Hotel, where she once lived with her ex-boyfriend's daughter, Mella Kaufman. Friends who knew Nyle had remarked at how much he looked like Susan's ex-husband, Mister Margulies.

According to those close to Susan, her relationship with Nyle had been volatile. Even so, in the last few years before her death, Brenner was the person with whom Susan spent the most time. They went to movies together, using Susan's free Writers Guild passes, and often went out to dinner. Brenner also drove Susan to a sundry of business meetings and doctor appointments. Brenner was overheard at her memorial service, which was held at the Writers Guild Theater, saying he would miss the free movies she treated him to with her Guild card.

After Susan's murder, Nyle regularly stopped by her house to pick up and open her mail, including her bank statements. Nyle later told police that he'd paid Susan's rent a few times and that Susan had paid most of it back. But because Susan still owed Nyle money, after her death, he tried to find out just how much money Bobby Durst had given her, hoping he could recoup the monies she still owed him. So, Nyle was checking her bank statements to see how much was in the accounts. After Sareb reprimanded Nyle for taking Susan's mail, Nyle returned the bank statements to Sareb and no longer went through her mail.

While police looked into the dynamics of the relationship, they stopped just short, at least publicly, of calling Brenner a suspect. Privately, as reported in the book *Homicide Special: A Year with the LAPD's Elite Detective Unit* by journalist Miles Corwin, Brenner was closely scrutinized. After an article appeared in *New York* magazine all but saying Nyle was under investigation and was a person of interest, LAPD's Lieutenant Clay Farrell, in October 2001, backed down, apparently afraid of a potential lawsuit. "Nyle Brenner is not considered a prime suspect," Farrell told reporters. "The only one calling him a suspect is *New York* magazine. *They said that, not us.*"

But behind the scenes at police headquarters, it was a different story. Detectives openly referred to Nyle as "*the* suspect," according to the book. Homicide investigators obtained a court order and searched Brenner's home. They confiscated his office files. If nothing else, Brenner was under scrutiny. But Nyle's house appeared to be more than scrutinized when a team of experts showed up to serve the court order and do a thorough investigation.

Then, on a dreary Wednesday afternoon in February 2001, Nyle Brenner, dressed in black cowboy boots, blue jeans, and a black button-down shirt, walked into police headquarters for an appointment at the Robbery-Homicide Bureau to be interviewed by the investigative team on Susan's case. The first thing detectives did was escort Nyle to the second floor, where he was fingerprinted. Brenner had promised to bring his calendar with him, but he told the detectives, "Sorry. I forgot." He told them that he had no appointments written down for the Friday Susan was believed to have been killed. Nyle reluctantly agreed to a polygraph, which was administered in a cubicle soon after Nyle arrived at police headquarters. Detectives Stephens and Coulter, who watched through one-way glass from an adjacent room, commented about Brenner's anxiety, how he tugged at an earlobe and crossed and uncrossed his legs. The lie-detector examiner asked Nyle Brenner questions about Berman's death.

"Did you shoot Susan Berman?" he asked Brenner. "No."

"Were you inside her room at the exact time she was shot?"

"No," Brenner said.

"Were you inside her house at the exact time she was shot?"

"No."

Brenner tapped his foot on the floor as he answered "No" to the rest of the questions. "He's fucking lying," Stephens said to his partner as they watched through a one-way window from an adjoining room.

Halfway through the test, the polygraph examiner excused himself to talk to Stephens and Coulter. "He's not telling us the full truth," the examiner told the detectives.

"My gut feeling is he did this, but something's missing," the examiner noted. From the test, he determined that Brenner was deceptive and, as a result, police could not clear him as a person of interest.

The polygraph examiner went back into the room where Brenner was waiting and told him, "You failed the polygraph. You have to cooperate."

"Is this a joke?" Brenner asked the examiner.

"No," he replied. "This is the worst trouble you can face in your life."

"This is absurd," Brenner answered.

"It's your life," the examiner said. "It's not going to go away."

In the next few minutes, Brenner, with his lip quivering, told the examiner, "How can I be blamed?" Then, as he recovered from the initial shock of being accused of murder, he said angrily, "I don't believe any of this for a second!"

The examiner left the room again and Stephens replaced him. "Is this for real?" Brenner asked Stephens when he entered the room.

"It's for real," Stephens told him. "I want to be fair to you. You can talk to me if you want. I'm not going to yell at you. Will you give me a handwriting sample?" Stephens wanted it to compare against the handwriting on the envelope of the letter mailed to Beverly Hills police station, telling them that a body was inside Berman's home. A handwriting expert determined there was a fifty-fifty chance it was Brenner's writing. But police needed to be certain.

Brenner responded with the statement detectives feared hearing, one that would bring the interview to a screeching halt: "I should probably speak to an attorney."

Stephens then presented Brenner with a search warrant for his home.

Stephens left Parker Center and hurriedly drove to Brenner's home, which was a tiny bungalow in the San Fernando Valley, thirty miles north of Susan's house. Nyle also maintained an office in his home. Stephens waited outside for crime scene investigators Rick Jackson and John Garcia, as well as criminologists, to join him in the physical search of the home and office.

The search turned up no additional evidence. It was long after the murder. Next, police obtained a search warrant for Nyle's phone records. The results of those records have not been made public.

As of winter 2012, Nyle Brenner had not been charged in connection with Susan's death. Witness accounts are that Nyle Brenner was irritated after Susan's death, making odd statements, criticizing her to her friends and family. Where was Nyle on that December Friday night when police believe Susan was killed? Did he have an alibi? Police were unable to find his calendar and took his word for it that he had made no appointments that day. Nyle told Susan's friends that on the day her body was found, he waited on the street for investigators to leave Susan's house, and then went through a kitchen window, taking some items, some of which have never been identified nor recovered, other than the bank statements he returned to Susan's surrogate son Sareb.

• • •

Susan Berman did not speak of her relationship with Nyle Brenner with just anyone. Stephen M. Silverman, an old friend who regularly talked on the phone with Susan, said he didn't know about her relationship with Brenner until after Susan's death. "Susan never even mentioned Nyle to me," he said.

But one friend she did discuss Nyle with was Ruth Bartnof.

"Nyle was very helpful to her in many ways," Ruth said in a telephone interview. "They had an unusual relationship. I don't know how intimate they were. I thought it was more of a companionship relationship. He would help her, go with her different places, escort her. I met him when I went to one of her book signings."

About two weeks after Susan's murder, a Reuters reporter interviewed Nyle Brenner and asked why he thought Susan was killed. "I'm entirely at a loss," Brenner answered. "I don't know that there was anything she was working on that had any relevance to the [current] Mafia." He did note, however, that before she was killed she was working on "several other projects" having to do with Las Vegas. "She had been talking to a lot of people in Las Vegas recently, people who'd had a past there." Susan, he said, was sought out by people in the publishing and film industries for her expertise on Las Vegas. "She was such a gentle person," he noted. "It's a mystery. I just don't know what to think."

To friends, and at times to reporters, Brenner's tone was more harsh, criticizing Susan and telling people they had no idea what she'd put him through. Friends said he was openly bitter and verbal about her, saying he was "done with her."

With Brenner lawyered up and no hard evidence discovered during the search of his home to charge him with a crime, the best detectives could do at the time was sit back, watch, wait, and listen.

• • •

The third person on the LAPD's list of possible suspects was Robert "Bobby" Durst, Susan's old college friend from UCLA. According to Bobby's attorney Dick DeGuerin, a detective talked to Bobby on the phone but never officially interviewed him. Later, after Bobby was arrested for murdering a seventy-one-year-old Texas man, they changed their minds about formally interviewing Durst. In retrospect, it was a missed opportunity for investigators.

"Mr. Durst is a person who knew Berman, and he's involved in a murder in Texas, so obviously he's under suspicion," said Sergeant John Pasquariello, an LAPD spokesman in the department's public relations office. "He has been arrested for murder, but beyond that there is no direct connection between Durst and the [Berman] murder."

Back in New York, officials there were relieved to learn about Durst's arrest.

"It's good news," said Anne Marie Corbalis, spokeswoman for the Westchester County District Attorney's Office, where Durst had been under investigation for the disappearance of his wife Kathie, "because we have what we believe to be a dangerous person out of harm's way for people." Still, she said, the New York investigation was continuing. "We'd like to bring closure for Kathleen Durst's family. We still have a missing person's case open."

• • •

There were no solid answers—just speculation—on why Susan died. And the trail was getting colder as time progressed. Los Angeles police looked for motives in Susan's death. Just after Susan's murder, Sareb Kaufman told police that Bobby had called him, offering to pay for both the funeral and a private investigator to look into the murder.

Sareb Kaufman told the *Los Angeles Times*, "It's shocking right now. She was a gentle woman who lived life with great caution. She loved a lot of people and she had no enemies, because if she didn't like you she would not let you get close. Nobody had the opportunity to develop a grudge."

To Reuters, Sareb said, "She would have done nothing intentionally to put herself in danger."

Somebody, however, had developed enough animosity toward Susan Berman to want her dead. Police from the start said the murder was not a random act of violence. Susan had been the intended, premeditated target.

Berman's friends had become alarmed when they could not reach her. Of course, they would later learn, by that time it was too late to help her.

"I tried to call Susan," said Ruthie Bartnof, who telephoned Susan's house not knowing she'd been killed. "Nobody answered. I kept calling and calling." Then Ruthie called her son, who was good friends as well with Susan. "I said, 'Kevin, Susan isn't answering and her machine isn't picking up.' He said, 'Mom, there's something wrong.' She was having her eyes checked for glaucoma. I told him she probably had that done and wasn't home. He started making phone calls to her friends. The information he got (from Susan's friends) was, 'Don't discuss anything on the phone. Don't talk about anything.' I didn't know what *not* to talk about. Later I said, 'How come it's not in the paper? The whole thing was bizarre. They [police and her friends] assumed it was an underworld thing. Why would they [old mobsters] care? They're in their hundreds."

It wasn't in the newspapers because the police had not yet announced the death to members of the press. Rather, Susan was buried *before* the media were informed about the murder of a daughter of an infamous Las Vegas mobster. The omission was curious. The code 187 radio call—denoting a homicide—went across the police scanner, routinely monitored by crime reporters and city desk editors. If reporters had heard it, they no doubt would have responded to the scene. But it was a holiday and newsrooms operate with skeleton crews on those days. No one knew that Susan Berman, an author, journalist, screenwriter, playwright, and mob daughter was dead. The public would not learn the news for another eleven days.

But at the scene of the crime, it was a different story. Soon, Benedict Canyon Drive and nearby Clear View Drive would be crowded with detectives, uniformed officers, emergency personnel, curious neighbors, and passersby. When the media don't pick up on certain calls, the ensuing press releases inform them of the crimes they missed. In this case, however, the release was not issued for ten days. Then, it didn't hit some newspapers for an additional couple of days.

Gilberte Najamy, Kathie Durst's best friend from college, questioned the duration of time between Susan's murder and notification of the death to the public.

"The interesting thing about Susan's murder," said Najamy, "is the time elapsed from when she was found and when police told the media. The time span gave Durst two weeks to construct an alibi. It didn't hit the papers until January 5th. I'm very curious about those two weeks. I think it's because of who he is. He does what he does best, and that's to keep himself out of trouble. As soon as I heard Susan was murdered, I said, 'Do ya think?'"

Police, however, denied anything other than the usual handling and processing of a murder investigation. Once police released details of Susan's murder, they were deluged with questions from reporters about the woman the media dubbed the "Mob Princess."

With Durst back home in New York, after flying there from California, gone forever was the opportunity for police to take residue tests of Durst's clothing, hands, and shoes. It was another lost opportunity for police and a fatal error in the case.

Publicly, Los Angeles Police Department spokesman Lieutenant Horace Frank told reporters that "investigators had no suspects and did not know the motive. Nothing appeared to be missing and there was no sign of forced entry and no signs of a struggle."

Susan Berman, struck from behind, had no reason, it appeared, to fear her would-be assassin, until it was too late.

Nearly every reporter asked police about a mob connection.

Lieutenant Frank remained neutral when it came to the Mafia. At a news conference, a reporter asked, "Was it a mob hit?"

"At this point," Frank answered, "we have no reason or evidence to support linking the murder to mob involvement. But at this stage, we would not discount anything. We are going to look at everything."

Los Angeles Police Department spokesman Eduardo Funes added, "It's a terrible homicide. A motive hasn't been established yet."

Funes, however, hinted that police had some leads to follow up on: "They are looking into several clues, but nothing I can tell you about at this time."

Detectives worked the case from the third floor of Parker Center. The Los Angeles Police Department's headquarters. Named after former chief Bill Parker, it's located in the heart of Los Angeles's downtown command center at 150 North Los Angeles Street. The Robbery-Homicide Division, at that time, was where murders in the City of Angels are chronicled by investigators.

With the May 2001 high-profile arrest of actor Robert Blake in his wife Bonny Bakely's murder, the LAPD was looking to clean up its image and get down to the business once again of solving cases. With the heavily publicized

Rampart corruption and ensuing scandal, the LAPD's image was tarnished. They were unsuccessful in solving the murder of rapper Notorious B.I.G. (a k a Biggie Smalls) and received some negative ink with that case. With the Blake arrest, as one TV talk-show pundit put it, "The LAPD got him." They appeared to be turning around their image and concentrating on crime solving, especially high-profile murders, instead of putting out fires with internal investigations.

LAPD Sergeant John Pasquariello explained the delay in solving Susan's killing: "It's a murder case," he said. "They take a while to investigate. There is no imminent arrest."

While detectives looked for evidence at the crime scene, Susan's body remained at her house until 6:30 p.m.

Her body was then taken to the Los Angeles County Morgue on Mission Street near downtown L.A. Susan Berman became county coroner Case No. 2000-08986.

Two days later, at 8:30 a.m. on December 26, Susan Selser, a medical examiner and doctor, performed the autopsy, according to Craig Harvey with the Los Angeles County Coroner's office.

At the time of Susan's death, the coroner's office was conducting about 6,500 autopsies a year, 2,400 of which were handled as homicides. Susan's examination fell into that category; her death was listed by the medical examiner as "a homicide with a pending investigation." It was noted on the autopsy report that she had brown hair, brown eyes, was sixty-six inches tall (or five-feet, six-inches), and weighed 151 pounds.

She was not wearing jewelry—no watch, and no earrings. No scars, marks, or tattoos were indicated by the examiner. The only property brought in was her driver's license. Susan's body was positively identified by her driver's license, not by a friend or a family member, Harvey explained as he showed me her death certificate during my visit to the coroner's office (later, a source within the police department gave me a copy). Then, the coroner's office mailed Susan's license to the California Department of Motor Vehicles to be destroyed.

Four days later, on December 28, 2000, according to the death certificate, Susan Berman's body was released by the county morgue and taken in a van to the Hillside Memorial Park on Centinela off the 405 freeway in Culver City. The body was formally released to mortuary officials there. Because she was Jewish, they did not embalm her body, per Jewish tradition.

On the last day of 2000, Susan's funeral was held at Hillside. Deni notified as many people as she could find.

After a few cloudy days, the sun was out for the service, as if it were meant especially for Susan. Her body was laid out in a long, black, velvet dress with white trim that had belonged to the grandmother of Sareb and Mella Kaufman, her ex-live-in boyfriend's children whom she raised as her own.

Deni Marcus went early to the funeral home to comb Susan's hair and prepare her for the memorial, also a Jewish ritual. Susan's trademark bangs had been cut back by the coroner's office during the autopsy examination. But Deni did the best she could.

About fifty friends and a few relatives crowded into the small chapel, which is owned by Temple Israel of Hollywood, where Susan was a member. Deni paid for her cousin to be laid to rest, declining an offer by Bobby Durst to cover the cost.

Immediately following the service, a mortuary van took Susan's body, in her casket, across town to the Home of Peace Memorial Park on Whittier Boulevard in East Los

Angeles's Boyle Heights, where her father, mother, and uncle were entombed.

Two days later, on Tuesday, January 2nd, a smaller group of Susan's friends—maybe a dozen—gathered to inter her cremated remains in the expansive mausoleum at the Home of Peace cemetery. Formerly a Jewish community, the neighborhood is now a *barrio*. Just one Jewish-owned family business remains in the nearby retail area that was once a thriving community cultural hub. Susan's cousin, Donna Berman, who owned the remaining family crypt at Home of Peace, gave it up for Susan's body. It was originally meant for Donna's mother Marge, who, when she passed away, was instead buried in Las Vegas at the Palm Mortuary. Susan's casket, placed at the end of a row of crypts, in the mausoleum's Eternal Life corridor, next to her parents and her Uncle Chickie.

At long last, Susan was home again. She was with her family.

"Fortunately, [Susan's vault] is on the second level," her friend Kim Lankford, an actress who played Ginger Ward on "Knot's Landing," told a reporter. "And there's nobody on the other side to annoy her." Those gathered sang "On the Sunny Side of the Street," written by Dorothy Fields and Jimmy McHugh. Susan's favorite lyrics, and the favorite of her father, were, "If I never had a cent/I'd be rich as Rockefeller/Gold dust at my feet/On the sunny side of the street." Susan's father had taught her how to play the song on the family's piano. A rabbi chanted a Jewish hymn for the dead.

Susan's treasured photo collection of friends and family were placed inside the casket with her body.

"We put all her favorite people in there," Kim Lankford noted. "(We) couldn't fit everybody in."

Susan compartmentalized her friends, as she did other facets of her life. So while many of her friends knew *of* each other, most had never met, although they said at the services that they felt as if they'd known each other for years, because Susan had often spoken about them. They were a loyal group. After Susan's death, they got to know each other better. They had a common bond and goal, to help police bring Susan's killer to justice.

After the service, Susan's friends could not help but look around and ask, who among them was it? Chatter at a get-together following the service inevitably turned to that nagging question. Police had said it was obvious from the evidence that it was someone Susan knew well enough to allow into her home. *It's one of us,* many of her friends thought. *But who could it be?*

Sareb Kaufman, Susan's surrogate son, had organized a memorial service for Susan the first week in February at the Writers Guild Theater. It was set up in the screening room, at 135 South Doheny Drive in Beverly Hills, some six miles from Susan's Benedict Canyon home. A dozen friends gave eulogies and read from Susan's books.

Conspicuously absent from the mortuary service, interment, and memorial was Susan's long-time friend Bobby Durst. That fact did not go unnoticed. Susan's friends found it curious, but that was about it. Investigators found it noteworthy, especially since Sareb had gone to great lengths to make sure the media were not informed in advance, so Durst would not be inundated from flashing lights and microphones in his face. Still, Bobby stayed away.

Detective Jerry Stephens, who had been given Durst's cell phone number by one of Susan's friends, called him. Stephen's had made arrangements to meet Durst at the service, so he and his partner could interview him. Stephens planned to get both handwriting samples and fingerprints from Durst and also ask him to take a polygraph exam. But that wasn't going to happen that day.

She was placed in a crypt next to her family, in the large mausoleum on the grounds, which is Los Angeles's oldest Jewish cemetery. Also buried there were MGM film director Louis B. Mayer, singer and theatre actress Fannie Brice, and "Curly" Howard of the Three Stooges. Susie consistency, her friends said, would have been pleased about that.

It was at that time that the murder investigation was moved from the West Los Angeles police station to the Robbery-Homicide Division at Parker Center in downtown L.A.

On January 4, two days after Susan was buried and eleven days after her body was found, police, in a press release, finally announced Susan Berman's death.

Once the media got hold of the story—even though it was delayed by police—published stories were fast and furious. In the days that followed the announcement of her death, headlines blasted the front pages of the *Los Angeles Times*, *Daily Variety*, *The San Francisco Chronicle*, *Las Vegas Review-Journal*, *New York* magazine, *New York Times*, *New York Post*, and The Associated Press, UPI and Reuters wires. The headlines screamed: "Author shot dead at home," "Mob Writer Susan Berman Found Slain," "Mob Scribe Berman Slain in West L.A.," "Writer of Mob Book Found Dead," "Did Mob Author Die For Writing What She Knew?" "Mob Daughter Turned Author Found Slain," "Execution-style killing of one-time Mafia princess is a mystery," "Who Killed the Gangster's Daughter?" "Final hit for Mob scribe," and "Screenwriter's death a mob hit?" Lieutenant Clay Farrell with LAPD's Robbery-Homicide bureau, tried to explain the nearly two-week lapse in time between Susan's murder and the news release outlining her death.

"On the Berman case, West Los Angeles [detectives] investigated that for ten days or so," Farrell explained. "Robbery-Homicide made the announcement to the media once the case came into our jurisdiction. The case was reassigned to us when it became apparent it would take longer [to solve]. There was an opinion that it would overwhelm the resources of West L.A."

Detectives Roberts and Phillips were officially off the case. It was reassigned to Robbery-Homicide detectives Jerry Stephens and Paul Coulter.

It was never made clear why the Robbery-Homicide division wasn't called into the case from the start, the day Susan's body was found at the scene of the crime. Did police assume it was a mob hit, and probably unsolvable, surmising there was no need to transfer the case to the elite Robbery-Homicide division? As a result, by the time the case did finally make its way to Robbery-Homicide, the trail was already cold.

On the afternoon of January 4, 2001, a Thursday, LAPD released their belated statement from the West Los Angeles detective bureau to the media at large—eleven days after Susan's body was discovered. They asked that news outlets hold off reporting Susan's murder until 5 p.m., just in time for the evening news and after business hours, so they wouldn't get any calls about it until the next morning. The press release read:

Media Relations Section
Office of the Chief of Police
150 North Los Angeles Street
Los Angeles, CA 90012
213-485-3586
213-847-1760 Fax

LOS ANGELES POLICE DEPARTMENT
PRESS RELEASE
Thursday, January 4, 2001

Writer Susan Berman Murdered

West Los Angeles—On December 24, 2000, at approximately 12:30 p.m., West Los Angeles patrol officers responded to a radio call of an "open door" on the 1500 block of Benedict Canyon. The officers entered the location and discovered the victim in a bedroom of the residence. The investigating detectives determined the suspect(s) shot the victim one time in the head. The motive for the murder is still unknown and no suspects have been identified.

The victim has been identified as Susan Berman, the daughter of David Berman. David Berman and Ben "Bugsy" Siegel were business partners who co-owned the Flamingo Hotel in Las Vegas until Siegel's death, leaving Berman in charge.

Susan Berman was a book author, producer, investigative journalist, and screenwriter. She wrote several books including *Easy Street* and *Lady Las Vegas*, and was a dual writer/ producer at the San Francisco radio station KPIX. Berman also wrote as a journalist for the *New York* Magazine and the Francis Ford Coppola Magazine. Her latest work was a screenplay for "Sin City," Showtime's version of the HBO hit "The Sopranos."

Please contact West Los Angeles Homicide Detective Ron Phillips at 310-575-8408 if you have any information that may assist in this investigation.

The following press release was prepared by Officer Danielle Lee, Media Relations Section at 213-485-3586. For Release 5:00 pm PST

On January 11th—more than two weeks after the murder—Detectives Jerry Stephens (since promoted) and Paul Coulter (now retired and a private detective) had caught the case in the Homicide Special Unit in the first murder case of the year. Two weeks after a murder is an eternity for a homicide investigation. They had a lot of catching up to do.

For a week, the pair studied the West L.A. detectives' paperwork. As one investigator on the case said at the time, because it was Christmas Eve and a holiday, law enforcement personnel "got sloppy."

Stephens and Coulter learned from the West L.A. investigators' reports that the detectives had not ordered a criminalist from the coroner's office to go to the scene and collect hair and fibers from Susan's body. In other words, CSI investigators were not called to the scene to collect possible vital trace evidence that could have been used to track a suspect. Hair and fibers were eventually collected at the examiner's office, from Susan's body, but that's not considered as effective as taking them directly from the scene.

That misstep was especially troubling for the new team of detectives, because Susan's body had been rolled over by the killer after she was shot and fibers and hair from the killer could have been left behind.

Also, a sexual assault test was not done to see if Susan had been raped. Her fingernails were not clipped and examined for DNA from the killer. Microscopic skin samples from the assailant could have been left behind; that possibility for forensics, however, was forever lost. Even though the body had no defensive wounds, examining under fingernails is considered common practice by medical examiners. Paint chips were on the floor next to the door jamb near where Susan's body was found. But the chips also were not gathered up during the initial crime scene processing.

A month after Susan's murder, detectives filed for a search warrant with the Criminal Courts Division of the Los Angeles County Superior Court for Berman's phone records. Through paperwork at her house, they learned that there was a small insurance policy connected to her membership with the Writers Guild.

Detectives Stephens and Coulter planned to ask LAPD technicians to return to the scene and search for possible fingerprints using more sophisticated methods. They also planned to ask technicians to apply ninhydrin—a chemical substance that highlights blood residue—to the walls near the location Susan's body was found to see if the shooter might have braced himself after firing the shot. They discussed the possibility that the killer might have left a print on the shell casing while loading the gun. Superglue is an effective method for lifting hard-to-get prints. From that second trip to gather evidence from Susan's house, criminalists picked up a palm print from the wall of the spare room Susan was killed in. They also submitted the bullet casing to the FBI's database in hopes the ammunition could be traced to the store from which it was purchased.

The new team of investigators hadn't ruled out someone breaking into Susan's house instead of knocking at the front door for her to open it. "There was a possibility," Coulter said. "The kitchen windows had little slide locks. (But) it would have taken a little work to get in." That, however, no doubt would have alerted Susan's terriers, whom neighbors said were barkers. Later, detectives would learn that Nyle Brenner had entered Susan's home through a kitchen window the day Susan's body was discovered and after police left the scene.

This much was clear: The killer had the intent to kill

Susan. "This was one single gunshot wound. It was clean, to the head, and that's it," Detective Coulter said.

• • •

In a notification to students and alumni, the *North Gate News*, a newsletter at UC Berkeley, published an article titled "Alumna Susan Berman Found Shot Dead in L.A." Kamika Dunlap, a journalism student at the time, wrote, in part, "As a journalist, Susan Berman capitalized on her life as the daughter of a Las Vegas mobster. . . . When Berman, 55, was found shot dead on Christmas Eve in her rented West Los Angeles house, newspapers from Los Angeles to London writing about her life, raised questions, but no answers, about a possible mob killing. Police found no sign of robbery."

On January 27, 2001, investigators with LAPD's Robbery-Homicide bureau put a security hold on the Berman case at the Los Angeles County Coroner's Office. The hold said simply that it was done by "the investigating agency," coroner spokesman Craig Harvey said. It meant no forensics or evidentiary details and no death or crime-scene photos would be released. In other words, the case was sealed.

The same day, "America's Most Wanted," a FOX TV crime show, posted a "Wanted" poster on its website, seeking tips in the murder of Susan Berman.

A few weeks into the investigation, Detective Brad Roberts told the *Los Angeles Times*, "We still got nothing on this one. No real leads."

Paul Coulter, by now the lead detective on the case, said he would have done things differently had homicide detectives been involved from the beginning of the Berman investigation, instead of the West Los Angeles office. His office was not given the case until thirteen days after the murder and, coincidentally, a couple days after reporters across the globe began deluging the LAPD with telephone calls. By that time, the trail had turned cold.

"It's very difficult, because we weren't there from the get-go," said Coulter, a burly middle-aged investigator, during a telephone interview.

Jerry Stephens, Coulter's former partner on the case, retired in mid-2003. Another detective, Jesse Linn, was at first assigned the case with Coulter but later dropped from the investigation.

In the book *Homicide Special: On the Streets with the LAPD's Elite Detective Unit*, author Miles Corwin writes that "when a gangster's daughter, brought up in Las Vegas, takes a bullet, veterans Jerry Stephens and Paul Coulter trace clues scattered across the country to one of Manhattan's wealthiest real estate magnates."

In fact, police had not interviewed Durst about the murder, although they spoke with him on the phone. Coulter said LAPD detectives instead interviewed Durst's attorney, Dick DeGuerin, several times.

In addition, Coulter said he shared information with out-of-town investigators on the other cases linked to Durst. "Obviously, we've been exchanging information," he said. "New York has their case, we have ours, and Texas had theirs." When asked if he and his partner were any closer to finding Berman's killer, Coulter responded, "Closer? Maybe a little. I mean, it's an old case."

It was a cold case as well.

"Things move at a snail's pace sometimes," Coulter continued. "But, hopefully, eventually you get there."

He worked the investigation, he said, in between his

other homicide cases. "I'm not actively working on this case," he noted. "I'm working on one from the weekend. But, yeah, I do work on it."

As for Durst, Coulter said, "We've always called him a person of interest."

Meanwhile, the property owner repaired the Benedict Canyon house that Susan complained about, but only after her murder, so that it could be rented out. Dee Schiffer replaced the windows and had the house painted inside and out.

"She had a helluva time renting it out, because she had to disclose the murder," Susan's neighbor Marvin Karp said. "It took her months. She finally found someone, an English fellow, to lease it."

By October 2001, ten months after Susan's death, Homicide-Robbery Detective Stephens said in a telephone interview, "We haven't made an arrest and won't be making one soon. But we're not finished with this investigation." He said Nyle Brenner, Susan's manager, was not considered a prime suspect. Was he *any* kind of suspect? "No comment," Stephens said.

Had detectives' interest in Nyle Brenner caused them to let Durst slip away? Nyle had a troubled friendship with Susan, so, instead of looking to Bobby Durst for answers, they pursued Nyle. They say no, that wasn't the case. Yet, they did not seek a formal interview with Bobby Durst or look at him as a serious suspect until Durst was arrested for another murder, this one in Galveston, Texas, nearly a year after Susan's death. Durst was charged with killing Morris Black, Durst's elderly neighbor.

Then, in March 2002, two years after Susan's murder, a headline in *The New York Post* screamed, "New Durst Shocker: L.A. Cops Seek Link to Murder of a Longtime Friend."

A month later, in April 2002, Lieutenant Clay Farrell acknowledged that investigators were "still doing the Berman investigation" but said detectives assigned to the investigation had other cases to work on besides the Berman murder; hers was just one of many, Farrell said.

"We just keep plodding along," the lieutenant said. "The guys working the investigation have other cases. There's less activity at times. Generally speaking, it averages out to be two detectives working on it at any given time. But it varies, depending on what we're doing on the case. There's nothing imminent happening."

It was an unusual admission, that officers were moving on to other cases, with Susan's file just one in a stack of many.

After Durst's arrest for the Morris Black murder, reports surfaced that Galveston Police did a ballistics test of the gun confiscated from Bobby Durst's car at the time of his arrest. The test was to see whether the 9-millimeter pistol found in Durst's car matched a bullet used to kill Susan Berman. Police compared the gun with the bullet casing collected at the scene of Susan's murder. Police did not release the results. But LAPD Lieutenant Farrell issued this statement: "We're acutely aware of the gun results and ballistic results. And we are not commenting on the ballistics. It's been reported that they [Galveston police] have a 9 millimeter weapon. Their agency, not LAPD, is testing the gun. We're continuing to interview people."

However, Dick DeGuerin, Durst's lead defense attorney, said the 9 millimeter pistol had been ruled out as the gun used to kill Berman. In actuality, the ballistic testing done by Galveston authorities came back inconclusive, which did not rule the pistol either in or out. It is not clear why the LAPD did not use their own lab to conduct a second test.

Even so, with Durst's arrest in the unrelated Morris Black murder, the LAPD still considered Durst a person of interest in Susan Berman's murder.

"The circumstances surrounding Durst now, of course, mandate that we take a look at him and evaluate the circumstances surrounding his recent arrest and any other evidence or issues that may or may not pertain to Susan Berman," Farrell said. "This is a murder where there involves a crime inside of a residence, and naturally we're very reliant upon evidence at the scene and information derived from interviews with her friends and associates. We have to look at all this evidence with considerable circumspection. And we have not publicly identified any suspects. We are continuing to assess information derived from those interviews and evidence."

Detective Jerry Stevens commented to me about Bobby Durst. "Mr. Durst is just another person we're interested in talking with," the investigator said. "I can't get into the merits of the case."

An insider at LAPD said an attitude common in dual murder investigations is that detectives look at the possible perpetrator as already facing prison time for an unrelated murder. In other words, he's going to get prison time, one way or the other, and it doesn't matter for which crime. It's a lot of work putting together a case against a suspect. So why bother? Let someone in another jurisdiction put him away, the source said.

Still, Lieutenant Farrell said that Durst "certainly appears to have shown a propensity to violence. His recent criminal behavior puts a burden on us to take a look at him." Meanwhile, Galveston police detectives probed the murder of Morris Black, whom Bobby Durst had admitted killing.

Later it was revealed that the LAPD had been in possession for more than a year of a handwritten envelope sent anonymously to the Beverly Hills Police Department shortly after Susan's murder. The envelope, on which Beverly was misspelled, contained a single sheet of paper with Susan's address handwritten on the sheet and the single word *CADAVER* all in caps. It was mailed before Susan's body was discovered, which was a key piece of evidence in the investigation. Detectives believed the note was written by the killer, because it was mailed before her body was discovered. The writing on the envelope and letter was analyzed by an LAPD handwriting expert.

Once news of the anonymous letter hit the airwaves, investigators still publicly insisted they had no suspects. Behind the scenes, however, police pursued three persons of interest.

The criminologist who tested a handwriting sample from the guest book of Susan's funeral compared it with the cadaver note sent to the LAPD. The expert, who determined earlier that there was a fifty-fifty chance the handwriting was that of Nyle Brenner, but police were still looking at Schiffer, Susan's landlord. "We figured maybe the landlady didn't want a rotting corpse ruining her hardwood floors and smelling up the house," Detective Ronald Phillips told author Miles Corwin for his book, *Homicide Special: On the Street with the LAPD.* "Another thing that interested us was that the landlady left on a vacation right after the murder and was driving a rental car. When we talked to her, she said the vacation was pre-planned and her car was being repaired. But it seemed odd."

It was not odd enough apparently to prompt police to verify Schiffer's alibi or to look into her further as a person of interest. Instead, investigators closed in on Robert Durst

51

by requesting that a judge order Durst to also undergo a handwriting analysis.

Durst's attorney, Dick DeGuerin, insisted it was not his client's writing. DeGuerin, who once represented the survivors and families in the Branch Davidians' wrongful-death lawsuit against the government, called any comparison similar to "reading tea leaves."

"We gave them [LAPD investigators] handwriting samples this week [the first week in May 2002]," DeGuerin said. "We asked to see what they had. They didn't want to show it. We gave them a sample anyway. What I originally told them was Mr. Durst makes no bones about having written to Susan and having given her money in the past. They corresponded back and forth. It sounds like they're trying to either tie it to him or eliminate him. Being the cynic I am, I assume they're trying to get some kind of evidence that my client wrote the note. He didn't."

"Besides," DeGuerin added, "he's got an MBA and he knows how to spell Beverly," referring to the misspelling on the envelope of the city of Beverly Hills where Susan lived.

Durst's attorney also commented on what he described as "clever machinations" by the police. "They did interview Mr. Durst by telephone once, right after Susan Berman was killed," DeGuerin said. "My client has cooperated. He offered to cooperate and they finally made a formal request through the courts in Galveston for handwriting examples. We didn't oppose that. We just wanted some ground rules laid down. The judge granted most of our requests for ground rules." DeGuerin said he made himself available to police. Instead, LAPD investigators requested Durst's handwriting samples through the court system.

"Bob Durst wants to cooperate in every way that he can with the LAPD, because he doesn't have anything whatsoever to hide," DeGuerin said. "I asked to have the L.A. police contact me directly. They've never contacted me. I've been sitting here waiting for them to contact me. I have yet to receive a single call from them."

DeGuerin said police had not formally named his client as a suspect in the Berman case. "He's never been told that," he said.

DeGuerin also said his office had hired "our own handwriting expert" to analyze the cadaver letter and envelope. Detectives, however, never provided DeGuerin with a copy of the letter so that DeGuerin could have it independently analyzed.

As for a connection to the Morris Black murder and Berman's, DeGuerin said, "The judge in the case has said that Susan's killing may not be mentioned during the Galveston trial. The LAPD have never contacted me, even though I offered to meet with them."

In the meantime, the then-investigators on the Susan Berman case, detectives Roberts and Phillips, looked to see whether Susan's murder was mob-connected.

Roberts told reporters, "She has a history of family involvement in the Mafia. (But) I have no idea at this time. We are still conducting our investigation. There have been no arrests at the moment."

"We have pretty much ruled out a home-invasion robbery," he continued. "It looked like she was the target, as she had nothing in the house worth stealing. She was on hard times. It looked like the target of the murder was Susan. Was it a mob hit? We have to look at every angle, of course."

# CHAPTER 3

# THE MOB-RELATED THEORY

*No one got killed that wasn't supposed to be.*
—Debbie Reynolds, *The Real Las Vegas*

FIVE DAYS BEFORE she was murdered, Susan Berman told a friend she had "information that was going to blow the lid off things."

"What do you mean?" said close friend Kim Lankford, in retelling the story to *New York* magazine.

"Well, I don't have it myself," Susan answered, "but I know how to get it."

The next question could have been, "Get what?" But no one ever learned the details Susan was referring to. After her death, they could only speculate. During their conversation, Lankford warned Susan to "be careful."

Susan's life, her friends said, revolved around one drama after another breathless drama. So when Susan talked like that, as she often did, they didn't take her seriously—like the boy who cried "Wolf" one too many times. Susan's friends assumed she was referring to a mob case. In retrospect, after her death, friends said they wished they'd paid more attention.

The mob-hit theory in the Susan Berman case turned out to be nothing more than interesting. Susan's friends were vocal to police and the media about their doubts in the theory from the start.

Detective Roberts told a pool of reporters, "We are looking at a few different things, even the Mafia, the mob thing, but it seems so remote and far removed. She was a mob daughter, and that was how she was making a living. But in talking to her family and friends, she had no connections now whatsoever."

Mob hit or otherwise, Susan's murder looked orchestrated. "Normal people don't kill each other that way," Jonas McCord, a Hollywood director and one-time writing partner of Susan's, told *Entertainment Weekly*. "They go crazy. They shoot five or six times. They use really big [caliber] guns. This was, I believe, a professional killing."

Dick Odessky, a journalist who worked in public relations at the Flamingo beginning in 1961 and knew Susan well, doubted her murder was a mob hit.

"When this all broke," he told me, "everybody was trying to lay it on the mob. Forget that. First of all, just in talking to her, she wasn't really afraid of anything, and, second, if it had been the boys coming to her for something that her father did or didn't do, the people who would have wanted to do that are either dead or so close to death that they wouldn't have been able to hold a gun. It almost had to have been someone she knew. It doesn't make any sense."

Odessky, who authored the book *Fly on the Wall*, which included Mafia life in Las Vegas, talked to Susan on the phone for between one and two hours about two days before her body was found.

"As far as the mob is concerned," Odessky said, "the mob as we knew it is gone."

Sareb Kaufman, Susan's surrogate son, agreed. "There's a theory going around that the mob did it," Sareb told *New York* magazine, "but I don't think so. I don't think they would have anything to do with this."

Susan often talked about the mob to friends. "But she was very careful about what she wrote," her friend Ruthie Bartnof said.

Several weeks into the Berman investigation, police said the mob theory was, unofficially, ruled out. An unnamed entertainment industry executive told the UPI news agency, "I heard initially that she was doing a tell-all and naming names and stuff. I think the mob got tired of hearing about her."

But the theory of Chicago Mafia-style contract hit was ruled out as well. Chicago mob murders historically go down using a 22-caliber weapon fired at point-blank range to the back of the target's head. Susan was killed at close range—not point-blank with a barrel against her head—from a 9-millimeter pistol. Former mob attorney Oscar Goodman pointed out that a 22 typically "is used in Chicago-style" killings.

John L. Smith, a columnist for the *Las Vegas Review-Journal* and an author, on January 7, 2001, had this to say about the manner in which Susan was murdered:

"As Susie told it, she was the Las Vegas version of *Little Miss Marker* who meandered through her father's glamorous, gaudy world as a princess in ponytails. Until (her father's) death in 1957, Dave Berman was a big man in Las Vegas at a time when the city was operated by characters straight out of *Guys and Dolls*."

Smith wrote that "Susie Berman crafted a successful

career as an author and screenwriter out of that image. In her book *Easy Street*, she painted a neon-hued memoir of her young life with her family, including her uncle, Chickie Berman, that betrayed her wisecracking exterior and revealed Susie as a not-so-tough girl who still longed for attention from her daddy.

"When I heard she had been murdered on Christmas Eve in her Benedict Canyon home in West Los Angeles, I anticipated someone would attempt to link her fascination with the mob with her demise. . . . That she was shot with a single bullet in the back of the head only added to the mystery of a potential mob hit on the former Mafia princess."

The theory, Smith pointed out, wasn't plausible. "A mob hit on Christmas Eve? Not even Hollywood writes such awful stuff. Even cat burglars take off Christmas Eve."

"Truth is," he continued, "Berman didn't know two things about the mob and had very little knowledge of her father's world. That's what made her memoir so touching."

The type of writing that can generate death threats wasn't Susan's style of writing. "As one person who knew her well recalls," he wrote, "she probably had never called an FBI agent or covered a mob trial."

Smith predicted that "when LAPD detectives make an arrest, most likely it will be someone Berman knew and not some mysterious La Cosa Nostra button man in a fedora and overcoat. The fact that the case is being handled by West L.A. detectives and not LAPD Robbery/Homicide, which investigates mob-linked murders, is a giveaway. California police sources confirm their investigation is leading away from something as nefarious as an organized crime killing."

In a later newspaper column, Smith wrote that the case was a murder mystery that Susan Berman would have loved to have written about.

*Casino* author Nicholas Pileggi worked with Berman a couple years at *New York* magazine. The year before her death, Susan called him to discuss projects she was working on. "It's so befuddling," Pileggi told Smith. "It just doesn't make any sense at all, and it clearly doesn't make any sense in association with organized crime. She wasn't an investigative reporter. Her interest was in the social mores of that world and what it was like being a girl raised by the cast of *Guys and Dolls*. That's the way she looked at her father."

Pileggi continued, "She was very smart, very deft, and a very good writer. . . . And she was a little girl right out of that Damon Runyon world."

Susan's cousin, Deni Marcus, was also skeptical about the mob theory. "Whoever committed this act of violence," Deni told *The Good Gambling Guide* in the UK, "maybe they did it this way to make it look suspicious, to keep people guessing at some silly notion."

That theory was what the evidence was beginning to point to.

Eleven days after Susan's body was discovered, detectives attended Susan's funeral hoping to gather more clues. "We had a presence there," Lieutenant Clay Farrell said in a telephone interview.

It is common practice for police to attend funerals of murder victims to see who's there and who is not. The LAPD detectives assigned to investigate the Berman murder stood on the sidewalk in front of the memorial park, closely observing mourners. Nearby, an officer, standing behind some trees and bushes so he would not be noticed, snapped photos. What was striking about the service was that Bobby Durst, one of Susan's dearest friends, was conspicuously absent. It was noted by her friends, but, more importantly, by detectives. What was Durst afraid of? Detective Coulter, for one, noticed: "The fact that as close a friend as (Durst) had been to Susan for several years, that he was not at the memorial, you start looking into who is Bobby Durst."

Former Nevada Governor Bob Miller, who knew Susan as a child, was unable to attend the service. He had this to say about the LAPD looking for answers with Robert Durst and even the mob: "Her level of information about the mob wasn't to the point where someone would want to kill her. The initial reports about it being a mob hit didn't make sense. Later, when the Bobby Durst circumstances came to light, that made more sense."

Miller said that Nyle Brenner, Susan's quasi manager, informed him of Susan's death.

"I first heard about her murder when her business manager called me," Miller said from his Las Vegas law office. "He told me about the circumstances surrounding her death. I told him, 'God, that sounds bizarre.' Her son (Sareb Kaufman) called me about the services. I spoke to him a couple of times. I couldn't go to her funeral."

Following the second service, this one a memorial held February 2nd—ironically, on the forty-second anniversary of Susan's mother's death—a flurry of speculation arose during an after-party. The memorial was held at the Writers Guild Theater in Doheny Plaza in Beverly Hills, near Wilshire Boulevard. On stage were two large heart-shaped red floral wreaths next to an easel with photos of Susan and her parents. Displayed on a nearby table were her book covers and writing awards.

Sareb had explicitly banned members of the working press if they were not there as friends of Susan. He wanted Durst to be able to attend without being bothered by the media. Durst, however, failed to show, just as he had been absent for Susan's funeral the month before. Once again, it looked as if Bobby distanced himself from the death of a woman who had been his best friend for more than three decades. He attended her college graduation, he gave her away at her wedding, he gave her large sums of money, and he provided her moral support over the years, but he conspicuously did not make it to her funeral or to her memorial service. That inaction did not look good. A police detective, expecting Durst to be there, pulled his cell phone from its holster and called Durst from the memorial service. Durst didn't pick up. The detective left a message, asking where he was. Nyle Brenner, however, did attend the service, accompanied by an aunt. He, along with dozens of others, signed the guest book. Police afterward confiscated it for handwriting analysis, hoping to make a match with the cadaver letter sent anonymously to police.

At the memorial service, the first speculation among her friends arose, according to *New York* magazine, with talk of Durst and whether he'd murdered his wife Kathie and her mysterious disappearance January 1982.

Mystery writer Julie Smith was alarmed when one of Susan's friends said, "Susan used to tell me it all the time. She would say, 'Bobby did it, but that doesn't mean we don't love him. Kathie's gone. There's nothing we can do. And we love Bob.'"

The unnamed friend said he pressed Susan at the time, asking how she knew. Susan replied, "Because he told me." Her friend wasn't the only person Susan had revealed that to on more than one occasion, that she provided Bobby's alibi the night Kathie disappeared. It explained the mysterious phone call from a woman to Kathie's medical school dean. At the same time, Susan insisted to friends, it did not mean that she thought Bobby was guilty of killing Kathie, just that he knew what had happened to her. Susan went so far with another friend to say she thought she was the only person who knew what really happened to Kathie. It was a revelation, but something Susan had not shared with police. New York State police, however, had an inkling that Susan knew more, which is why they wanted to talk to her.

Another friend of Susan said that Susan and Bobby had a mutual understanding to continue keeping that information a secret between the two of them. For twenty years, Bobby Durst apparently felt comfortable with that pact. But as police closed in, his confidence in Susan appeared to waver.

Two of Susan's cousins agree. They believe Susan knew too much about Kathie's disappearance, Bobby feared she would talk to the cops, and it got her killed. "If Susan liked you, you were a friend for life, no matter what you did," said Dave Berman, who was a year older than his cousin. "Knowing Susie like I did, I believe at the time of Kathleen's disappearance, Susie—as Bobby's publicist—helped him with his alibi."

Dave and Susan's cousin, Rosalie Bruce, who lives in Las Vegas, agreed. She too has felt strongly that Durst killed her cousin. "I think Susie put too much pressure on Bobby," Rosalie said. "She knew too much and I think she held it over his head." Berman, she added, could be "pushy." Maybe, Rosalie said, Durst couldn't take the pressure and wanted to silence Susan.

Speculation arose at the memorial service about Nyle Brenner, another person of interest, and what some considered odd behavior. After giving the bad news to Sareb Kaufman, on holiday in the Netherlands at the time of Susan's death, Brenner picked up Sareb at the Los Angeles International Airport. Nyle reportedly badmouthed Susan to Sareb. He continued to do it, friends said, the night of the memorial. That's when several friends either had a conversation with Nyle or overheard bits and pieces of his unsettling conversations with others. "At least I won't have someone calling me ten times a day," Nyle reportedly told one attendee. "She sucked me dry," he told another. One friend stopped by the homicide office the day after the memorial and told detectives that Nyle told someone at the service, "This is the only way it could have ended between Susan and me."

Nyle admitted to Susan's friends that he had broken into and climbed through one of Susan's kitchen windows, gaining access to the house, after police left the scene. He saw black soot on the floor but said he did not notice anything out of the ordinary, nothing out of place. He completely missed the dried blood and lock of hair on the spare-room floor where Susan's body once lay. Nyle also said he played Susan's phone machine and heard a message that a neighbor had one of Susan's dogs at her house. Later, he told a friend of Susan's, "It seems very much like a professional job. It was very quick." How did Nyle know her death was quick? Did Nyle think that everyone believed it was a mob hit? Susan and Nyle were known to talk every day, but he told detectives he had not been in touch with her. And there were no messages from him on her answering machine.

When I reached Nyle Brenner by telephone at his office, seeking comment, he at first was friendly and said he could loan me photos of Susan. Then, he said, "Everybody says they're going to write something and use photos. No one ever does. Forget it. The Associated Press said they were going to and they didn't," and he hung up. In a later telephone conversation when I tried once again to interview him, Nyle told me, "Anything about Susan doesn't interest me. I'm way past that. I just can't take it anymore. She wasn't the easiest person to get along with. I'm done with her."

"I have work to do and I can't be bothered," he continued.

"I have a business to run. I don't want to talk about Susan."
He hung up the phone once again without saying goodbye.
His business was managing and representing mostly B-grade
actors, according to information listed about him on the
Internet. Susan couldn't afford to pay Nyle as a business
manager and was never an official client.

Sareb asked nine people to speak about Susan at the
Writers Guild memorial service. Friends later said the
anecdotes were touching and humorous. The room was
full of some of Susan's favorite people: mystery writers,
screenwriters, and journalists, people who knew, like Susan,
how to turn a phrase.

# CHAPTER 4

# POOR LITTLE RICH GIRL

*Whatever I am now, and whatever I become,
I will always be, first and foremost, Davie and
Gladys Berman's only child.*
Susan Berman
from *Easy Street*

"I LIVED IN LAS Vegas, the center of the world, and my dad owned it," Susan Berman wrote in *Lady Las Vegas: The Inside Story Behind America's Neon Oasis*. "My strange Vegas pedigree allowed me to be raised in wealth and glamour by a man who owned the town. . . ."

Hers was, in fact, a childhood of luxury, with live-in mobster bodyguards serving dual roles as playmates and a full-time housekeeper and cook acting as a mother in a comfortable, opulent setting. It was the 1950s in a well-to-do downtown Las Vegas neighborhood.

Susan's life was both connected to the mob and sheltered from it. She was lavished with gifts and spoiled by her father, Davie Berman, who was given the name Don when he was born in 1904 in Odessa, Russia, to David and Clara Berman. Davie's father, and Susan's grandfather, was an assistant rabbi who blessed kosher meat while living in Russia. Susan's grandmother was born to one of the wealthiest families in Odessa.

The family left Russia for America. They landed at Ellis Island, in New York City, and Dave found work at a laundry. When he learned that a special fund had been set up to help young Jews get land grants in North Dakota, David sent his wife and three young children, which included Davie, to Ashley, North Dakota, where they homesteaded a plot of land.

The farming experiment, however, soon failed when their sod hut burned to the ground. They were poverty stricken and had little food for their children. To make matters worse, their boys had head lice.

Susan wrote about the trying times in her memoir. "I found two Jewish graves of my father's younger brothers who had starved to death. They moved to the United States under a socialist living experiment."

At ten years old and the only surviving child of the Bermans, Davie's family relocated to Sioux City, Iowa. It saved the family financially, but it also forever set Davie's path in motion. Sioux City was also, Susan once wrote, where her father "discovered the life of organized crime."

Davie started out as a newsboy, buying newspapers for one cent apiece and reselling them for two cents each or three for a nickel. To get an early start each morning, he started sleeping in the *Sioux City Journal*'s print shop.

His boyhood friends remembered him as always looking for angles to earn more money. He turned the money over to his mother. On the street, he noticed gambling men who appeared to have money. He started hanging around the basement at the Chicago House Hotel at Fourth and Jones streets in what was known as a gangster-rough neighborhood of Little Chicago.

Davie became friendly with the gamblers and began running errands for the them. They taught him the tricks of the trade. He learned how to play poker, mark cards and how hide a tiny mirror in the palm of his hand, and to roll loaded dice. At just fifteen years old, Davie could beat boys his age at their own game. His games of choice were pool, poker, and craps.

His new gambling skills prompted him to drop out of high school. At sixteen, Davie went to work full-time for Sioux City's gamblers. Because he was tough, they used him to collect gambling debts. He put together a gang of boys and hired them out to the gamblers. To collect, they often had to rough up the debtors. Before he turned seventeen, he had rented and moved into his own apartment. He bought fancy clothes and his friends started calling him "Davie the Jew." He started a bootlegging syndicate to earn even more money, making liquor deliveries to Minnesota and the Dakotas.

Just before his twentieth birthday in 1923, Davie Berman was arrested and convicted for holding up a poker game at the Grand Hotel in Watertown, South Dakota. He served eight months in jail. Even though he served time in jail, his unsuspecting family believed he was nothing more than a businessman. In 1925, he graduated from bootlegging to robbing post offices and banks. A gang of Jewish hoodlums who worked for him. That first year, he made $180,000 from one job and $280,000 from another.

While still a teen, Berman worked full-time as a robber, eventually moving his operation from Sioux City to Chicago, and ultimately to New York City. In 1927, Berman was arrested in Wisconsin for a U.S. Post Office robbery. He refused to give up those who were involved. He was convicted and sentenced to seven-and-a-half years in the Sing Sing penitentiary.

Around that time, when Davie's father died, he permanently took the name Davie.

Berman later became an integral member of underworld Las Vegas. His family still did not know exactly what Davie did for a living, only that he worked at casinos and appeared to be in a high position. Whatever it was, Susan's mother, Elizabeth "Betty" Berman, whose stage name was Gladys Evans, knew it was dangerous. It threw her into episodes of deep depression and seclusion. The same anxiety would plague her daughter in her adult years.

Susan Jane Berman was born in Minneapolis, Minnesota, on May 18th, 1945, on a Friday. She was given the middle name Jane after her mom's older sister, Jane. Two months later, in July 1945, Susan's life in Las Vegas began when her mother took her from the Tri Cities to southern Nevada by train, aboard a Union Pacific coach car, because Susan's mother was afraid of flying. Her father had moved to Las Vegas months earlier, just after Susan was born, to prepare for his family's relocation to the desert. Las Vegas had a population of just 16,000 and was on the brink of becoming a gambling boomtown.

The Bermans moved into the El Rancho Vegas, in a bungalow, the only place where hotel owners like Davie could get a war-rationed telephone installed. El Rancho was said to be the original luxurious hotel-casino in the desert outside town, a landscaped and waterfall resort complex covering 66 acres. It was on U.S. Highway 91, which later became known as the Los Angeles Highway, and, ultimately, the Las Vegas Strip.

The family lived at the El Rancho for several months until Susan's mother found a quaint and comfortable house downtown, at 721 South Sixth Street. Susan would spend the first twelve years of her life in that house. Susan's parents went to the pound and got their daughter a dog they named Blackie.

The Berman home was a cozy two-bedroom, two-bath, tan stucco single-story English Tudor with a dining room, large living room, two-sink front bathroom, a large brick fireplace, cedar-lined closets, air conditioning—a real luxury in those days (other residents, if they were lucky, had swamp coolers)—a one-car garage, and trees in both the front and back yards. At the back of the lot, hotel construction workers built a large custom-style playhouse for Susie about the size of the home's single-car garage.

It was a comfortable house that became a meeting place for Davie and his crew. They spent their time either in the dining room, which was the first room as they walked into the house and was off of the kitchen, or they walked down the hallway to the living room, with its brick fireplace and cozy atmosphere.

By Las Vegas standards in the 1940s, the downtown neighborhood was considered upper-class. The Berman home sat on one-sixteenth of an acre and was built in 1937, one of the earliest houses in Las Vegas, and listed as parcel number 139-34-410-212 with the Clark County tax assessor's office. Davie paid $7,000 in cash for the property, but he ultimately spent nearly $8,000 in renovations and improvements, for a total investment of $15,000 (in 1983, the last time the house sold, it went for $105,000). The house was later included in a book of landmark homes because it was one of the few English Tudors in the area.

Susan's father summoned a contractor to move the

windows of the bedrooms, including Susan's, high off the ground so kidnappers could not grab her. (Her father's phobia carried over into Susan's adult years, when she was afraid to stand next to windows in high-rise buildings.) The height was also intended to prevent a drive-by shooting during mob unrest. Davie had the second bathroom added, with full-length mirrors on the bathroom doors, and huge cedar-lined closets in the bedrooms and in the hallway. A hotel gardener planted grass, and stucco bird baths were added.

Susan grew up riding horses from a livery stable on Fifth Street, next door to the Last Frontier hotel, and loped across the desert in western togs from Smith and Chandler Store, a western apparel shop on Fremont Street in Glitter Gulch. Each year for the Helldorado Days' western parade on Las Vegas Boulevard, Susie would ride on a float wearing a bright red sash across her chest that read "Flamingo Hotel."

Her parents took her out on Lake Mead in the hotel's boat where she would dive off the boat and into the bathtub warm water.

She walked with her bodyguard Lou Raskin to Cliff's market, the corner grocery just two blocks away. She played cards, swam in the Flamingo Hotel pool, retrieving dimes from the pool bottom, and counted money with her father in the casino's count room. It was the most sacred room in the casino, but little Susie had full access.

Weekend outings included the Del Mar Race Track in northern San Diego County, where "the turf meets the surf." The Bermans had box seats near Harry James and Betty Grable, each of whom owned thoroughbred horses.

Back in Vegas, Susan's father in the evenings would leave work to read to Susan before she fell asleep, and then he would return to the casino. He opened a casino house account in her name when she was just seven years old so she could go to a vacant room and order shrimp cocktails from room service. He also commissioned a portrait of her in pigtails that hung in the lobby of the Flamingo. Susan was a self-described tomboy, she wrote in *Lady Las Vegas*, a girl who was "short and scruffy" and "wore jeans, a Western shirt, and cowboy boots; my knees were always skinned, my nose was sunburned from living in the Flamingo Hotel pool." When Susan was nine, her parents took her on a five-day trip to New York City. They were met with a limousine and stayed at the Hampshire House on West Forty-seventh Street in the heart of Midtown Manhattan in the theatre district. They took in two Broadway shows, *Guys and Dolls* and *Wish You Were Here*. They went to Rumplemayer's on Central Park South for a Continental cuisine breakfast, and then shopped at Fifth Avenue's F.A.O. Schwartz where Susan's father bought her an expensive toy switchboard. It was during that trip that Susan fell in love with the City of Angels.

It was an unusual childhood, filled with celebrities. From the outside, she appeared to be spoiled.

Young Susie Berman lived in a world of privilege: the best schools, vacations to high-end Los Angeles hotels, meals at trendy, expensive restaurants, and tickets to shows with the best star entertainment the Las Vegas Strip had to offer. She was lavished with expensive toys and gifts from high rollers and famous clientele and possessed a name that afforded her deference in high society. Susan was born into Mafia royalty. Her father was, as she once wrote, "one of the founders of the Syndicate, a trusted partner of Meyer Lansky, Frank Costello, and Bugsy Siegel." Later, she would unabashedly called her family "the royal family of Las Vegas."

Susan loved her childhood. She didn't realize until later,

however, just how lucky she was. "The life (my father) gave my mother and me was glamorous, but it seemed ordinary to me," she wrote in *Lady Las Vegas*. "I lived with them, my dog Blackie, and intermittent middle-aged Jewish bodyguards my father referred to as 'best friends.'"

Her maternal grandmother, Florence, moved in and helped with chores and cooking, including preparing meals for mob associates who attended meetings at the Berman house. Susan's mother didn't cook or clean; a full-time housekeeper spent her days at the Berman house. After Grandmother Florence arrived, she took over the household, according to Susan's cousin, Tom Padden, Jr. "Florence was a domineering shrew who would often interrupt people before they got out a full sentence, so she could set the agenda. She had to have her way with just about everything. Betty (Gladys) was in the background."

Patrick Bailey, Susan's childhood friend, remembered Gladys as distant. "Toward me," he said, "she was aloof."

Bailey also recalled that Susan's mother was "a heavy smoker. She was tall and thin, and she used a long cigarette holder. It made her look more regal."

Susan remembered her childhood from the view of a starry-eyed twelve year old. During an interview for A&E network's *The Real Las Vegas: The Inside Story Behind America's Neon Oasis*, a documentary series Susan co-wrote and co-produced, she said, "There was an ebullience and exhilaration in the late 1940s and '50s. You were coming to Vegas. I knew everyone, and my dad owned it. You were coming to the center of the world, and it was terribly exciting."

Susan's mother, however, did not feel the same as Susan about their desert town. She became depressed and felt isolated. Susan's father sent his wife three times a week to

Los Angeles for treatment, which included shock treatments that left her mother unresponsive and reserved.

When Susan was ten, her mother had gotten better and she moved with Susan to an apartment in Westwood, California, so her mother could undergo therapy nearby. For the fifth grade, Susan enrolled at the Fairburn Elementary School on Overland Avenue. Her bodyguard Lou, who lived with the family in Los Angeles, walked Susan to and from school. When the school year broke for the summer, Susan returned to Las Vegas to be with her father. Her mother stayed behind to continue treatment.

Susan's father would plan get-togethers with kids from the casino. One childhood acquaintance was Bob Miller— Susan called him Bobby—who would go on to become a two-term Nevada governor. His father worked at the Riviera Hotel. It was in 1955 that Miller met Susan, shortly after Miller's family moved to the desert. His father was Ross Miller, a Chicago bookmaker said to be associated with the Outfit, who, with Davie Berman, ran the Riviera, which opened April 19, 1955. Twelve years later, in 1967, Riviera executives, including Ross, were indicted for skimming from the casino for the mob.

"We were young children together," Bob Miller said. "Our fathers were partners for a short while, in the 1950s. We were thrown together, as children, when our fathers would bring us to the casino and we would see each other. She remembered me more than I remembered her. But I remembered her father. I remembered his face. I knew that he was a partner with my dad. I honestly, unfortunately, didn't get to know Susan as well as I would have liked to."

He said they spoke about getting together. "We discussed on the phone several times what Las Vegas has become," Miller said. "We talked about getting together sometime to reminisce about what it was like when we were children. That never happened."

Susan recalled, in her book *Easy Street*, the outings with the children of her father's associates: "Every day, no matter what, my mother took me, in my early years, to the Flamingo pool, and then to the Riviera pool. . . . All the kids of the owners swam and dove in that long, blue pool all summer."

Susan contacted Miller while she worked on a TV special. It was the first time they had spoken since they were kids. "She did a telephonic interview of me [for an A&E documentary]," he said, "then sent a TV crew to interview me."

In her book, *Lady Las Vegas*, Susan described Miller. "He's Governor now," she wrote. "When I knew him he was tall, gangly Bobby Miller, my dad's partner Ross Miller's kid. . . . I didn't know Bobby well but I remember that he was a lifeguard by the pool and hung around the massage-parlor part of Mike Tulane's Health Club on the sixth floor of the Riv, with all the other owners' sons, hoping to get a glimpse of a showgirl coming out.

"Most people love him in town. They say he is totally committed to Las Vegas and will probably be a senator." After two terms as governor, however, Miller returned to practicing law in Las Vegas.

Susan often wrote about, and said in interviews, that her father started the first Jewish temple in Las Vegas so she could go to Sunday school and "the wiseguys would have a place to worship." The *shul* they attended was the Las Vegas Jewish Community Center, at Thirteenth Street and Carson Avenue, seven blocks from the Berman home. Also attending regular services at the synagogue was Hank Greenspun, an influential Las Vegas newspaper publisher.

"(My dad) built it for me," Susan would say. She once wrote that her father was "a Jewish role model" and "extremely proud of being Jewish. He felt that for a Jewish child to be properly brought up, there must be a synagogue, a rabbi, and a cantor in evidence."

In fact, it was not Davie Berman who built the temple. It was a group of twenty-five families who founded the temple, and the Bermans weren't one of them. If Davie Berman was involved, no one alive today remembers. "As far as I remember while I was on the board, he had nothing to do with it," said original board member Charles Salton. "I knew who he was. He was one of the boys on the Strip. But he did not have anything to do with starting the Temple."

In 1931, a group of people began worshiping behind a store, explained Sandy Mallin, past president of the board of directors of Temple Beth Shalom. "In the early '40s, they met in the rectory of the Catholic Church downtown at Bridger and Second Street," Mallin said. "In 1944 and 1945, they began raising money for a temple. In 1946, the temple opened at Thirteenth Street and Carson Avenue." It was Las Vegas's first Jewish temple and the second in the state, Mallin said.

Las Vegan Adele Baratz also remembered how the temple got started. "The Bermans came to town after the temple was organized," she said. "So did Hank Greenspun [publisher of the *Las Vegas Sun*]. They all were members. The original people who were behind it, Nate Mack, Harry Mack, and Louie Mack, got it off the ground. Davie Berman may have attended temple, but he wasn't a founder. He could have given money. The way it got started was that the Macks decided they wanted a temple. They went around to the Jewish people who lived here, in the 1940s. They asked if they would pledge so much, but [the founders] didn't want it right away. As soon as they started building the temple, they collected on the pledges. This was at Thirteenth Street and Carson, around 1945. It was called the Las Vegas Jewish Community Center. When it moved to Oakey, in 1956, it was called Temple Beth Shalom. My brother, Charles Salton, is the oldest living member of the Temple. I don't think there's anybody else here who's been a member since it started. Most Jewish people who moved to the town went to the temple to meet people. It started out as the Sons and Daughters of Israel. They'd have parties for some of the holidays."

After the temple moved to the Oakey location, Susan wrote in *Lady Las Vegas*, her father took her to the Friday night services.

Temple Beth Shalom moved in 1999 to Summerlin, a planned community in northwest Las Vegas, after selling its Oakey location to a Christian Church.

Ruthie Bartnof, a former Las Vegan and a close friend to Susan, said it was her understanding that Davie contributed money for the synagogue, quietly and behind the scenes. After Susan's murder and Ruthie's son's death six months later, Ruthie had a plaque installed for them at Temple Beth Shalom's new location.

"I went to the temple and put a plaque up in their names," Ruthie said. "That was their hometown. Davie was one of the founders. All those casino people contributed big money. Susan went to temple with me in Los Angeles. She followed the Jewish laws. Her mother wasn't Jewish, but her father was. I think it brought her closer to him."

Susan's first-class life in the desert opulence abruptly ended when her father died in 1957, then again with her mother's death eighteen months later. The home Susan had experienced so much happiness in was sold to a man named

Ellis Johnson and his wife Alline (today the house serves as a law office).

"To me," Susan wrote about her late father in *Easy Street*, "this is a story of a father who was a gangster, not a gangster who was a father."

Even knowing what she knew as an adult, Susan still saw her father through the eyes of a little girl. She adored him as a child, overlooking his faults, and continued to do so as an adult. Susan's father had dark hair, was 5 feet, 10 inches tall, weighed 165 pounds, but to Susan, he was larger than life, a giant of a man in her eyes. Now he was gone. For the rest of her life, Susan would be told how much she resembled her father.

During Gladys Berman's last year of life, when she was gravely ill and had another mental breakdown after which she was institutionalized, she sent Susan to Chadwick School on the Palos Verdes Peninsula in southern California. Judy Garland's daughter, Liza Minelli, was one year behind Susan.

"Everybody at Chadwick was the son or daughter of somebody famous," Susan wrote in *Easy Street*.

Susan *hated* Chadwick and later wrote in her autobiography, "Never had so many young egos joined under one roof." The only friend she made was Susan Amateau, daughter of Hollywood television writer and director Rod Amateau. "I stayed in my dorm room most days to avoid the sun and wrote," Susan said in *Easy Street*. Until she befriended Susan Amateau.

"I thought Susan (Amateau) was the most intelligent person I had ever met," Susan Berman wrote. "She read Shakespeare, used big words, and wrote poetry. She was the leader of the Bohemian crowd and I was terribly honored to be her friend. She called me Bermouse, because I was so silent, and included me in early morning poetry readings on the lawn."

Dean Martin's daughters Claudia and Gail lived in Susan's dorm. Yul Brynner's son Rock was in Susan's French class. And Jann Wenner, founder of *Rolling Stone* magazine, was editor of the school newspaper and president of the eighth grade. Susan's celebrity prep school also included on its roster of alums Robert Towne, Brandon Lee, and Mike Lookinland (of TV's "Brady Bunch"). The school was immortalized in the book and made-for-TV movie *Mommie Dearest* where Joan Crawford's daughter Christina attended with unhappy results.

After Susan's mother suffered a series of nervous breakdowns, Gladys Berman passed away while staying at a rest home in Los Angeles. The official cause of death was "suicide by drug overdose." Susan, along with family friends and relatives, believed until her own death that her mother was killed to prevent her from inheriting her husband's share in Las Vegas hotels.

After her mother's death, Susan lived, while on boarding-school breaks, with her Uncle Chickie, his wife Marge and cousins Dave and Donna. With his brother gone, Chickie was no longer a part of the Las Vegas mob scene. Chickie was given monthly stipends to support Susan from Davie Berman's interests in several Las Vegas hotels, according to Chickie's son Dave Berman, and tried to raise Susan in the opulent manner in which she had been accustomed. But Chickie gambled most of it away. "It was the only money my father had coming in at the time," Dave said.

With the stipend, Chickie was able to pay tuition for Susan to continue at the Chadwick boarding school, where her cousin Donna joined her. But the girls didn't get along. After a year, Susan transferred to St. Helen's Hall, an expensive Episcopal preparatory boarding school in Portland, Oregon, paid for by her trust. "Dad separated Susan and Donna," said her cousin Dave, whom Susan referred to as Davy. During holidays and summer breaks from school, Susan enjoyed horseback riding on her uncle's Lewiston property. Dave and Donna had horses of there own. When Susan moved in, her uncle bought her a purebred quarter horse cross.

"He was an older horse who was broke," Dave said. "He wasn't too much for her to handle. Susan was familiar with riding because she rode horses in Las Vegas." She and Dave often rode together, when Dave was home, on the family's seven-and-a-half-acre property, which had two long pastures, a corral in front of the barn, and a swimming pool.

It was at St. Helen's Hall that Susan began to learn of her father's mob activities. She read, over a boy's shoulder, a *Los Angeles Times* article about Gus Greenbaum's gangland-style murder. The paper reported that, on December 3rd, 1958, police discovered Greenbaum dead in his own bed, his throat cut completely through so that his head nearly fell off.

Down the hallway from Greenbaum's body, in a different bedroom, officers found Greenbaum's wife, her throat fatally cut as well. The wife had been knocked out with a heavy bottle which caved in the right side of her eye. Newspapers were piled around her to keep the blood from staining the carpet. Whoever killed the Greenbaums did not want it to be messy

Susan's classmate told her, "The gangsters, they run Las Vegas and kill each other and the way you know if you're going to die is they put a picture of a black hand on your bed."

The thought terrified Susan.

🖋 For the rest of Susan's life, the desert—the good *and* the bad—haunted her. She especially would feel robbed of the good life she'd felt was her birthright and one she'd been spoiled with as a child. She never got over losing her parents and being yanked out of the Las Vegas childhood she had so enjoyed. It would carry over into her later work as a journalist, author, and screenwriter. For the rest of her life, she would miss her father. She sought solace in a surrogate figure, a young man named Bobby Durst, whom she would meet during her college years who would become a big brother to her—a best friend—and would play a large role in her life.

Susan was haunted not only by her childhood and the void of not having parents, but by Las Vegas itself.

"The man I grew up with in Las Vegas adored the town, loved the town," Susan said during her A&E network interview. "I often looked at Las Vegas as an older sibling I had to compete with. All I know is, every morning she woke up and said, 'It's 80 degrees outside. How bad can it be?'"

In *Lady Las Vegas*, Susan wrote: "In the beginning, I adored her, that Lady Las Vegas, my fantastic, world-famous, older sister—who could ever compare? Even though my father, the famed Las Vegas hotel-casino pioneer Davie Berman, had her just one year before my birth; she had 40 years of sophistication, glamour and class on me. As I grew up, I began to envy her. Did my dad like her better, prefer her? She intrigued him, magnetized his interest, and earned his constant praise."

One summer, while still in high school, Susan's Uncle sent her to the prestigious Montecito-Sequoia Camp for Girls. While there, she befriended Julie Nixon, who played a lead with Susan in the camp production of *Little Women*. Susan also went to Camp Solomon Schechter in the Pacific

Northwest on Whidbey Island. That's where she met friend Anita Pinchev Dash. "We were roommates together for over six weeks and constant companions throughout the day," said Anita, who went on to sell real estate before going to work in the entertainment production business. They hung out together two summers in a row. "We were best friends. I was thirteen when we met, and she was one year older. We sent each other letters in between the first and second camps. We were roommates both years." The island, Anita said, was a beautiful setting for camp, which was sponsored by the Synagogues in Portland, Seattle and Vancouver, British Columbia.

Despite the setting, Susan still grieved the loss of her parents. "She used to cry at night in her sleep, like a puppy, and I'd go over and comfort her. She was very innocent. She liked to have the light on at night." In their cabin, "She was always looking out the windows and closing the blinds. She hung things from the door handle so if anybody tried to get in, she could hear them. She was paranoid. Just before camp, someone tried to get me in a car from a bus stop. I told her about it. She said someone tried to get her too.

"I met her a year after her mother had died. She told me that her mom was killed by the same people who killed her dad. She would start out saying, 'If you don't tell anyone, I'll tell you this.' I always figured she wasn't telling me the truth."

At camp, when Anita's parents sent letters, Susan asked to read them. "She didn't get letters from home. I was always afraid to talk about her parents, because sometimes she looked like she was about to explode crying. She had pent-up energy. The fact that she didn't have parents was sad. I tried to talk about other things."

After camp ended, Susan went home with Anita. By

that time, Susan had learned while in high school even more details about who her father worked for. Susan was sick at the end of camp, Anita said: "My mother told her, 'Sweetie, if you're not feeling well, just come home with us.' She stayed with us four or five days. My parents took her to a doctor. She had a touch of pneumonia. In the car, she told my parents that her father was in the mob and that she had lived at the Flamingo Hotel."

Even then, Susan was picky about the environment she stayed in. "Before she came to my house, she asked me if I had cats," Anita recalled. "She hated them. She could have been allergic."

Susan, despite her eccentricities, was difficult to forget. "She would bring people into intense conversations, as intense as you can be when you're fourteen. She had a quick way of ending sentences, and it was usually funny. She had a great personality. She would be the loudest one cheering and singing. I thought about her all my adult life."

And while Susan was still a child in many ways, "She had an air about her," Anita remembered.

Years later, they ran into each other. By then, Anita lived in Palmdale, California, and Susan lived in L.A. Susan immediately recognized Anita in the lobby of The Beverly Hilton. "I was with a friend. She walked up to me and said, 'Are you Anita?' We talked about camp, and she told me she'd gotten her master's degree, and then she went to New York. I told her what I was doing. We didn't have anything else to talk about after that. She asked if my parents were alive. I told her they weren't. I got her phone number, she got mine, and we never called each other."

Nothing was too good for Davie Berman's daughter, as Anita learned about her friend. Susan, in her father's absence, pampered herself. When she moved to Manhattan, she rented a studio on Beekman Place, an exclusive street in Manhattan's Midtown East. All she could afford at the time was a postage-stamp-sized studio, but she was determined to live there.

Back in L.A., after the live-in relationship with Paul Kaufman ended and Susan lost her house in Brentwood, she moved to Hollywood. It was meant to be temporary until she got back on her feet. Actress and singer Barbara McNair, with whom Susan was friends, lent Susan an apartment at no charge.

It was a generous offering. The unit had one bedroom, one-and-a-half baths, and a den. Mella used the den as her bedroom. It was located on Alta Loma Road in West Hollywood just off the famed Sunset Strip. The unit was at the Park Wellington Hotel, which had been converted to apartments and condos. Alta Loma suited Susan just fine. With its twenty-four-hour doorman, it was in keeping with her penchant for living in trendy, high-end neighborhoods. Alta Loma Road, just west of La Cienega Boulevard between Holloway Drive and Sunset Boulevard, is an exclusive celebrity-filled cul-de-sac that's just a block long.

Susan relayed a story to her cousin Tom Padden, Jr. about a trip to Sunset Boulevard to a store to pick up a barbecue dinner. "She walked to the corner market and there was a guy with a gun holding up the place," Tom said. "He told Susan to move to the side. She said, 'Get out of my way. I want my barbecued chicken.' She grabbed the chicken and walked out of the store. She really was fearless in some ways. She would tell that story and laugh."

"I remember the place on Alta Loma," said Dave Berman, Susan's first cousin. "She let me know she was living there for free. She said a friend offered it to her. She wasn't ashamed of living rent-free."

While in the apartment building's Jacuzzi one evening, Susan and Mella met Kevin Norte, an attorney who lived across the hallway from them. "She introduced the girl as her daughter," Kevin said.

Susan also befriended a sports agent, Norby Walters, who lived on Alta Loma too. She mentioned to friends that the two hit it off. Ironically, Walters at one point was alleged to be an associate of Michael Farnese, a known member of the Colombo crime family. Walters was sent to prison after his conviction in 1988 of fraud and racketeering because of signing college players to pro teams before their eligibilities expired.

Nyle Brenner lived in an apartment complex across the street from Susan. He walked his dogs on Alta Loma, as did Susan. She and Nyle often saw each other outside, and eventually the two spoke. A year later, Nyle became Susan's unofficial manager for whatever she needed done. He ran a small talent agency out of his home, and Susan was the only writer he represented.

Nyle may have been Susan's business manager, but he was not her literary agent, according to Norte. "She talked about Norby Walters as an agent," he noted. "She only mentioned Nyle once or twice, saying just that he was her manager."

While Susan preferred living in high-end neighborhoods, it didn't appear to be out of her wanting to impress friends. She never entertained. Those days ended when she left Beekman Place in New York. It was as if she'd wanted to live in upper-crust neighborhoods for the sake of having the address as a status symbol, not because she wanted to show off her home to visitors.

"We would invite her over for our Christmas parties," said Kevin, who lived at Park Wellington with Don Norton, his lifetime partner. "She would become the life of the party because she would tell her mob stories about old Las Vegas. It was always the same stories, about Frank Sinatra and Liberace at her birthday parties, but in front of a different group of people at each party."

For five years, Susan lived rent free with Mella in Apartment 117. When Susan left the place in disrepair, she and McNair, who passed away from cancer in 2007, had a falling out and never spoke again. Susan moved to the Benedict Canyon house. The homes was ironically just two miles from where her father's partner, Benjamin "Bugsy" Siegel, was murdered in 1947 in a Moorish-style Beverly Hills house rented by Virginia Hill, at 810 Linden Drive. Some have said Siegel's associates, including Davie Berman, ordered the hit. After Siegel's murder, newspaper reporters following the case wrote that Siegel "had an arrest record like a village phone book." It was front-page news across America. Nine bullets were fired from a 30-caliber Army carbine.

Vegas was a small town when Ben Siegel first rolled into the desert in the 1940s and started the Flamingo, with Meyer Lansky and Lucky Luciano's money. To run the Flamingo, Siegel had three partners: Moe Segway, Davie Berman, and Solly Sollaway.

Gangsters built Vegas in the real world and ran it until the FBI ran them out in the 1970s and '80s. It was a world Susie knew from the inside. Susan Berman was a mob princess in her childhood, with the Flamingo Hotel as her playground. Before he worked at the Flamingo, Davie ran the Plaza Hotel and Casino. When it was purchased by Benny Binion, Davie went to work with Bugsy at the Flamingo.

Siegel once described the Flamingo to a reporter as "the

goddamn biggest, fanciest gaming casino and hotel you bastards ever seen in your whole lives."

The Bermans lived a first-class existence. Theirs was the lifestyle of old, moneyed Las Vegas, the type of life portrayed in Universal Pictures' hit movie *Casino*, based on the life of Frank "Lefty" Rosenthal and the *Godfather*, which included passages about Vegas. Davie Berman coddled and protected his daughter from knowledge of his gangster life. Even Susan's mother in the early days believed her husband was simply a hotel manager. "Betty knew nothing about what Davie did," said Susan's cousin, Tom Padden, who followed the Bermans to Las Vegas to work for Davie at the Las Vegas Club. "Everybody else knew, so Betty eventually did too."

For Susan, it was not until years later that she learned the truth about what really went on behind her family's life in the desert. She would later spin her childhood tales of hobnobbing with Mafia players and high-rolling gamblers into a series of successful books and documentaries. Davie Berman couldn't do enough for his daughter. For her eighth birthday, he gave her a vintage slot machine stocked with nickels. As her school schedule allowed, he took her to work with him. It was almost as if he'd known that his days were numbered. He wanted to spend as much time with her as he could—and he did. Susie was constantly by his side, both in and out of the casinos. Employees took care of her while her father worked, taking her to the gift store and buying her whatever she wanted.

In those days, Davie was called the "ambassador of gambling." He worked in the pit overseeing the tables where hanging out were entertainers Jack Benny and Jimmy Durante, producer Harry Cohn, prominent businessmen, foreign dignitaries, and Las Vegas's highest rollers. Susan walked beside her father, a man who was forceful and feared, unknowingly living in a world that was dangerous and violent. The family didn't have a bank account; they paid cash for everything, and the money seemed endless. Davie Berman neither gambled nor drank. He invariably wore expensive pinstriped suits and Zizane, a French cologne. Hanging from his pocket was a ruby mezuzah on a gold chain. Davie greeted customers by their first names, making them feel welcome and at home in his joints. He was a respectable gangster casino operator. He drove a fancy new Cadillac. To his Susie, he was the world. To her cousin Tom Padden, he was family. And he was his boss. "He was a generous man."

What Susan did not know was that when mob families were feuding, her family was in danger. During mob unrest, Davie piloted Susan and her mother away to Los Angeles, flying out of McCarran Field to the Los Angeles airport, to the Beverly Wilshire Hotel for two or three days. He told Susan they were "short vacations." Bodyguard Lou Raskin lived with the Bermans in their house and traveled with them. Davie sometimes stayed home. With Raskin and Susan out of town, Davie often asked Tom Padden, Jr., Gladys' first cousin, to stay at the Berman home to watch over it while Davie worked at the hotel-casino. "He asked me to stay at the house," Padden said, adding that, even though Susan was away, Davie's enemies didn't know that.

"He was afraid someone was going to come in and kidnap little Susan. The routine was he would call from the casino and say he was coming home. I'd be waiting at the door with a pistol as he drove up, in case he was followed." As time went on, the pressure would become too much for Gladys. She became more withdrawn as time went on.

Susie, on the other hand, unaware of the danger at home, remembered the L.A. trips as wonderful outings.

Her mother, Lou, and Susie took off from the then-small Las Vegas airport. She'd run across the tarmac to the steps leading to the cabin. She'd sit by the window and chatter all about her own plans for L.A. A car waited at the airport to take them to their hotel.

She ordered coffee ice cream from MFK's drug store, delivered to their hotel room. During a shopping outing in Beverly Hills, Susie sipped from the lemonade tree at Uncle Bernie's Toy Menagerie on Rodeo Drive.

After a couple of days out of town, her father would "reappear," as Susan called it, and treat them to dinner at the famous Brown Derby. "We'd sit under Ingrid Berman's picture," Susan recalled. Susie sat on a red-leather booster seat so she was high enough to join in on the conversation at the table.

Susan's mother often told her, "If anyone asks if you're Davie Berman's daughter, say, 'No.' Run, scream for Lou, yell, use whatever you have to do to get away. You go nowhere with no one.'" Susan told A&E network, "It was almost an obnoxious drill to a kid, I heard it so many times." Lou, her personal security guard, was a large man her father hired to watch over his daughter. "Lou was always seated in the front room," Susan said. "I don't know if my father would have considered him a bodyguard, but he was basically my gin (rummy) partner. I was playing gin and beating him from the time I was three, and I thought that was his sole purpose."

Gladys Berman's worst nightmare, that her daughter would be kidnapped, became a reality in 1955 when Susan was ten. She was in front of the Fifth Street School, where she was enrolled, when a middle-aged man dragged a kicking and screaming Susan into a waiting car. He tossed Susan onto the back seat of the sedan with a bunch of comic books. Susan wrote the following in *Easy Street* about her abduction: "He [the man] had only driven a block when I hit him in the face and jumped out of the car yelling all the way. Two policemen heard me and brought me home. It was a blow my mother's friends say she never recovered from. There was no evidence it was a mob kidnapping; it could have been a crank or a pervert. But it happened to be a time of mob tension. My mother was convinced that I had just escaped death."

The kidnapper no doubt would have faced a death sentence had he been caught by Susan's father. A reporter once said that Davie Berman was "so tough he could kill a man with one hand tied behind his back." And an FBI file described Berman as "a trained killer" and a "stick-up man." Davie Berman had a notorious reputation in law enforcement circles because of his involvement in the kidnapping of a mob bootlegger and bank robbing spree in New York during Prohibition in the 1920s.

Susan's maternal grandmother, Florence, moved in and helped Gladys with cooking and chores. Her grandmother was a big influence on Susan, according to her cousin Tom Padden III. "Florence was a domineering person. She had to have her way with just about everything. Susan's mother was in the background."

It was a more than colorful life for a child. But Susan's parents went to great extremes to shelter their daughter from the seedy side of that life. The notorious Davie Berman was not the man Susan knew as a father. Davie was devoted to his family, and he made certain that his daughter was kept unaware of his unlawful enterprises. They sheltered her and spoiled her at the same time. Her being spoiled showed in tantrums she would sometimes have. Tom Padden, III often accompanied Davie to work, including on the days he'd take his daughter along. "Susan used to have big tantrums with her dad," Tom said. "Davie would be driving along with Susan sitting in the front seat, in the middle with me on the passenger side. She'd ask for something and Davie would say, 'We can't do that now,' and Susan would kick his legs and cry."

Susan's best childhood friend during her Las Vegas days was Patrick Bailey. "Did I consider Susan one of my best friends?" Patrick asked. "For a good part of my childhood, she was my only friend, certainly the closest in geographic proximity. The property immediately south of Susan's house was an orchard filled with fruit trees and owned by Old Lady Underhill, who lived in a house just north of the Berman's." Patrick lived at 711 South Sixth Street, just three houses north of Susan's.

The Carson family bought the orchard property and built a house on it. "Their nephew, Ronnie, was my age, and we became friends," Patrick said. "This was about the time Susan was kidnapped, and she became even more removed from sight. But her door was always open to me."

Besides time spent with Patrick, Susan's childhood was also spent around famous entertainers. Her father arranged for Elvis Presley and Liberace to sing at her birthday parties.

And there were other performers in her life. For a young girl, it was a fairy-tale existence.

"There were a few entertainers my father absolutely adored," Susan told A&E. "Danny Thomas, Jack Benny, Jimmy Durante. They were always over at our house, or we were talking to them [at the hotel]. In fact, my father had a silver dollar made. One side was a silver dollar and the other side said his name in Hebraic script, and he gave one to Jack Benny. He wore one, and he also gave one to Durante, who wasn't Jewish, but [Durante] wore it as a sign of interfaith or something."

Other top stars who played the Flamingo were the Ritz Brothers, the Andrew Sisters, Tony Martin, Frankie Lane, Kay Starr, Sophie Tucker, Spike Jones, Ken Murray and the Blackouts, Dean Martin and Jerry Lewis, Peggy Lee, Xavier Cugat, Ben Blue, the Mills Brothers, and the Ink Spots. And Susie Berman knew them all.

Susan preferred afternoons spent in the showroom watching the chorus line rehearse at her father's Flamingo Hotel over playing with her classmates from the Fifth Street School a block from her house. She often played dress-up backstage with the showgirls' costumes or swam in the Flamingo's pool. In the afternoons she took private dance lessons from Nancy Williams, a popular showgirl at the El Rancho. At home, she'd play the piano and sing "Sunny Side of the Street." When she told her father she wanted to be a chorus girl when she grew up, he told her, "You're too smart to be one. You're going to college."

"As soon as school was out," Susan wrote in *Easy Street*, "summer became The Pool. Every day, no matter what, my mother took me, in my early years, to the Flamingo pool, and then to the Riviera pool. My entire summer wardrobe was two bathing suits ('Hang the wet one in the bathroom, Susie') and a flowered swimming cap." Susan would jump from the high diving board. But, first, she'd holler from the high dive to the pool below, "Look at me, look at me!"

"Our mothers drank ice tea with a slice of orange and lemon on a toothpick in it," Susan wrote in her autobiography. "We swam laps, did back dives, frolicked in the water, and upset hotel guests, whom we laughed at because they burned so badly."

On Halloween, Susan couldn't go house to house like the other kids did. It was too risky. Patrick remember one Halloween in particular. It was 1953. "The City of Las Vegas usually decreed that we kids go trick-or-treating on October 30 as well as the 31st," Pat said. That year, however, Susan's mother, Gladys, hadn't read about it in the newspaper and was surprised when children knocked on her door the day before Halloween. She was unprepared.

"When my group of goblins from school rang their bell and said, 'Trick or treat,' Gladys appeared flustered. 'You children are a day early! I have no treats in the house,'" she told them. He and his friends returned the next night and "treats were in abundance" at the Berman house, Pat said.

On weekends in his spare time, if he wasn't golfing, Susan's father took her and her mother to the new floor shows that opened at the Flamingo every two weeks.

"My favorite second act was the Apache dance team," Susan wrote in *Easy Street*. "My father's favorite chorus line was 'Sioux City Sue.' He never missed a performance of a new rendition of that song and I used to wonder then why he liked it so much."

Susan's mother was engaged in her life, but aloof at the same time, Pat said. "She hardly ever spoke or smiled," he explained, "but she always offered Susie and me a glass of water or some cookies, baked by their cook. She was coolly cordial."

Susan lived in Las Vegas when the first atomic bomb was detonated for testing in January 1951, seventy miles northeast of town. Susie was just five, but she remembered it well. The blasts were offered up by the casinos and Feds as an evening of entertainment.

"The *Las Vegas Sun* ran articles, and also the *Review-Journal*, on how to treat your collectibles during the blast," Susan told A&E. "It was never thought it could hurt people."

According to their accounts, "Atomic dust fallout posed the biggest danger to your vases," she said.

Susan's father stressed education for his only child. She had vivid memories of her father teaching her math in the casino's famous counting room, using dice first, when she was three, then as she got older, coins and cards.

As a counting lesson, Davie divided the money this way: so much for her father, so much for the government, and so much for La Cosa Nostra boss Meyer Lansky. Susan unwittingly learned the ways—and the skimming habits her father practiced—of the underworld players. Skimming cash off the top was a way for casino operators to pocket tax-free profits from the daily takes.

"The skimming—of course, it was a crime, but it wasn't a crime like having to kill people. In their minds, they cheated the government," Susan told A&E.

"I was in the famous counting room, and I saw them go, 'Three for us, one for the government, and two for Meyer.' I helped them count the bills. My father taught me to count basically on dice, when I was very little, two or three, and on cards."

Not for one moment did Susie suspect that this doting father, thoughtful employer, and star citizen could possibly have been instrumental in running Murder, Inc. in Las Vegas for out-of-town mob bosses. Nor did any other family members question his activities. The generous Davie regularly distributed money to his unsuspecting relatives, paying particular attention to his aging parents and his sister, Lillian Berman Minter. When Lillian married, Davie footed the bill for the extravagant wedding. Susan never forgot the fairytale wedding and dreamed of growing up and having the same lavish ceremony.

It would not be until Susan attended college that the truth sunk in about her father and his lifetime association with the underworld.

Susan Berman's high-class, story-book life was shattered—and the glitz and glamour along with it—when her father's heart failed during surgery two days before Father's Day, on June 18, 1957.

Davie Berman had been admitted to the Rose De Lima Hospital in Henderson, an outlying suburban city southeast of Las Vegas, during a surgical procedure to remove a polyp from Davie's colon. According to the death certificate, he died an hour into the surgery from coronary thrombosis.

Davie always told Susie, "Nothing can hurt you. You're my girl." Now that he was gone, who would protect her? Her mentally ill mother, who for years had been in and out of a mental hospital? Her mother had been absent emotionally to Susan for several years. Susan was devastated, and she was alone.

A cloud washed over Susan's happy childhood. The rich Vegas lifestyle—and her security—slipped away along with the death of her father. Life as she knew it would never be the same.

A month to the day, on May 18th, before Davie Berman's death, her parents threw her a lavish twelfth birthday party at the Riviera Hotel. It was a night to remember and one Susan would recount many years later. Liberace sang "Happy Birthday" to her. To produce friends for the party, Davie compiled a list of children of other Las Vegas hotel executives and owners, kids Susan barely knew. Her father wanted to fill her party with boys and girls her own age, to make her happy. Susan's mother handled the details of the event—party favors, the cake, and the invitations. Patrick Bailey, Susan's neighbor and classmate, was Susan's age. He felt lucky to have ridden in the limousine with Susan to the Riviera for the party, and to previous parties as well. "At one of Susie's birthday parties, limos took us out to the Flamingo to see Spike Jones," said Patrick, referring to the flamboyant musician and bandleader who performed for Susan.

A month later, Patrick's mother read in the *Las Vegas Sun* that Davie Berman had died. She told her son about it. Davie's funeral was scheduled for the next day.

"It was summer, there was no school, and that meant I'd be spending at least a couple hours at the municipal swimming pool over on Bonanza," Patrick said. "It was a ten- to fifteen-minute bike ride from my house. When I got out of the pool, for some reason I can't remember why, I decided to forego my usual post-swim visit to the City Library on Mesquite so I could at least sign the guest book." He hopped on his bike and, wearing damp shorts because his swim trunks were under his shorts, he pedaled to the funeral home to attend Davie Berman's viewing.

"Signing the guest book was an important thing to do, according to my mom," Patrick said. "I parked my bike on the sidewalk at Bunkers Mortuary. There were two large men I didn't recognize who eyed me suspiciously but didn't say anything to me when I went in. I was wearing shorts and a T-shirt and tennis shoes—not quite kosher attire for such a setting."

Another gangster assessed Patrick, but he didn't say anything to Patrick either.

"I was aware of my appearance, and I figured maybe I really was over the line, but then an even *larger* man, whom I recognized as one of Susan's 'uncles,' said to one of his associates, "No, that's Pat. He's a friend of Susie's. He's okay."

Then to Pat, the man, who was Lou Raskin, Susan's bodyguard, said, "You here to see Mr. Berman, Pat?"

Patrick nodded, and Lou, with his arm on Pat's shoulder, escorted him into the viewing room.

"I had seen this man playing poker, blackjack, and gin with Susan and me, laughing and having all the appearance of really enjoying himself. Now, he was absolutely the most desolate man I had ever seen. Seeing Davie was sad, but seeing this man still alive but with a crushed spirit was even more sad."

The door to the viewing room was closed except for entering and leaving. "I remember it was distinctly cooler in there than it was in the rest of the mortuary, because they didn't embalm Davie's body."

Patrick peered into the casket.

"It was the first time I'd ever seen a Jewish man with all the accouterments—*tallis, tefillin*—and laid out for burial. I can still see it in my mind. After a few seconds, I asked if I could sign the guest book. My escort said, "Sure you can, Pat.""

Patrick signed the book and left the mortuary. He had not seen Susan for two days, when they saw each other on their street. As he left the mortuary, "Susie was coming in, and that's when I last spoke with her, trying to say how sorry I was," Pat said. "She was pretty much out of it, in tears, and deeply in denial that her daddy was gone. She was surrounded by her 'uncles,' and I don't think she was able to hear me through her crying.

"I never saw her again."

At the service the next day, Susan's Uncle Chickie held her in his arms and told her, "Susie, cry now, not later. You're going to have to be tough to survive."

"It was 1957 and I was twelve," Susan later wrote. "They said it was the largest funeral Las Vegas had ever seen. There were thousands of mourners."

Before the service began, Nick the Greek, the famed odds maker, and associates Susan described as "squat Jewish men" surrounded Susie and her Uncle Chickie inside the mortuary saying, "We don't expect trouble."

Davie Berman's funeral turned out to be peaceful. Susan was right; it was, at the time, the largest ever in Las Vegas. Berman, dead at fifty-four, lay in an open casket. Susan, not yet out of grade school, stood stoic next to her beloved father's casket, alongside mourners in the crime syndicate's royal family. As the service ended, Susie broke down.

"I cried for the life I would know no more," she later explained, "cried for my father who would not live to see his only child grow up, and cried most of all because I forgot to tell him I loved him, and now it was much too late."

Then Susan tried to climb into the casket to drape herself over her father's lifeless body. The pallbearers stopped her.

In *Lady Las Vegas*, Susan wrote that her father's death caused her to despise Las Vegas. "By the age of twelve," she wrote, "I hated her [Las Vegas] with every fiber of my being and I held her responsible for the terrible tragedy that befell my family and orphaned me."

Davie's partners and associates served as pallbearers. They included people like racketeer Gus Greenbaum, later decapitated; convicted extortionist Willie "the Ice Pick" Alderman (also known as "Little Auldie" and "Izzie Tump Tump") who eventually died serving time in Terminal Island on a mob extortion rap; gambler Nick "The Greek" Dandolos, a famed odds maker; and Davie's business partner Joe "Bowser" Rosenberg, known as Davie's onetime mouthpiece.

Susan wrote about what happened next.

"After my father's death," she wrote, "the whole town [Las Vegas] went crazy. First they thought he had been murdered. One man told me, 'There was an emergency meeting of all of us. When we heard Davie went down, we were furious. If some bastard had killed him we planned to murder him and his family for this. Nobody could kill Davie Berman and get away with it. He belonged to us. He was our mainstay here, he was number one. It was a bad time for us, real bad, I remember that day, men I had never seen shed a tear were crying. In our business we don't really love each other, but we all loved Davie.'"

During the funeral, Rabbi Arthur Leibowitz told mourners, "It is a sad day for all of Las Vegas. Davie Berman, one of our original pioneers who made this city bloom, is dead. There will never be anyone like him. Davie Berman had a vision. He saw a boom town where others had just seen desert. He was Mr. Las Vegas. Davie Berman, beloved by all of Las Vegas, beloved husband, and beloved father, is gone."

Years later her father's friends told her, "Davie, boy, was he crazy about you!"

After the service, mourners grabbed Susie, kissed her, and told her, "Susie, your dad was the greatest gangster that ever lived. You can hold your head up high." It would mark the first time Susie would hear her father referred to as a gangster. Another mourner told her, "Your dad was a stand-up guy."

She didn't know then that "stand-up guy" meant someone who would not crack under pressure, someone who would not rat out his friends.

The men's words would haunt Susan for the rest of her days. She would spend her life writing about Las Vegas and researching her father's ties to the Mafia.

Susan's world instantly unraveled. It would never be the same again, not without her precious daddy.

The day after Davie's death, obituaries ran on the front page of the *Deseret News* in Utah, the *Las Vegas Sun* and the

*Las Vegas Review-Journal* in Nevada and inside the pages of the *Los Angeles Times* in California. In the June 19th edition of the *Los Angeles Times*, the obit was headlined "Las Vegas Hotel Man Dave Berman, 53, Dies." It read:

*David (Dave) Berman, 53, Las Vegas hotel-man and one of the principal owners of the Riviera Hotel there, died yesterday morning after surgery in Rose de Lima Hospital, Henderson, Nev. Mr. Berman had been ill only a week.*

*Funeral services will be conducted in Las Vegas at 11 a.m. today and a memorial service will be conducted in Los Angeles at 2 p.m. tomorrow in the Home of Peace Mausoleum Chapel.*

*Mr. Berman was active in the Nevada hotel business for many years and was (in) the group that owned and operated the Flamingo Hotel in Las Vegas prior to his connection with the Riviera.*

*He leaves a widow, Gladys, and daughter, Susan, 12, of Las Vegas.*

And on the same day, the *Las Vegas Sun* ran its own front-page obituary:

*Funeral Rites Here Today For Dave Berman, 53 Funeral services will be conducted at Bunker Bros. Mortuary at 11 a.m. today for Dave Berman, 53, one of the pioneers in the Las Vegas casino business, who died of a heart attack yesterday at Rose de Lima Hospital where he was recovering from a glandular operation.*

*Berman was one of the active owners and operators at the Riviera Hotel where he was associated with Gus Greenbaum, Benny Goffstein, Joe Rosenberg, and Willie Alderman. Moving from the Flamingo to the Riviera, Berman and his associates took over the floundering hotel and made an outstanding success of the venture.*

*Following the local services to be conducted by Rabbi Arthur B. Leibowitz, Berman's body will be sent to Los*

Angeles where services will be held at 2 p.m. tomorrow at the Home of Peace in Boyle Heights. He is survived by his wife, Gladys, his twelve-year-old daughter Susan, his brother Charles Berman of Lewiston, Idaho, and sister Mrs. Maurice Minter, of Minneapolis, Minn.

Berman entered the Henderson hospital last Wednesday for major surgery and was making a satisfactory recovery at the time of the heart attack. Doctors said that there was no connection between the heart condition and the surgery. He succumbed about 7 a.m. yesterday.

Berman was well known for his philanthropies—many of them performed anonymously—came to light later only by accident. One of them, for example, was the little known occasion when Berman won a luxurious Cadillac after buying many $100 tickets on a Variety Club drawing. He refused to accept the car, telling the officers to sell the Cadillac and put the money in the club to help handicapped children. He was always willing to help out charitable organizations. In addition to being a member of the Variety Club, he was a major fundraiser for the City of Hope Hospital.

Berman had an outstanding war record. In 1942, he tried to enlist in the U.S. Army but was rejected because he was a convicted felon. So, he and Minnesota friend Nathan Gittlewich entered the Canadian Army's Eighteenth Regiment—nicknamed the 12th Manitoba Dragoons, which was a reconnaissance outfit. Serving in a reconnaissance unit overseas, he fought with distinction at Anzio, Sicily, and throughout the entire Italian campaign. Davie was honorably discharged in 1945. When he returned to Minnesota, the rackets he had been running had been broken up by Minneapolis Mayor Hubert Humphrey. Berman quickly relocated with members of his crew to Las Vegas and worked for Moe Sedway, a Genovese Family associate.

He became part owner and an associate in four clubs, in addition to the Riviera. In 1945, he was connected with the El Cortez Hotel. In 1946 with the Las Vegas Club and El Dorado (now the Horseshoe); and in 1947 he became interested in the Flamingo Hotel.

Berman watched Las Vegas grow from a fledgling gambling town to one of the world's most glamorous resort centers. It was partly through his vision and industriousness that it became what it is today, according to his close associates.

Berman was born Jan. 16, 1903, in Ashley, North Dakota.

(Both obits incorrectly reported Davie's age as fifty-three. He was fifty-four.)

Within hours of Davie Berman's funeral, the same men who acted as pallbearers at his funeral cleaned out the Berman home and gave away most of Susan's toys. Susan was then abruptly sent to Chadwick School, an independent Kindergarten through twelfth grade boarding school located on the Palos Verdes Peninsula in Los Angeles County. It was away from the only home Susan had ever known. Her mother, Gladys, returned to a rest home in Los Angeles, where she was being treated when Davie died. Susan took with her just a single trunk load of clothes, mementos, and Las Vegas souvenirs—the things her father's partners had packed up. In the trunk was the family Bible from her mother's side of the family, her mother's evening gowns, photos of Susan growing up, Susan's childhood diary, and some of her books. Also included was an audiotape of Susie, at age 6, singing, with her parents encouraging her from the sidelines. It was the only audiotape she had of their voices.

Susan Berman never learned what happened to the rest

of her family's belongings, and she was not asked what she wanted to take with her, nor was she asked who she wanted to live with. Gladys's cousin, Tom Padden, Jr. said there was no choice, and Susan's maternal relatives were not consulted. It was understood, Padden said, that Davie's associates were in charge. No one protested when Susan was skirted from Nevada to live in California.

Then, on February 2, 1959, just twenty months after her father's funeral, Susan suffered another devastating blow when, away at boarding school, she was notified that her mother had died from a heart attack. Betty "Gladys" Ewald Berman was just thirty-nine years old. Gladys was placed in a casket, still wearing her engagement and weddings rings, and interned next to her husband Davie at the Home of Peace cemetery in Whittier.

Susan eventually learned that Gladys overdosed on drugs. The official cause on her death certificate said, "Suicide by overdose." Gladys, who had suffered several nervous breakdowns while the couple lived in Las Vegas, was overcome with grief at the loss of her husband and, as a result, or so Susan was told, Gladys had taken a lethal dose of barbiturates.

But Gladys's cousin, Tom, who worked at the Las Vegas Club at the time of Gladys' death, was not convinced. He was adamant that his cousin did not take her own life. He insisted that the mob murdered Gladys because they did not want to pay out Davie Berman's shares in the hotels to Gladys. She unhappy with the offer they made to her. Instead of paying her more, Padden insisted, they killed her, and then made a smaller payout to Chickie Berman to offset support expenses for his niece Susan. Chickie became Susan's legal guardian after Gladys's death.

At just thirteen years old, Susie Berman was an orphan. Chickie had whisked her away permanently from Las Vegas the year before, only to be taken away again, this time from Los Angeles where she had been staying off and on to be near her mother, and removed from the only two towns—Las Vegas and Los Angeles—that she was familiar with, towns that felt like home. Susan, now parentless, was shuffled off to Lewiston in Northern Idaho to live with her uncle Chickie, her father's younger brother, his wife Marge, and their two teenage children, Dave and Donna.

The life Susan had spent as mob royalty, unknowingly surrounded by the Mafioso, was over. Her Uncle Chickie, while she loved and respected him, was not her father. He also was not a mob boss. He had worked for her father as a low-level member of the mob.

Susan desperately held onto her visions of the desert oasis she grew up in. Her images of her mother were vivid. She remembered that each New Year's Eve, her glamorous former tap-dancing mother, famous in St. Paul for her "Pennies From Heaven" routine, sparkled as she performed on a Las Vegas stage in one of Davie's casinos. The memories of Susan's father were that of a quiet, hardworking casino operator who doted on and adored his only daughter.

Chickie was a once-notable gambler and bookie. Although her uncle was good to her and Susan adored him, she missed her parents terribly.

Not long after Susan moved to Idaho, her bodyguard Lou Raskin visited her, along with a chef from Minneapolis. Susan relished the attention from the bodyguard who helped raise her.

"They stayed one night with us," said her cousin Dave.

Shortly after, Lou committed suicide—at least that's what they were told. He was found with one gunshot wound to his head. Now, one more person close to Susan was dead.

As time went on, Susan's Uncle Chickie became a broken man, never fully recovering from the loss of his brother. Along with Davie, he lost his job working for the mob. Davie Berman was the brains of the Las Vegas affiliate. He brought his brother Chickie into his inner circle of gangsters. Without Davie, Chickie was no longer needed.

Chickie had always been a compulsive gambler. Now, no one was left to help him out of scrapes, like the time Davie bailed out Chickie, after he gambled away hundreds of thousands of dollars from Benny Binion's high-stakes poker game at Benny's Vegas horse ranch on Bonanza Road, west of downtown. Benny, who founded Binion's Horseshoe Club, was known for breaking legs and shooting men if they didn't make good on their gambling debts. Davie was always there for his baby brother, regardless of the trouble, and he settled things peacefully with Benny.

The Binion family was loyal to Davie Berman. Binion's oldest son Jack told Susan years later, "I remember we saw your dad the day before he went in for that operation that killed him. He was always so nice to me. I was just a kid. My dad says to him, 'If you're having stomach problems it's because your money belt is ingrown.' Your dad laughed. When we found out he had died, we just couldn't believe it."

Chickie ended up living in cheap Vegas motel rooms and in and out of hospitals, where he eventually died. But throughout his gambling sprees, he set aside money the mob gave him, from Davie's interests, for Susan to continue attending an expensive boarding school alongside children of means and wealth, and then later sent her to college. That was what Davie would have wanted.

Susan Berman's education, technically speaking, was financed by the mob. But Susan wouldn't learn where her Uncle Chickie's money came from until years later.

# CHAPTER 5

# DAVIE BERMAN AND THE JEWISH MOB

*He passed on to me his greatest quality:*
*strength. Strength, because maybe he knew that*
*one day I would find out who he had really been*
*and then I would need every bit of strength I*
*had to survive.*

—Susan Berman

from *Easy Street*

WITH BUGSY SIEGEL'S arrival in Las Vegas in 1945, Jewish gangsters began running the desert town.

Back in the 1940s and 1950s, "The Jewish mob *was* Las Vegas," said Myram Borders, who grew up a decade before Susan Berman in the same neighborhood, and who, like Susan, became a journalist. "The Jewish mob ran this town. No one had even heard of the Italian Mafia."

Author Norman Cantor agreed in his book *The Jewish Experience.* He wrote, "It was the Jews, by and large, not the

Italians, who created what was later called the Mafia. In the 1920s, the Italians began to replace the Jews in the New York organized crime industry, but as late as 1940 if you wanted a spectacular hit you were looking for a representative of the Lepke Buchalter Gang, also known as Murder Inc. Jews were also prominent in the gambling trade and developed Las Vegas in the 1940s. It was a Jewish gambler who fixed the 1919 baseball World Series—which became known as the Black Sox scandal."

And in Wallace Turner's book *Gambler's Money*, he quoted what he described as an "anonymous high government official" as saying, "Some of the places in Las Vegas today are really controlled by the Mafia and we know this because we see some of their muscle men around. But the front men are almost always Jews."

Robert Lacey, in *Little Man: Meyer Lansky and the Gangster Life*, wrote, "Las Vegas offered Meyer Lansky the second great chance in his life to go legit, but he made no special effort to take it. Several dozen former bootleggers, bookies, and carpet joint operators flooded into Las Vegas from different corners of America in the late 1940s, seizing the opportunity to sidestep their pasts—and most of Ben Siegel's co-investors in the El Cortez fell into this category. Gus Greenbaum was an Arizona bookmaker. Willie Alderman and the Berman brothers, [and] Davie and Chickie, had run carpet joints in Minneapolis."

In fact, Davie Berman's criminal career began with bootlegging in Iowa, and quickly evolved to bank robberies in the Midwest to a kidnapping in New York, from heading a gambling syndicate in Minneapolis, to running hotels in Las Vegas for Meyer Lansky and Frank Costello and partnering up with Benjamin Siegel.

Despite his notorious background, Davie kept a low

profile in Las Vegas. He became one of the most influential post-World War II mob barons in Las Vegas, but he didn't want his daughter to know it.

Unlike their Italian counterparts, no Jewish mobster wanted his children to follow his example and go into "the business." Davie Berman was no different. In contrast to retired Italian Mafia leaders, Jewish mobsters were loath to grant interviews to the media. They did not like to see their names in print. In part, it had to do with the awareness that their activities could bring shame to their families and the Jewish community. It explained why Davie Berman, an important part of Las Vegas history, intentionally stayed out of the limelight.

Jewish gangsters did all they could to keep their offspring and families totally separated and uninvolved in their illegal enterprises. As an example, Meyer Lansky kept his family ignorant of what he did for a living and was proud of the fact that his younger son, Paul, graduated from New York City's elite Horace Mann School and from West Point. Longy Zwillman was painfully aware that his family and children suffered because of who he was and what he did for a living. He dissociated his relatives from his activities, finding them jobs in legitimate businesses.

Bootlegger Waxey Gordon made certain his family remained ignorant of his unlawful enterprises and sent his children to the best private schools and universities. And the FBI acknowledged that the notorious Louis "Lepke" Buchalter was devoted to his family, kept them unaware of his activities, and provided for his stepson's college education. West Coast hoodlum Mickey Cohen spoke for that generation of Jewish mobsters when he maintained: "We had a code of ethics like the ones among bankers, other people in other walks of life, that one never involved his wife or family in his work."

The Last Frontier casino opened in 1942. Next came the Flamingo, and with it Bugsy Siegel and organized crime to Las Vegas. During the 1950s, hotel building took off at a feverish pace. Each hotel owner tried to outdo its predecessors in opulence. The unbridled growth of what would later be called the Strip divided Las Vegas casinos into two basic categories: "carpet joints" and "sawdust joints." Sawdust on casino floors was ultimately replaced with wall-to-wall carpets.

The Flamingo had redefined gambling joints. It was a high-class carpet joint. Gone were tobacco-chewing men in cowboy hats and boots. People, instead, dressed up to gamble. Las Vegas was becoming sophisticated. Davie Berman helped run the higher-end carpet joints.

Despite their gangster backgrounds, Davie and the Jewish mob brought glamour and class to the casinos.

The Mafia needed Las Vegas for two reasons: to take control of legal gambling, and to launder money from their varied and nefarious enterprises. In the early days, there was no Strip, just downtown's seedy Glitter Gulch and a few small casinos sprinkled along the two-lane Los Angeles Highway. The town was small, and when the wind kicked up, it was a dust bowl. The streets of downtown were still dirt, except for parts of Seventh Street and Fifth Street. Sixth and Seventh streets were where mob-connected families like the Bermans chose to live. It was considered a nicer section of town.

With the nod from their East Coast bosses and the promise to give them 25 percent of everything they took in, the partners bought their first downtown club, named the El Cortez. Davie Berman brought in his best friend, Willie Alderman, and joined another old friend, Moe Sedway, in the partnership. Bugsy, in turn, brought in Gus Greenbaum, a leading bookie from Phoenix. The partners bought and ran two other downtown casinos: the Las Vegas Club and the El Dorado. As the pit boss, Davie owned 11 percent of the combined take. Bugsy owned 25 percent. Gus and Willie each had 10 percent. The rest belonged to the bosses. Each day, Davie watched over the shares, set credit limits for gamblers, and supervised the games.

As soon as word spread that Vegas was a success, gangsters from Chicago, Detroit, Cleveland, and Los Angeles began to muscle their way in. There was an influx of mobsters from Los Angeles because of the constant police crackdowns there. Davie became known as a mob diplomat, setting up liaisons between aspiring opportunists and East Coast bosses. But he had to fight constantly to protect his and his partners' home-town turf. Las Vegas was their town and they made sure that outsiders understood that and kept their distance.

Early on, Bugsy Siegel had convinced Meyer Lansky that he could expand south, away from downtown, by putting a hotel out on the two-lane U.S. Highway 91, later called Los Angeles Highway, and transform it into a gambling palace. It was a strong draw for tourists worldwide, including Hollywood celebrities. Lansky bought out all but a few shares of William Wilkerson's interest in a new half-built hotel. It was called the Flamingo and was surrounded by desert on the south end of the highway. Bugsy got the nod from his bosses, finished construction, and opened the Flamingo in 1946. But the hotel was still unfinished and in debt. It was draining the mob of money.

Making matters worse, Hollywood stars could not attend the grand opening because of a violent rain storm in Los Angeles. The so-called opening was a public relations disaster. As a result, Bugsy never showed a profit. Before Bugsy could prove himself and turn a profit, he was shot and killed gangland style in June of 1947. His murder was never solved. It was widely believed that the syndicate bosses had ordered Bugsy to liquidate and cut his losses. When Bugsy refused, Meyer Lansky, Bugsy's boss and his childhood friend, ordered his death, according to accounts in the books *Greenfelt Jungle* and *Augie's Secrets: The Minneapolis Mob and the King of the Hennepin Strip.*

Several people in Las Vegas, including Davie Berman, were at one time rumored to have pulled the trigger of the gun used to kill Bugsy. That was impossible, though, because within five minutes of his death, while Los Angeles police were still arriving at the house in Beverly Hills, and long before any official news of Bugsy's murder reached Las Vegas, four men—Dave Berman, Gus Greenbaum, Willie Alderman, and Moe Sedway—marched into the lobby of the Flamingo and took control of the casino. Fierce sandstorms tore through the sky that night, and the casino was half empty. In honor of Bugsy Siegel, the casino stopped operations for five minutes. The next day, a meeting of the mobsters was called to decide ownership of the hotel. Then control of the Las Vegas syndicate fell on Davie and his partners. Within six months, the Flamingo was showing a profit. The partners continued using whatever force necessary to retain their hold on their empire.

On the outside, Davie appeared to be a generous philanthropist and a model citizen, promoting Las Vegas and engaging in civic and Jewish activities. He moved in the same circles as top entertainers and powerful people, such as the mayor and the town's sheriff. Davie had become an integral member of the Jewish mob, Meyer Lansky's first lieutenant, and confidant to Frank Costello, but also a well-respected casino mogul.

Susan Berman's life in the underworld began in Las

Vegas in 1945, still an isolated, dusty desert town. After they arrived, Davie, Gladys, and Susie stayed in El Rancho Vegas's yellow and blue hotel, which was more like an expanded motor inn. With its then-towering windmill on the Strip, it attracted hordes of guests and celebrities. The Bermans stayed there for several months until Susan's mother found a house at 721 South Sixth Street, which they purchased. Most mob and casino operatives lived on South Sixth or nearby, buying up small houses spread over a couple of blocks. Susan regularly climbed a big tree in the front yard and played in a large playhouse—practically the size of a small bungalow—at the back of their property, behind their house. Her father was set financially and gave his only child whatever she wanted.

Vegas has no memory—only the present—and Davie Berman, a convicted and notorious kidnapper-robber-gangster from the Syndicate in Minneapolis, took advantage of his new town's unusual trait. He gained respectability.

One way the mobsters back then did this was to put their names in the phone directory, just like every other citizen in town. Davie was listed under "Berman, Dave," with his street address and telephone number Dudley 4-1941 next to it. Even Willie Alderman was in there, at 1400 South Sixth Street, a block up the street from the Bermans. Joe Rosenberg lived at 1800 South Fourth Place (the house has since been torn down).

According to the FBI's records, file number 52755, Davie once used aliases of "Dave Berman, Charles Gordon, Charles Gorden, and Dave the Jew." In Las Vegas, he was called Davie, although he referred to himself as "Dave." Even though he was a notorious gangster, Davie was considerate of those he robbed.

A reporter for the *New York Times*, after a 1925 bank

robbery and kidnapping in Wisconsin where Davie was implicated, wrote about Davie, saying: "The bandit was termed a gentleman *yegg (robber) by* his courtesy for his captive."

Davie had gone to New York in 1927 after he was summoned there to help kidnap wealthy men involved in illegal activities. Davie's job was to hold the men for ransom after his fellow mobsters kidnapped them. That same year, Davie and an associate, Joe Marcus, kidnapped a bootlegger named Abraham Scharlin. They held him for a $20,000 ransom. A couple days later Davie was arrested for the kidnapping during a dramatic shootout near Central Park.

It went down like this: Davie and Joe were hanging out on West Sixty-sixth Street when two cops approached. Joe drew his gun and a detective fatally shot him. The cops tried to squeeze Davie, but he wouldn't give in and talk. His response to police, which was later published in the *New York Times,* was, "Hell, the worst I can get is life." Scharlin was later found in Brooklyn, but he refused to finger Davie as his kidnapper. Davie, who was armed when he was arrested, was charged with felony assault. New York authorities also nabbed him for violation of the Sullivan Act, a state law that requires a permit to carry a concealed weapon.

It was 1927 and Davie was just twenty-three. He went to Sing Sing, the state prison in Ossining on the banks of the Hudson River just south of the farmers dock at Sing Sing landing.

A 1939 FBI memo described Davie as "tall, lean, giving the appearance of a great quantity of nervous strength. Quiet to the point of being noticeable. High cheekbones tended to accentuate the peculiar steadiness of the eyes.

Berman in his conversation, as well as mannerisms,

clearly reflected that he spent a great deal of his adult life in prison confines . . . Inasmuch as he had tasted confinement for a considerable length of time, he is a most dangerous type of law violator, due to the great price he is willing to pay in order to avoid another taste of confinement. Had a great ability to control his emotions, and where before to being sent away to Sing Sing Prison for a lengthy term he was considered tough, subsequent to his release he was considered vicious."

Another entry in Davie's FBI file read, "The notorious Dave Berman has a reputation as a stick-up man and killer. Both Dave and Chickie Berman, his brother, associate with Philip alias Flippy Scher, notorious Minneapolis killer who was recently discharged from the Army and presently operates a gambling joint at 319 Nicollet, Minneapolis."

Yet another FBI entry said, "Davie Berman was arrested 5 May 1927 for the kidnapping of bootlegger Abe Scharlin. He received on 24 November 1927 a 12-year sentence. He would do 7.4 years in Sing Sing. He got free 15 August 1934. Berman then became the gambling czar of Minneapolis replacing Isadore Kid Cann." Cann, a mob bootlegger, was identified by the FBI in 1942 as "the overlord of the Minneapolis, Minnesota, underworld."

Davie was in fact released on parole after serving seven-and-a-half years of an eleven-year sentence. The warden released him on good time, noting on his record that it was because of his high IQ and "total rehabilitation."

Author Robert Rockaway, in *But He Was Good to His Mother: The Lives and Crimes of Jewish Gangsters*, wrote about "the Berman brothers, saying, "Originally from Sioux, Iowa, prominent Jewish gangsters in Minneapolis included 'Kid' Cann (Isadore Blumenfeld), Yiddie Bloom, and the Berman brothers, Davie and Chickie. Cann is believed to have been responsible for the murder of Walter Ligget, publisher of *Midwest America*, for a series of articles the paper printed about the Minneapolis criminal underworld. Ligget was gunned down in front of his family while Christmas shopping. Much of illicit [Minneapolis] business was managed by Isadore 'Kid' Cann. . . . Blumenfeld and his all-Jewish syndicate."

Once Davie relocated to Las Vegas, the Feds tagged Davie's FBI file, along with Gus Greenbaum's and Bugsy Siegel's, with the words "the Nevada Project."

Susan proudly described her father's crimes to public radio's "This American Life." "He was the brain kid who engineered one of the first kidnaps for ransom, escaped death in a Central Park shoot-out, and was described by a detective on the front page of *The New York Times* as "the toughest Jew I ever met."

Davie, Chickie and their cousin Ed "Barney" Berman were members of Kid Cann's mob gang based in Minneapolis and Las Vegas between the 1930s and '50s. Davie was said to have used his crew to intimidate and terrorize members of the racist Silver Shirts, driving them out of Minneapolis.

By 1941, Chickie Berman was fingered by police, as reported by the *Detroit Free Press*, as part of a ring that "drew (Minneapolis) city officials and administrators into its web with bribes and payoffs." Chickie was arrested and charged with "operating a vice resort."

Years later, it took Susan nearly a year to get her father's FBI files, which also included information about her uncle's criminal past, through the Freedom of Information Act. Prior to receiving the files, a clerk at FBI headquarters in Washington, D.C., was assigned to read through them before releasing redacted copies to Susan.

Susan asked the clerk about her father.

"At one point," she wrote, "I asked timidly, 'Do you have any information that he killed anyone? 'Oh, yes,' the clerk answered in her cheerful impersonal way, 'He was a trained killer.'"

Later, Susan wrote in her memoir, "(My father) told his friends that I must never know the secrets of his past because the knowledge might destroy me." Her mother, Susan said, "remained fanatical about keeping me away from anything that might mention my father—newspapers, detective magazines, books." Her mother's friend, Ethyl Schwartz, told Susan that her mother used to say, "What if Susie reads something one day on her own?"

Instead of bothering Susan, she seemed fascinated by her father's gangster lifestyle. Susan described him in *Easy Street:* "He lived in the midst of a world that was dangerous, violent and severe. But he fabricated a childhood for me that seemed all-American and completely normal, disguising his real career as carefully as he managed it."

Las Vegas was a chance for a new start for Davie, as well as for Chickie. Susan commented in her A&E documentary, "My father and all his friends were criminals from the time they were eleven or twelve years old," she wrote. "He had served eight years of hard time in Sing Sing. So I think for many of these men, Las Vegas was their last chance, Las Vegas was their *only* chance, and they were determined, in their forties, to do it right. They didn't want any trouble with the government and they didn't want any crime in Las Vegas."

After Pearl Harbor, Davie Berman tried to join the service, to fight for his country. But he was an ex-felon and was denied. So he and his associate Charles Barron, a bootlegger and gambler from Chicago, drove to Winnipeg and enlisted in the Canadian Army's 18th Armored Car

Regiment of the 12th Manitoba Dragoons, a reconnaissance unit nicknamed "Princess Pat." He also enlisted and served with Minnesota friend Nathan Gittlewich. Davie earned the rank of lance corporal. He served at Anzio, Sicily, and he was also sent to Britain with the 1st Canadian Division Support Battalion as a machine gun loader and wireless operator.

Susan's mother's past was less dramatic than her future husband's. She was born Elizabeth Lynel Ewald on September 7, 1919, in New York to Jerome and Florence Ewald. Her mother was full German, her father Scotch Irish, Dutch and English. Jerome was a carpenter and mason who built three houses for his wife, eventually settling into the third home, which was a brown stucco, two-story house on Hubbard Avenue in St. Paul, Minnesota, where their daughters were raised. "It was a nice house," said Shirley Ward, who was Florence's niece. "It had a dining room, three bedrooms, a bath upstairs, and a big porch across the whole front of the house."

As a child, Gladys' mother enrolled her two daughters in a dance studio. Gladys' cousin, Tom Padden Jr., who referred to Gladys as Betty, remembered it well. "Betty's mother insisted that her daughters take dance lessons," Padden said. "She wanted them to be famous dancers." By the time Gladys was eighteen, she and her sister Jane were tap dancing at venues in Minneapolis, including the large hotel-casino Davie Berman had invested in. Jane and Betty, using her stage name of Gladys Evans, met Davie while they performed inside his casino.

"Dave liked the looks of Gladys," Padden said. "He adored her. She was cute—a pretty girl." From then on, Davie called her Gladys. "He knew her as Gladys Evans, not Betty. To him, Gladys was her name."

After a year of courtship, in 1939 they were married. Gladys was just nineteen.

Soon after, Davie joined the service. During his absence in the Canadian military, Gladys joined the Women's Army Corps, along with 150,000 other American women who served their country during World War II.

Davie was injured in action in Anzio, Sicily, behind German lines, and honorably discharged on August 16, 1944. He was shot in his legs. The Canadian government awarded him the Italy Star, the Defense Medal, the Canadian Volunteer Service Medal, and a plot of ground in Canada, which Davie donated to a Jewish organization.

Davie, now a war hero, returned to Minneapolis, to his wife, and to the rackets. He never recovered from the gunshot injuries to his legs. "The wounds never healed," said Gladys's first cousin Tom Jr. "He couldn't run. I saw the injuries once. They looked awful."

The next year, in 1945, Susan was born and the family soon after relocated to the Nevada desert, where Davie invested in casinos, starting on May 10th, 1945. He borrowed a million dollars from his mob associates and purchased the newly renovated El Cortez Hotel. His co-owners were Meyer Lansky, Benjamin Siegel, Moe Sedway, and "Ice Pick" Willie Alderman, a mob associate from Minneapolis. Davie soon became known as a "Mob Diplomat."

Davie's brother, Chickie, stayed behind in Minneapolis to deal with a criminal case. After it was dismissed for lack of evidence, Chickie, too, relocated to the desert and became an associate for the Vegas underworld as an employee of his brother.

In Las Vegas, gangsters' pasts could be shed like a lizard skin on the desert floor. Comedian Alan King, who worked in Las Vegas in the 1950s, told A&E, "No one talked about the background of the owners or the casino managers, or whatever. Vegas was like another planet. All of a sudden, the things that were illegal all over the country became not only acceptable, it was what drove the town."

It was the start of Las Vegas's glory days. Mobsters, billionaires, politicians, gamblers, and movie stars sought solace in the desert. The Flamingo represented the new and enticing Las Vegas

"Las Vegas could not have been Las Vegas if it had not been for the mob," Dennis McBride, a historian and author who grew up in the desert town, told A&E.

Rod Amateau, retired from TV writing and instead directed, agreed, telling A&E that the mob comfortably moved alongside entertainers. "Those were the days of the Reds," he said, "Red Skelton, Redd Foxx, and Red Buttons, and large, heavy Jewish men with little-boy names—Henny, Snooky, Youngie, Beepy, Booky, Boppy. You know, little names. Little names for big guys."

After meeting Ben Siegel for the first time, someone walked up afterward to Amateau and told him, "You know, he's a gangster." Amateau replied, "Well, you know, as long as he doesn't shoot me, I'm not gonna judge him; everybody's gotta make a living."

Violent crime in the gangsters' new town was committed outside the state line. "There was to be no killing in Las Vegas," Susan said in her A&E documentary. "The story is always told, and I'm sure it's true, about two men who robbed the casino. All the owners followed them to the state line and killed them because there is no crime in Vegas."

Susan was right: Las Vegas was an unofficial no-kill zone. Mobsters could continue their skimming while local lawmen turned their heads, just as long as they didn't commit murder inside the Nevada state line. With the Nevada-California state line just forty miles south of Las Vegas, the order was easy for mobsters to follow.

Bob Stupak, a casino operator who developed the Stratosphere Tower, chuckled when he told A&E, "Back then, it was like we had two police forces. We had regular police and then we had the boys. [It was] one of the few cities in the country that had two police forces, you know, and that took care of everything."

Debbie Reynolds, a mainstay Las Vegas entertainer from the Rat Pack days, explained it most succinctly when she told A&E: "I don't say I respect how they got their money. It's none of my business anyway. That was for Elliot Ness to handle. [But] no one got killed who wasn't supposed to be. And we never were frightened or anything of that sort." She commented that she missed "that loyalty, that respect," because of the courteous way "the boys" treated female entertainers in the early days.

Because Nevada had legalized gambling in 1931, for people like Davie Berman and Benjamin Siegel, it was a desert oasis with a promising and lucrative future. Davie was convinced that it was the only place to be. He could pursue the American dream, get a second chance for his family, become respectable. And he did.

Susan's father was a good friend and business partner of Siegel's, the notorious gangster whose mob power base spread from Los Angeles across the Mojave Desert to Vegas. Davie Berman, Siegel, and Meyer Lansky were gangsters from a mostly Jewish crime syndicate. The trio pioneered the development of Las Vegas from a sleepy desert cow town to a thriving gold mine. But they soon found themselves in an uneasy alliance when the *La Cosa Nostra* firms moved in. Davie, along with his partners, ran the Flamingo after Siegel was shot to death.

With Siegel's death, the Flamingo partners regrouped: Gus Greenbaum bought 27 percent interest; Elia Atol, 17-

1/2; Joe Rosenberg, "Little Icepick" Willie Alderman, and Davie Berman, 7 percent each; Charlie "Kewpie" Rich, 2 percent; Sidney Wyman, 10 percent; and Jack McElroy, 4 percent. Then Gus gave Benny Goffstein 2 percent and named him vice president.

"Rosenberg was made casino manager and Dave Berman, who could kill a man with one hand, was suddenly everywhere, barking orders, scowling ferociously, and getting things done in a hurry," according to the book the *Green Felt Jungle*. During the first year the new partners managed the Flamingo, it showed a profit of $4 million dollars. Ten years later, Davie Berman was dead. Three years after that, Gus Greenbaum was murdered.

In 1971, the Flamingo Hotel was purchased by the Hilton Hotel Corporation and renamed the Flamingo Hilton. The mob no longer ran it.

The late Dick Odessky, a former journalist-turned-author, went to work as a public relations man for the Flamingo in 1961 and remembered its heyday. Before he worked at the hotel, he was a newspaper entertainment columnist who covered hotels and casinos. He got to know the players.

"I went back to Los Angeles as a newspaper man at the L.A. *Herald Examiner*, then in '61, I went to work at the Flamingo," Odessky said in an interview from his California home before his death in 2003. "Morris Lansburgh had just taken it over. It was still a Lansky property. Lansky kept it until Lansburgh left in '67. With the Jewish mob back then you never knew with them who was big and who wasn't. Lansky was boss. He was boss of the Mafia. Lucky Luciano was the *big* boss. When he was deported, he put Lansky in. Davie and the boys were operators for Lansky. There were different organizations and we didn't learn of some of them until much later.

"The Jewish mob was very heavy into book making. The Italians were in with the Jews. It was a co-arrangement. They weren't fighting each other."

Odessky knew Davie Berman. "I had met Davie Berman," he said. "I stayed away from the Flamingo earlier because Gus Greenbaum scared the heck out of me. He was as frightening looking a man as I'd ever known. One day I was told Gus wanted to see me. I tried every possible way not to have to see him. I saw him. He told me they were going to build a silo out in front that could be seen from the California border. They built it and it could be seen only from Tropicana [Avenue on the Strip]. Davie stayed in the background. During that whole time the big guys, the hoods, were all my friends. They were all looking out for me. I wasn't even old enough at that time to *be* in the casinos. I was 19. They kind of adopted me. Ned Day [the late reporter who covered the mob] always would come to me when I was still writing at the *Valley Times*. He'd come to me and say, 'How do you get in to see these people?' I told him, 'You don't just walk in. You've got to get respect from them.' He said, 'You walk into every door in this town.' I told him, 'Notice where I *don't* walk. You never see me with the feds, do you?' The boys don't like that. You can't play one side against the other.'

"The feds tried to court me going all the way back to '53. They wanted me to watch for somebody. I told them I wouldn't do it. Because of that, the boys had a lot more respect for me." The mob "boys" on the Strip who respected Odessky included Davie Berman.

After Susan learned about her father's role in the mob, she wrote in *Easy Street*, "My loyalty to him is just as strong as his loyalty was to his way of life, whether or not my attitude is rational. He was involved in a kill-or-be-killed world. I have more questions about my own ethics in not being able to judge him in any way for those acts than I do about his committing them. . . . It's a dilemma I will be struggling with for a long, long time."

# CHAPTER 6

# THE COLLEGE YEARS

*After fifteen years in journalism writing other people's stories, writing my father's was the toughest assignment I ever picked.*
—Susan Berman

SUSAN CHOSE TO live an honest life, far removed from the one her father had led in Vegas. Susan graduated in June 1963 with honors from St. Helen's Hall High School, taking home a certificate from the National Honors Society.

For graduation, Susan's Uncle Chickie sent her a ticket to Lewiston, Idaho, under the guise that it was to visit him and his family. Once there, however, Chickie surprised her with a plane ticket to spend the summer at the United Synagogue Youth Pilgrimage tour. Susan was thrilled. She caught her plane and headed for Israel. She blossomed in the environment. While there, she wrote her first book, a novel titled *Driver, Give a Soldier a Lift.*

After the Israeli tour, Susan returned to the states to attend college at the University of California at Los Angeles, located in Westwood, a pedestrian-friendly college town developed in the 1920s after the UCLA campus relocated there, near where Susan attended the fifth grade while she and her mother escaped mob unrest in Las Vegas. Westwood is located at the entrance to the giant UCLA campus and its Mediterranean-inspired architecture.

Susan was accepted into UCLA's Letters in Science College, the largest academic unit in the UC system. As a sociology major, many of Susan's classes were held in the Life Science Building (now called Franz Hall), which was built in 1940. At that point, she had already made up her mind she was going to be a journalist and took undergraduate writing classes in the Humanities Building.

It was a time of change for the country, what with civil rights protests of that era. UCLA was near the heart of it when the Watts Riots broke out in Los Angeles in the summer of 1965. Discrimination, equal rights, women's rights, and civil rights all became major issues.

During Susan's sophomore year, her uncle called to let her know that he was "going away," as he put it. He was about to be incarcerated at the Terminal Island federal penitentiary. A New York Times headline at the time read, "Four Imprisoned for Stock Fraud: United Dye Case is Rested by U.S." It said that Charles Berman, forty-nine at the time, had pleaded innocent but had been convicted anyway: "Four brokers and a corporation were convicted Monday of defrauding the public of $5 million through a conspiracy to sell 400,000 shares of unregistered stock of United Dye and Chemical Corporation." Federal Judge William Herlands said the conviction "brought to a close the longest trial before a jury in the history of a U.S. District Court in the country." The article identified Chickie Berman as a broker and dealer from Lewiston, Idaho.

Chickie was sentenced to six years in prison and ordered to pay a $35,000 fine. The U.S. attorney called the defendants "classic examples of financial parasites" who had a total disregard for the small investor in their fraudulent dealings.

*Fortune* magazine also wrote about the scam, describing it as "The Great Sweet Grass Swindle," noting that "selling watered stock has become a difficult and intricate business. But the boiler room boys are still at it. Here's the story of a classic operation in which the victims paid $16 million for oil stocks now worth $4 million." Chickie was pinpointed as the brains behind one of the stock schemes. "Charles M. Berman," the article continued, "who for nearly twenty years had run a string of pinball machines and juke boxes in Minneapolis where he was twice arrested on charges, later dismissed for lack of evidence, of making book on the side."

Chickie was imprisoned at a maximum-security penitentiary in Lewisburg, Pennsylvania, and then at La Tuna, Texas. He ultimately was transferred to Terminal Island in San Pedro, California where Susan visited him on weekends.

Back at college, Susan joined a sorority at UCLA but got kicked out after six weeks for piercing her ears. While Susan had been an honors student in high school, she was an average student in college who regularly cut classes and spent much of her spare time writing. After four years, she squeaked by and, on June 13th, 1967, earned her undergraduate bachelor of arts degree in education, after switching majors from sociology. Davie Berman would have been proud; his Susie was the first Berman to finish college. Then, in September, Susan began graduate school in the education department at UCLA.

Bobby Durst had also enrolled in a graduate program at UCLA, majoring in economics. After their first meeting on the campus's quad, they spent time together, mostly socializing with other friends. Susan, with her long, thick black hair reaching her shoulders and dark, almond-shaped eyes, was striking. And she always had a smile on her face and something funny to say. The subdued Bobby, who had a boyish charm but was quiet, seemed mysterious to Susan. During their years at UCLA, Susan and Bobby grew closer.

Susan left UCLA's graduate school in March 1968 after five months and one-and-a-half quarters to transfer 350 miles north to the journalism program at the University of California at Berkeley.

She wanted to pursue a career as a writer, and UC Berkeley's J-school program would help her reach her goal. Bobby continued at UCLA until the end of June 1969. Susan and Bobby stayed in touch with each other. Bobby eventually walked away from UCLA without getting a graduate degree, according to records kept by the campus registrar.

In the meantime, Susan adjusted to graduate school. It was 1969 in the San Francisco Bay Area in the midst of flower power and the hippie generation. A year earlier, Martin Luther King, Jr. had denounced the Vietnam War in a speech on campus at Sproul Plaza, in front of the College of Journalism building where Susan attended classes. Berkeley during the 1960s was home of the Free Speech Movement and student radicalism. Years later, Susan would learn that the FBI had continued to track her, even after her father had died, noting in Davie Berman's file that Susan was "a member of the San Francisco women's liberation and pro abortion debater." In fact, Susan was a member with classmate Sandra Sanders-West in Students for a Democratic Society. It was Susan's boyfriend, Alan Neckritz, who was the antiwar activist.

"She and Alan were joined at the hip," fellow student

Elizabeth Mehren said. "He was a character too. He was an activist."

Back then, especially at Berkeley, anti-Vietnam protests were commonplace. Activism was rampant on campus, with anti-war and free speech rallies. Tom Hayden, who helped launch the Students for a Democratic Society—which became the largest student organization of the New Left—called for a demonstration protesting the Vietnam War.

According to news accounts, on the afternoon of May 15, 1969, nearly 6,000 students and residents moved to reclaim People's Park, a university-owned plot of land along Telegraph Avenue that students and community members adopted as a park. Berkeley exploded. The university brought in police to repossess the park. In the ensuing riot, police and sheriff's deputies fired tear gas and buckshot at the crowd, blinding one observer and killing another. Then-Governor Ronald Reagan ordered the National Guard into Berkeley. Students continued to gather on campus and march in the days following the first riot.

"We all protested the war," said Elizabeth Mehren, who graduated with Susan. "It was a popular thing to do."

It was 1969, the year Richard Nixon was inaugurated into office. The year before, Robert Kennedy and Martin Luther King Jr. were assassinated.

One professor, an elderly instructor, took his journalism students, including Susan, to the balcony of Sproul Hall, overlooking sit-ins, speeches, protests, and rallies. "He taught us how to count people in crowds," Mehren said. "I still use it today."

Elizabeth remembered Susan well. "She had this glamorous patina, the daughter of a mobster," she said. "Who can forget the girl who had the white Mercedes Benz at Berkeley? Here we were in Berkeley, in 1969, with National Guard troops on campus. The rest of us had crummy cars. People were driving beat-up Volkswagens. She drove a white Mercedes sedan. It was a college graduation gift [from her Uncle]. It was such a bad status symbol at Berkeley. It was almost comical. She gave you the illusion of having endless resources."

"She was an orphan," Elizabeth continued. "We all knew about the Riviera and the Flamingo. We all knew about Uncle Bugsy. They were part of her lore."

With student groups discussing the issues on and off both the UCLA and UCB campuses, Susan grew intellectually. Once at UC Berkeley, Susan changed her major from education to journalism and enrolled in UCB's Graduate School of Journalism, on the north end of the campus, in preparation to pursuing a career as a writer.

Among Berkeley's distinguished faculty were Nobel laureates, members of the National Academy of Sciences. Many Berkeley faculty were on the *New York Times* best-seller lists. The J-school program was an intimate one with small classes—a working collegium that put students under the direct tutorship of a group of permanent faculty, lecturers, and teaching fellows. No marketing, advertising, or public relations classes were taught there, which meant Susan was learning strictly journalism. Most of the instruction was done by journalism practitioners who continued to publish in the nation's biggest and best newspapers and magazines while teaching.

Susan honed her writing skills and was taught the craft of journalism and traditional forms of news gathering from the best in the business.

By 1969, students were demonstrating—and still being arrested by the hundreds—demanding the creation of a "Third World College."

Still, as graduation approached, Susan concentrated her time on a job search. She interviewed with a daily newspaper in San Francisco. In June 1969 she received a master's degree from UC Berkeley as part of the J-school's first graduating class. She had just earned a journalism degree from one of the best universities in the country. Her future looked bright. Susan's classmates thought the same, that she was on her way to a brilliant writing career.

While at Berkeley, Susan befriended Edwin Bayley, the Graduate School of Journalism's first dean, beginning in 1969, and a professor emeritus. She also got to know Bayley's wife Monica, who died in April 2002. Even then, Susan was networking, looking for ways to excel, befriending influential people who could help her. Bayley retired from UC Berkeley in 1985 and moved to Carmel, California, with his wife.

Ed Bayley saw Susan's work differently than her classmates who viewed her as a potential star. As her dean, Bayley had a different perspective, as she often went to him to discuss her journalism future, he said.

"My relationship with Susan was more of an advisor than anything else," Bayley said. "She was the kind of kid who needed a *lot* of advising. She was a big baby in a way. She put on a tough, flippant attitude and played the role of a gangster's daughter, but she was really just as soft as a baby inside. She needed a mother. She liked my wife a lot."

It was a small community of students in the J-school program, Bayley said, and everyone knew each other. "My wife and I lived in Berkeley and students came over to our house a lot," he said. "It was a smaller school. We admitted about fifty or sixty students at any one time."

"To be honest," Bayley continued, "I was critical of her because she was always trying to find the easy way out, using gimmicks. That was the only thing I was critical of. I think she was lazy mentally that way without having to do the hard, grubby work. Then, of course, using her father's gangster status. She had a picture on her fireplace mantle of her Uncle Chickie and his girlfriend in a nightclub in Havana. Most of the time she was just a student. She had a very nice boyfriend, Alan Neckritz. He was a law student and they lived together. They were like a settled-in married couple. They used to entertain and invite faculty and other students over."

Susan lived on Hillegass Street, about eight blocks from campus. Later, she moved in, with Neckritz in his house at 2555 Le Conte. Neckritz eventually practiced law in Walnut Creek, California. Susan also once rented a small Spanish-style house on Euclid Street on the north side of Berkeley, near the university, with roommate Sandra Sanders-West, who went on to become a police officer in the Bay Area.

Susan's personality was engaging, which made her popular on campus.

Elizabeth Mehren said Susan, however, tried to take short cuts during college. "I hate to speak ill of the dead," Elizabeth said, "but Susan was a spoiled little girl who didn't know how to deal with life. She was marginally talented. She balked at doing a master's thesis. She didn't like the fact that she had to research topics. I was in journalism school with her and there were maybe thirty or thirty-five people in that class. It was very intimate. Everybody knew each other."

Mehren, too, said Susan was well liked during college. "She had a wonderful sense of humor," Mehren said. "There was something very appealing about her. She had this vulnerability. At the same time she had this toughness.

"I'm very blonde and very California. I look like a

cookie-cutter California girl. So Susan and a couple of other kids in the class felt sorry for me because I didn't know anything about Jewish culture. They made me a glossary of Yiddish terms. They gave it to me for my birthday at the end of the year. However, they forgot to make it phonetic. So I mispronounced everything."

Ed Bayley said Susan struck him as being sad, even though she appeared to want for nothing. "My wife felt sorry for her," he said. "She was lonesome. She wanted to make us her mother and father. In the last letter she made a point about how much she loved us both. My wife felt sympathetic toward her more than anything else. Susie was not happy. She was a lonesome kid who wanted a lot of comforting. Everything she did seemed to go wrong."

After Susan was murdered, "My wife was very upset," Bayley noted. "She really liked Susie."

Lou DeCosta was in the journalism program with Susan. DeCosta, who now works in Hollywood as a story editor and writer on documentaries, also remembered Susan and her days at Berkeley.

"I was a year behind Susan," he said in a telephone interview from his L.A. home. "She was the star. She was like the golden girl. She was a great writer. She was very outgoing and self-promotional. Her reputation in school was that she was the bright star or, at least, had the potential to be the bright star if she put out the effort. . . . The brutal truth was that she was not an attractive woman. She was homely. But she was almost arrogant. I remember when I found out about her dad, it was like a huge shock."

Susan made friends and business connections in journalism school at UC Berkeley. Later, she "used the J-school connection to pitch stories to Richard [Zoglin]," Lou DeCosta said.

According to DeCosta, Richard Zoglin, formerly a TV critic at *Time* magazine who became a freelance editor, dated Susan briefly. "I remember having a discussion with him," DeCosta noted. "He said he hadn't seen her for a while but that she had pitched him stories."

Susan enjoyed San Francisco and the Bay Area, its culture and aliveness. She thrived in the hustle and bustle of a metropolitan city. It reminded her of L.A.

The ink was still wet on her diploma when she went straight from journalism school to the staff of the then-Hearst-owned *San Francisco Examiner*, where she worked as an entry-level features and news reporter. She worked in the city at the paper's newsroom in the Hearst Building, in the middle of the block at Third and Market Streets, which housed both the *San Francisco Chronicle* and the *Examiner*. The *Examiner's* newsroom, which was separate from the *Chronicle's*, was a large rectangular room, with the women's department, where Susan worked, to the right as people entered that floor. "Susan didn't like having to go upstairs, but she had no choice. The *Examiner* was upstairs."

During her stint at the *San Francisco Examiner*, Susan's career flourished.

Former classmate DeCosta noted, "The fact that she was immediately working as a reporter out of school sort of made her a hero to us."

To top it off, in 1971, while she was at the *Examiner*, Susan co-wrote and published her first book, *The Underground Guide To The College Of Your Choice*, which was released with a warm reception as a mass-market paperback by Signet Publishing. The subtitle read, "The only handbook that tells you what's really happening at every major college and university in the U.S.A."

*The Washington Post* reviewed the handbook in its January 1979 Sunday edition. "There is something refreshing about anything that calls itself underground. That applies to *The Underground Guide to the College of Your Choice* by Susan Berman," writes Stephen L. Goldstein. "For high school seniors, it holds the promise of telling "where it's happ'nin'." For the rest of us, it promises to lighten the shadows of a mysterious other existence— the college world.

"It dismisses one college ('It finally went coed, but it didn't help.') and another ('Politically it's a hotbed of opathy.') But the *Guide* is balanced enough in its judgments to find one place 'composed of thinking liberals' and another that is 'calm and sane.' Under the heading 'Bread,' it reports that the costs at one college are so high 'It's impossible to scrounge here . . . Nothing is cheap, even Xerox.' At another college, 'dates are cheap because guys are in the minority and can usually get the chick to go dutch.' The mental environment of one college is summed up by the observation that 'people read textbooks,' presumably for pleasure, while the campus of yet another college is described as 'a quad of chipped salmon-colored structures.'"

"Published in 1971, the *Guide* is well behind the times," the article continues, "but there is still a remarkable measure of truth to its perceptions of a number of colleges. Written against the backdrop of student protest in the 1960s, the book is like an archaeological find chronicling a bygone era." Susan should have been on top of the world. The *Examiner* was an excellent opportunity for a cub reporter, and her book was getting national notice. As an up-and-coming writer, on the surface, the future looked bright. During the course of a year, however, Susan went from being cheerful to depressed. She became frustrated with her job. She liked being the center of attention. At the *Examiner*, she was just another writer.

It could have been because, around that time, Susan was told that her mother might not have killed herself, that she could have instead been murdered by the mob after being forced to take an overdose of pills for not accepting a settlement on her father's interest in the Las Vegas hotels he had skimmed from for his East Coast bosses. No evidence pointed to that scenario, although her mother's cousin, Tom Padden, Jr., felt the same. As a former employee of Davie Berman, and Gladys's cousin, Padden was asked by a mob associate to be the middleman and make an offer to Gladys Berman of a payout for Davie's share in the hotel-casinos and investment properties he was a part of. "(Gladys) was angry," Padden said in an interview. "She told them, 'No.' A week later she was dead."

Suspicions about the circumstances surrounding her mother's death threw Susan into a long period of agoraphobia and manic-depression. She had friends, money, a good job, and a promising career. According to her friends at the time, San Francisco was good to Susan and she appeared, at least on the surface, to be happy. She was bubbly when she greeted people and was active socially. Yet, in her memoir, she portrayed those years in a completely different light.

She wrote that when she lived in her Pacific Heights home she had emotional difficulty just walking the six blocks to her therapist's office. On top of that, she was suicidal. But something forced her to stay alive. "I was all that was left of a whole family that I didn't know," she wrote. "If I died now, their lives would mean nothing. . . . Then one day I got better, suddenly I could drive, I could smile, I could write. I still remember that day after my analytic session when I knew I was going to make it. I ran out, walked with confidence for the first time, hugged my dog, kissed my parents' pictures, yelled, 'I'm alive again!' I opened the blinds on my life after a year of a deathlike depression."

• • •

Davie Berman was still listed in 1962 with the Nevada Gaming Commission as a licensed partner with 4.5 percent shares, in the Riviera Hotel, which explained what Susan called her "trust-fund payments."

The payouts began in the early 1960s, continued throughout college and into adulthood. At one point, the payments ended after a lump sum was paid to her. Susan eventually went through the money. She never disclosed to anyone what the amount was. Besides the Flamingo, Riviera, and El Cortez, Davie Berman had interests in and ran the Las Vegas Club and El Dorado. Her cousin Dave, along with his sister, knew what the amount was, because his father told him. Susan was given a grand total of $5.25 million, which did not include support throughout the years by the mob through her Uncle Chickie. The payments to Susan began when she turned twenty. She received a final payout ten years later on her thirtieth birthday.

Elizabeth Mehren, Susan's classmate from UC Berkeley, said, "She appeared to have unlimited resources. Unlike the rest of us, she always had money."

According to her friends at the time, San Francisco was good to Susan and she seemed happy. She was bubbly when she'd greet people and was active socially.

Because the *San Francisco Examiner* hired Susan for entry-level beat coverage, filling in as a temporary court reporter in a musty press room on the fourth floor of downtown's City Hall, Susan, her friends said, felt insulted and underutilized. She was not well suited as a beat reporter and was unhappy. Still, she lasted at the paper from 1971 to 1975.

"Her career there was not exactly meteoric," mystery writer Julie Smith told *New York* magazine. Julie was a *San Francisco Chronicle* reporter at the time. "If anything, she was not employable because she was so independent," she said. "She just couldn't work for a big company, and so she began to freelance. This is when she really came into her true flamboyance and independence. She had a great eye for the flamboyant, and she knew what would sell."

Her writing career began in San Francisco.

# CHAPTER 7

# BEYOND COLLEGE

SUSAN THRIVED IN the Bay Area. She enjoyed the fast pace and her growing high profile as a staff writer at one of two prominent newspapers in the Bay Area. She made new friends and she dated a lot. Susan was in her element, excelling both professionally and personally.

One of her new friends was Bachmann. Said Marcy: "We became friends in the early seventies when both of us worked at the *San Francisco Examiner*. I was freelancing, filling in for people who were on vacation. I would work for maybe six weeks at a time. That's where I met Susan. We hit it off after she kind of latched onto me."

While at the paper, Susan moved from Berkeley to downtown San Francisco, mostly because she disliked crossing the Bay Bridge to get to work. It was one of her many phobias. "She used to hate to come to work in the city. She was convinced that one day she would stop her car and jump off the bridge. She would say, 'I'm afraid I'm going to throw myself off the bridge.' I would laugh at her," Marcy said.

Because she didn't yet know very many people in the city, Marcy introduced Susan to her friend Juline Beier, who lived in the same San Francisco neighborhood as Susan. They too became fast friends.

Marcy described Susan as "a delightful person." Still, Susan had quirks that not everyone at the paper accepted, like her constant wearing of what some called a "ratty raccoon coat."

"I was the only reporter in our department prepared to accept her eccentricities," Marcy noted. "The thing about Susan, she was ahead of her time. The way she wrote, she used to write from the gut.

"A lot of these women intensely disliked Susan. She looked like a big loveable kid, I guess. When she walked into a room, you couldn't help but notice her. I always felt that the other writers were jealous of her. She was really good. I would tell her all the time how good she was. She was an instinctive writer. She was very emotional and she knew how to get it out of her head and onto paper. A lot of writers there were hack writers, quite frankly, and they were envious of her."

Susan's closest friends overlooked her quirkiness because she was fun to be around. "One Fourth of July, she organized several carloads of her friends at the last minute," Marcy said. "We took off for Stinson Beach where we spent the day sprawled on towels, gossiping, sipping sandy Cokes, and basking in the sun."

Marcy described her friend as "a giving person, especially when it came to holidays. Her heart was huge. One Thanksgiving, she had a large potluck dinner at her home, a large Victorian painted purple with bright-red gingerbread trim. There must have been four or five turkeys, at least. She invited all of her single friends who had nowhere else to go."

Susan's home in the Heights, in the park-like neighborhood with scenic views, Marcy said, "was absolutely gorgeous."

Susan's first house in the city was on Clay Street, and, as Marcy pointed out, "It was pretty bare. People lived above her and below her in the house. She lived in the middle part, on the second floor. It was a huge house. She didn't like to be alone. She'd say, 'Come over and bring anybody you're with.' But her apartment in Pacific Heights was absolutely gorgeous. It was very comfy and lovely." One friend described the area as "the part of town the rich and famous lived in."

On the heels of her success at the *Examiner* and tired of the daily grind, Susan yearned to expand her horizons. She had bigger and better things in mind for herself besides cranking out stories for a daily. She'd made contacts that helped her land new freelancing gigs. After four years in the newsroom, she left the *San Francisco Examiner*. Her friends say it was a mutual decision.

Leaving the *Examiner* launched her freelance career. She had no problem finding work.

First, she landed a job as a newswriter-producer at San Francisco's KPIX-TV Channel 5 on the "Westinghouse Evening Show," a CBS affiliate. But because Susan wanted to be a magazine writer, she left Westinghouse a short time later and freelanced as a writer at famed filmmaker Francis Ford Coppola's *City of San Francisco* magazine, which failed shortly after Coppola took it over. *City* magazine, a glossy alternative weekly, hired Susan as a regular contributor.

The magazine published Susan's most famous article, an idea which she thought of while out one night at a bar in the city with girlfriends. The piece was headlined "Why Women Can't Get Laid in San Francisco." It caused a stir in the Bay Area because it openly talked about sex in the still-conservative seventies, as well as very publicly pointing out the growing gay population in the Bay Area. It sent sales at the magazine from 20,000 circulation to 42,000 sold editions, according to a September 1, 1975, article about the piece in *NEWSWEEK*.

"Inside, the story dwelt at somewhat lurid length on the problem of male passivity," *NEWSWEEK* wrote. "According to writer Susan Berman, the dilemma transcends San Francisco's high population of homosexuals. It's the straights who seem to be leery of sex. 'They drive themselves so hard during the day,' testified a mini-skirted secretary, 'and then drink to get to sleep so that they don't have any libido left at all.' Forthright sexual approaches by women, Berman reports, meet with 'extreme stress manifestations.' According to a TWA stewardess, men 'were raised to think that we women want emotional commitments and relationships—and when we just want one good night of sex they can't relate to it.'"

While still in San Francisco, Susan met and dated Warren Hinckle, an editor at the time for *City* magazine. When the magazine failed—although critically acclaimed—Hinckle went to work for the *Chronicle* as a columnist, then eventually hired on with the *Examiner*, moving to its New York City bureau. An *Examiner* editor who said she knew both Susan and Warren described the liaison as "a sexual relationship."

Susan's friend Stephen M. Silverman remembered that she had dated her editor. "She was involved with Hinckle, as I recall," Silverman said. "Hinckle was the editor of *City* at the time she wrote her 'Laid in San Francisco' article. But she used to say she wouldn't sleep with Francis Coppola, who was the publisher. As a rule, she didn't date casually."

Susan also dated Morgan King, who knew Susan's friend Marcy Bachmann. While visiting Marcy at her apartment,

Morgan admired Susan's author photo on the back dust cover of one of her books. "He jumped at my offer to introduce him to the author," Marcy said. "He and Susan wound up having a brief, albeit passionate, affair." King, an attorney who later married and had children, still had fond memories of Susan years later.

"One word I would describe her as was spontaneous," said Morgan, who went on to become an attorney. "She loved to have fun. I was single at the time, and she was just the kind of friend I really enjoyed having. I found her interesting." Still, he noted, "She seemed very lonely. I guess a part of me really felt sorry for her. About certain things, she was very childlike."

Morgan King recognized some passages in the article as similar to his relationship with Susan. Even though he was intimately involved with her, Susan's sex life remained a mystery to him. He explained that after their first night together, "She jumped out of bed and said, 'I've finally joined the 20th century.'" Yet, King also learned that Susan had been flirting for weeks with her editor at *City* magazine and ended up having an affair with him. "My impression at the end of our relationship was that something was developing with (Warren) Hinckle," King said.

Despite Susan being involved with two men around that time, according to their mutual friend Marcy, "Morgan insisted that the 'getting laid' story was about him."

By the time Susan left the *Examiner* to write for *City* magazine, Marcy had moved on to the San Francisco *Tribune*. She and Susan stayed in touch, which meant Susan gave Marcy regular updates and juicy details about her social life. "Susan used to call me occasionally when I was at the *Tribune* to tell me what she did the night before," Marcy said. "She once called and told me about having sex with the city editor under his desk. 'How could you do that with *him?*' I asked her. She laughed and said, 'I think it saved my job.'" In the early seventies, Marcy said a short relationship wasn't considered promiscuous. "Everybody was doing it," she pointed out.

Her dalliances appeared to have helped Susan build a name for herself and make a splash in Bay area journalism circles.

She was becoming a media darling. She was often mentioned in Herb Caen's gossip columns in the *San Francisco Chronicle*. She regularly lunched in North Beach at the Washington Square Bar and Grill, a restaurant affectionately known as the "Washbag." In its heyday in the 1970s and '80s, the Washbag was a favorite for attorneys, advertising execs, publishing professionals, and celebrity patrons. Susan enjoyed hobnobbing with the city's movers and shakers. It made her feel like a princess again.

Susan's former classmate, Lou DeCosta, noted that she "really made her mark in the Bay Area in an amazing article called 'Why Women Can't Get Laid in San Francisco.' It was so bold, the nature of the article and the fact that it had been written by a woman. And the play she got with 'Why I Can't Get Laid' was huge. It made her name."

Her dean at UC Berkeley remembered the story well. "The 'Get Laid' article," Ed Bayley said, "made a big splash at the time."

"People were attracted to Susan," Bayley pointed out. "She was lively. She seemed to like other people. She would come in to see me quite often and ask my advice. She wasn't a student of mine. I remember being sorry that she left the *Examiner* and thought she needed more newspaper experience. I remember thinking if I'd had her in my classes, I would have taught her discipline. That's what she needed. I think she probably had the idea that she was interested more in magazine than news writing right from the beginning." Fellow UC Berkeley alum Harvey Myman also recalled Susan's reputation. "She was an interesting writer, a smart writer, I thought," Harvey said. "She was never in mainstream media. She had a high profile right out of the box."

After the success of the *City* article, while people were still abuzz about it, Susan drove to Los Angeles to pitch some ideas to magazines. One editor she contacted was Silverman, who eventually went to work for *People.com* and as an adjunct professor at New York's Columbia School of Journalism.

"That's how we met," Silverman told me. "I was a young editor of a magazine in L.A. called *Coast* magazine. Susan had just written the cover story for *City* [magazine]. She telephoned, then came barging into the office unannounced. She introduced herself as 'the world's best writer.' She always did that."

Stephen told Susan he could give her an assignment, but she turned him down. "She never did write for *Coast* magazine," he noted. "We didn't pay enough for her."

Susan's writing credits were growing, and they were impressive. In the 1970s and '80s, she worked as a print and TV journalist in San Francisco and New York, and, later, she became a contributing writer for *New York* magazine, *Cosmopolitan*, and *Family Circle*.

In 1976, the year after Susan left the *San Francisco Examiner*, her second book, titled *Driver, Give a Soldier a Lift*, was published, this time by Putnam, a large New York publishing house. It was a novel about war in Israel and a Berkeley woman's quest to find a husband.

The jacket read, "With an irrepressible wit and the sharp eyes of a keen observer, Susan Berman has written a wildly funny novel of present-day Israel—and the story of a young American girl who goes to the land of milk and honey in search of love, ending up with more than she bargained for."

The publisher, calling Susan "a fresh new talent," wrote that the book was based, in part, on Susan's personal experiences "while she lived in Israel."

The publisher was referring to Susan's summer spent in Israel when she was eighteen and met her first boyfriend. Susan also later spent nearly a year writing the book, beginning while she was still in Israel. She dedicated it to her parents, a few friends, relatives, her shrink (Dr. Edward Alston), "and to the great state of Israel—may it carry on with strength forever."

Susan felt particularly connected to Israel because her father had traveled there when she was a child. "Outwardly," she wrote, "he was the first citizen of Las Vegas promoting his town and engaging in civic and Jewish philanthropies. Inwardly, he was in torment. He decided suddenly in the fall of that year (1955) to take a trip to Israel. He had never been there but had many Israeli friends from the days when he donated so much money to the Irgun. . . . He wanted to take me to Israel with him but said my mother would worry too much."

Susan loved the stories her father told her about his trip. "He was gone for two weeks and called me every night," Susan wrote. "He told me about Jerusalem, saying, 'I know this sounds crazy, Susie, and I never told you I believed in God, but I do now. I felt something today when I walked the streets here.'"

Susan had a book launch party in San Francisco for *Driver, Give a Soldier a Lift*. Marcy Bachmann, whom Susan had worked with at the *Examiner* and became good friends, bought a copy. Susan autographed it with, "To Marcy, We're independent glamorous women together—ain't it fun! Susan."

Marcy placed the book proudly on her coffee table.

It was about this time that Susan started getting antsy in San Francisco. She wanted to move to New York City, where the large national magazines were. And she wanted to move there to be closer to where her best friend Bobby Durst lived.

So, in 1977, she left San Francisco and relocated to New York City, 2,900 miles away and on the opposite coast, where she'd told friends she hoped to become a "real" writer among those she considered to be true *literati*.

Susan also yearned to live in the city her father had moved to exactly fifty years earlier, in 1927, when he was just twenty-three, when he'd gone to Manhattan to execute, for the mob, the kidnapping of a bootlegger.

For Davie Berman's daughter Susan, it was the late seventies when she moved to 34 Beekman Place in Manhattan's Upper Midtown. Stephen Silverman ended up moving into the building next door to Susan, at 32 Beekman, while he worked the celebrity beat for the *New York Post*.

"I was thinking about moving to New York," Silverman said. "She called and said there was an apartment available next to her building. It was on Beekman Place, an exclusive street in Manhattan on the East Side in the fifties. I moved into a small apartment. Susan lived in a studio. Both our apartments were tiny." Later, Susan bought an apartment nearby at 30 Beekman Place, in a pre-war doorman co-op building.

Susan hung out with Stephen as well as Bobby Durst, who took her with him when he got together with his friends, including Bobby's wife, Kathie Durst.

Gilberte Najamy, who met Susan through Kathie Durst, said Susan often entertained at the Midtown Manhattan apartment. "She had a beautiful place," Gilberte said. "At the time, Susie was right up there, hanging out at the Studio 54, the Parrot, Xenon's—all the hot clubs. We would go out to dinner a lot. Susie was very friendly and introduced us to her circle of friends in the literary community. The Susie I knew was social, friendly, generous."

A college classmate, Harvey Myman, said he got to know Susan better in New York than he had while they attended UC Berkeley. He, too, visited Susan on Beekman Place, with a fellow classmate.

"By the time I knew her better, it was in New York," Harvey said. "She had written a couple of books, the one about Israel [*Driver, Give a Soldier a Lift*], and the one about growing up in Las Vegas [*Easy Street*]." Harvey learned through Susan's memoir that she'd had what he called "a bizarre, fucking childhood."

He remembered Susan always hustling for new ideas. "There was a lot of chasing projects, movie this and movie that," he said.

Harvey was good friends with another fellow journalism student, Richard Zoglin, who had also known Susan at UC Berkeley.

"Richard lived in New York," Harvey said. "I was there at her Beekman Place apartment with Richard. It wasn't like Susan had said, 'I found a nice place in a nice neighborhood.' It was more like, 'I'm *going* to live on Beekman Place. *This* is the street I want to live on.' My vague sense of the apartment was that it was nicely appointed and very specifically furnished."

Susan began getting assignments from top magazine editors.

"She was writing," Stephen Silverman said. "She wrote

a cover story for *New York* magazine on Bess Myerson. It upset Bess Myerson. [The magazine] titled it 'Queen Bee.'" Susan then went to work for *Us* magazine when it was just getting started in the early 1980s. Then CBS started a *People* magazine TV show, and "she went to work for *People*," Silverman said.

"When we were in New York, she called up a top editor," he continued, "and made a luncheon date. She asked me to go with her. For a while, I was her audience. I was like the kid brother. She'd invite me to her various appointments, as a bystander. She told the editor, 'I'm the world's best writer.' At the end of the lunch, Susan asked the editor, 'Am I going to write for you?' The editor very curtly said, 'I have lots of the "world's best writers" right here in New York, without you.'"

Silverman wasn't surprised. "Susan was a steamroller," he said. "Sometimes it worked to her advantage, and other times it didn't. 'I can write rings around so-and-so,' was Susan's mantra." Stephen said he remembered the luncheon as being "exhausting. You'd go to a restaurant and the poor waiter would get a lecture immediately."

Even so, in those days, Silverman said, he enjoyed Susan's company. "We were pals," he explained. "She lived at 34 Beekman Place. I was at 32. They were two adjoining brownstones that had been converted into studio and one-bedroom apartments."

"They were owned by a frisky older man," Silverman continued, "who mostly liked to have sexy young women stay there. Susan's apartment was on the ground floor, because she hated heights. Mine was on the second. These were really tiny apartments. They made the apartment on the 'Mary Tyler Moore' Show look like the Taj Mahal. As I recall, my rent was $325 a month. I think Susan's was a bit more. She had white walls without much on them. She never used the kitchen. She later bought a nice condo, on a low floor, at 30 Beekman Place. It was a very nice apartment, though by then I had moved away, so I wasn't there often."

For *New York* magazine, Susan wrote mostly gossip and entertainment items. And she hung out with a posse of successful writers and publicists, many of whom she'd met through her best friend Bobby Durst. They included original "Saturday Night Live" cast member Laraine Newman, publicist for the stars Liz Rosenbert, record company executive Danny Goldberg, New York writer Julie Baumgold, journalist Judy Licht, and Bobby Durst. "She was certainly the most brilliant person I ever knew," Rosenberg told *New York.*

Life for Susan was good, despite her phobias. Besides writing for some of the top publications in the country and hanging out with well established writers in the literary community, she enjoyed living on Beekman Place, a tiny, two-block historic neighborhood of luxury dwellings. The short street is sandwiched between First Avenue and the East River, and Fifty-first and Forty-ninth streets, on the fashionable East Side of Manhattan. It was named for the Beekman family, whose mansion stood there during the revolutionary war period. By the early 1920s, the striking views of the East River that Beekman Place offered attracted the well-to-do to the area. Mrs. William K. Vanderbilt, Anne Morgan, and Elizabeth Marbuary were credited with turning over Beekman Place to polite society. However, it was Emily Eaton Hepburn who was considered the grand Old Lady of Beekman Hill. A New Englander by birth, she was the wife of banker Barton Hepburn, and when John D. Rockefeller built One Beekman Place in the late 1920s she built Number Two across the street.

Some of the most illustrious people in society and show business at one time or another have lived on Beekman, including Katharine Hepburn, John D. Rockefeller III, Billy Rose, Irving Berlin, James Forrestal, Katherine Cornell, David Lillienthal, Huntington Hartford, Henry Luce, to name a few. Susan Berman chose to live there too.

The walkup Susan lived in was at the end of Beekman, across the street from Peter Detmold Park, a small but well-maintained neighborhood park with trees and benches.

During those years, "Susan spent money like there was no tomorrow," said her old friend Stephen Silverman. "For my twenty-fifth birthday, she took me to dinner at Elaine's. She had a trust fund. She was writing, but she didn't have a lot of money [coming in from writing]."

The first summer Susan lived in New York, in 1977, she received a phone call from a reporter. At the time Susan lived in her tiny one-room basement apartment with her dog, Oomi, and wrote for *People* magazine's TV show. A fellow writer called her and said he was writing a book about her father. The next day Susan met him at Sardi's, at West Forty-fourth Street in the heart of New York City's theatre district. He showed her multiple FBI reports about her father. Page after page were about criminal activities involving her dad.

"Did you know your father was a killer?" the reporter asked her.

Susan got up and walked out of the bar.

In September 1978, while still living on Beekman Place, Susan's Uncle Chickie died. He was seventy. Just five people, including Susan, attended the funeral in Idaho. Charles "Chickie" Berman had died, "indigent and bereft," Susan later wrote, "a broken man living in seedy motels in Las Vegas."

Chickie first had depended on his brother, Davie, for

money, and then on Susan because he was trustee of Susan's payments for her father's interests in hotels until she turned twenty-one, which is when the trust-fund payments went to Susan instead of Chickie. In addition, when Susan turned twenty, she was given a large lump-sum payment from her father's interests.

What her friends did not know was that she'd had money in the form of her trust fund and another large payout of mob proceeds from her father's interests when she turned thirty. She had gone through much of the money, squandering by overspending and making bad investments. She dressed in expensive St. Laurent blouses from Saks Fifth Avenue and pricey leather boots she bought in sets of two. She purchased three homes over the years and lost them all. She wasn't good with money, her cousin, Dave Berman, said, which prompted Susan, when she found herself broke again, to ask her friend Bobby Durst for help.

To those in her inner circle, Susan tried hard to keep up the pretense of having money. She still wanted to be treated as if she were wealthy, as if she were mob royalty. At some point, during those stressful years of having money and then being penniless, Susan went on prescription psychotherapy drugs, which she continued taking until her death. But her eccentricities continued.

"She could be plumb broke, but she'd be wearing $400 shoes," her cousin Dave said. "She'd walk into a restaurant, and she'd act like everybody should bow and scrape to her."

Through it all, Susan Berman became part of the celebrated stable of writers at New York magazine during its heyday. Also there was Nicholas Pileggi when the magazine first began publishing in 1968. Pileggi was still writing for New York when Susan signed on with the magazine in the late 1970s.

Even with her career looking up, "Susan was never quite satisfied with her lot in life, always looking for something better," said Stephen Silverman, who lived on Beekman from 1977 to 1979. "I can't say they were halcyon days for her."

While living in New York, Susan befriended Danny Goldberg, a record producer and a former CEO of Artemis Records who went on as president of Gold Village Entertainment. "I had a PR company, called Danny Goldberg and Associates," he said in a telephone interview from his New York offices. "One of my clients was the Electric Light Orchestra [band]. Susan was at *US* magazine and I was pitching her about doing a story about them. That's how we met." Susan introduced Danny to movie producer Lynda Obst. "Linda and I were partners in the development of what maybe could have been a movie *Easy Street.*"

Ed Bayley, Susan's dean at UC Berkeley, and his wife Monica visited her in Manhattan.

"We were in New York at the same time Susie was living in New York," Ed Bayley explained. "Susan was far from the world's best writer. I'd hoped she'd get a job at a newspaper. I think she was a competent writer but not much more than that."

Susan's writing stints in New York and her earlier reporting position at the *San Francisco Examiner* would be the only full-time positions she ever held. Everything else was freelance work.

In February 1979, death again visited Susan's life when her Aunt Lillian died. Susan attended the tiny funeral on March 2, 1979. Only three people were there. After the service, a friend of the family handed Susan a necklace—a medallion—her Aunt Lil left to her. It was a silver dollar with an etching on one side of the Star of David and the word *Zion*. The other side said *Davie Berman*. Susan later bequeathed the prized medallion to her best friend Bobby Durst.

The friend told her, 'Susie, only you are left now. Maybe some day you can make the world understand that your father Davie was a good man who acted out of the most basic desire, to see his family continue and survive."

Susan responded by telling her, "I intend to try."

Just about everyone Susan knew in those days encouraged her to write about her Las Vegas roots, because she talked about it so much. To them, it was colorful enough for a book. So she did.

The result was Susan's memoir, *Easy Street*. It would be the highlight of her career.

She would have more successes after that, but they were spread out, causing her financial difficulties off and on for the rest of her life.

It was the late 1970s and Susan began seriously delving into her father's background, which she described as his biography. It ended up being recognized as Susan's own memoir. *Easy Street* officially released on October 16, 1981 with a retail price of $13.95 a copy.

During her research for the book, the Superior, Wisconsin, Police Department sent Susan a mug shot, taken of her father when he was booked in their jail. She put it in her wallet and proudly showed it to everyone she knew.

An advance press release from Susan's publisher, The Dial Press (later purchased by Random House), dated August 31st, 1981, stated, "As a journalist, Susan Berman has a reputation for getting the 'impossible' interview. In 1977 she assigned herself the toughest investigative reporting job she had ever taken on—to find out the story her parents never wanted her to know, about her father's life as a mob gangster. For more than two years Susan Berman traced her family history and interviewed members of the mob to learn the truth about her father, Davie Berman. On October 16, 1981, the Dial Press will publish the most sensational personal story of the year, *Easy Street: The True Story of a Mob Family.*" The book included sixteen pages of black-and-white photos.

Her best buddy Bobby Durst threw her a lavish book launch party at a New York restaurant to celebrate what would be the first of five books by Susan. At the party, photos were taken of Susan and Bobby cheek to cheek, mugging for the camera. In the background was Bobby's wife.

The praise for *Easy Street* was impressive. Amy Wilentz with the *New Yorker* described it as, "A fascinating memoir." And *Publisher's Weekly* called it "a sensational story."

Susan, looking professional in a business suit, appeared on set at NBC in 1981 for an interview with Jane Pauley for NBC's *Today Show.* The TV piece was titled "Discovering Dad Was a Mobster."

Pauley introduced Susan by reading from a passage in Susan's memoir: "As the years passed, the little girl grew up, and only when she was an adult did she learn that her beloved father was one of the most powerful gangsters in the world."

Susan told Jane Pauley that she discovered her father's underworld life after a friend from UCLA suggested she go to the library and look up her father's name.

Then Pauley asked her, "You must have very mixed feelings. Is there a perverse sort of pride that your father was as big a guy as he was and an incredible shame that he was a pretty bad man?"

Susan wasn't put off by the question. She was proud of her dad, regardless of what he did.

"I feel no shame, Jane, because I was never motivated by hunger or starvation or the things that (my father) went through," she told Pauley. "I feel tremendous sadness that his life was so painful and the life of organized crime led in many ways to his early death and my mother's early suicide. I have sadness that their lives led to me living without parents."

"So, if anything," Susan continued, "I feel so sad that they had that type of life because of what he thought was really a free lunch but always turns out not to be."

As Susan continued researching background for her book, she told Pauley she went "underground off and on for three years" and dealt with "violent, unpredictable men." Her mother's fears, she relayed to Pauley, became her own "when I went on the road and found my mother's relatives in St. Paul.

She told Pauley that her parents had married when her mother was just nineteen, naïve about her father's life in the mob, and "totally in love. They were always madly in love. She had no idea that he was anything other than, really, an owner of gambling clubs in Minneapolis. She had no idea he had tentacles to organized crime."

"I was raised in the lap of luxury, where my dad was a hotel owner," Susan continued, speaking quickly. "There was no sign that (my father) was anything different. We were the 'First Family.' We road in the Helldorado parade. We went to all the openings, the celebrations. Jack Benny, Jimmy Durante—they were always at our house. There was no hint of this other life that he'd had before I was born."

The NBC interview was in the midst of Susan's national book tour. She looked tired, with bags under her eyes and too much makeup covering the dark circles.

Upon its release, an excerpt of *Easy Street* appeared as

a cover story in *New York* magazine—one of the benefits of being a staff writer at the increasingly popular monthly magazine. *New York* was relatively new at that juncture, competing with *The New Yorker*. The glossy *New York* magazine included news features about the city as well as restaurant reviews and coverage of entertainment and the arts. According to the publisher's press release, the *New York* magazine excerpt was "the longest in the magazine's history."

A second excerpt of *Easy Street* appeared in *Us* magazine (now *Us Weekly*), another one of the publications Susan worked for while she lived in New York. The excerpt coincided with the October 1981 official release date of the book.

Such national TV appearances and printed excerpts in New York publications are an author's dream. The publicity could not have been better for Susan. It generated a lot of buzz for the book.

It was all part of her month-long book tour that began October 16, 1981, with back-to-back interviews beginning with the New York media. Then she moved on to Philadelphia, Boston, Washington, D.C., Baltimore, Cleveland, Chicago, Minneapolis, Seattle, and San Francisco, ending November 18 in Los Angeles. Curiously, the tour did not make a stop in Las Vegas, although the two Las Vegas daily newspapers picked up the publisher's press release and wrote about it. Las Vegas was not a large market at the time, with very few book stores, and the publisher decided not to include it as a stop on the tour.

The publicity paid off. *Easy Street* was received with critical acclaim. The paperback rights sold as well. But hardcover sales were not as swift as expected. Even so, the book continued to receive national attention.

Herbert Mitgang, a writer for *The Montauk Fault*, wrote in his review of *Easy Street*: "I found it completely enthralling as a family story—so sad in its way, yet such an adventure in loyalty. The early life on a Jewish farming homestead in North Dakota especially should come as a complete revelation to many people; the search for roots there gives the book a depth beyond Las Vegas and the gangsters."

*Publisher's Weekly*, a prestigious literary publication, covered the book. The review, in part, read: "The author's struggle to reconcile the caring father and husband of an invalid wife—and a much-decorated war hero—with the ruthless mobster provides the real drama of this sensational story."

With the release of her book and the positive reviews, the 1980s were mostly good to Susan and her career. She went on to sell the movie rights for *Easy Street* to Universal Studios for $350,000, a good chunk of change in the early 1980s. The pair of producers working on the movie project were Alan Carr and Ray Stark, both heavy hitters in the film industry. Three years earlier, in 1978, Stark won a Golden Globe for producing *California Suite*, and Carr won a Golden Globe for *Grease*.

Susan's friend, Danny Goldberg, an executive in the music industry, helped Susan iron out some of the details of the movie deal.

"I worked with her briefly," Goldberg said. "Susan had asked me, when *Easy Street* came out, to be involved with the sale of the film rights. Although I was in the record business and not the movie business, I had some contacts there. She liked the idea that she thought she could trust me to look after her interests. She introduced me to Lynda Obst, who is a movie producer. Lynda and I were partners in the development of what maybe could have been a movie *Easy Street*."

After being paid the large fee for the movie rights, the project failed. "Most screenplays never get made into a movie," Goldberg pointed out, adding that it goes with the business. "In that sense, like many writers of unmade films, I think Susan was disappointed."

On the other hand, Stephen Silverman pointed out that Susan had put demands on the producers. "She insisted she had to write the screenplay," he said. "The movie fell apart. She was the queen of pushy."

The movie also never got off the ground because it had became overshadowed by the bestselling novel and box office blockbuster *The Godfather*.

Within two years, in 1983, Susan left New York City. Once again, Susan got antsy. Boosted financially from the payment for the movie rights—which she did not have to return even though the film was never made—she decided to move to Los Angeles to embark on a screenwriting career in the heavily competitive Hollywood arena. To do that, she was told she needed to be on the West Coast where the action was. She told friends she wanted to become "a famous Hollywood screenwriter."

She sold her co-op apartment on Beekman Place, and left the Big Apple for life in the City of Angels that she remembered with fondness as a child: the expensive lunches at the Brown Derby with her father, and shopping sprees with her mother at the best shops on Beverly Hills' Rodeo Drive.

Her friend Liz Rosenburg drove her to the airport the day she left New York for good. "I remember putting my coat over her head as I drove her to the airport because you've got to go through a bridge or tunnel to get to an airport in

New York," Liz said. She was deathly afraid of bridges and tunnels and had a lot of phobias. She was screaming and very, very freaked out. The fear was very real."

Liz also recalled it as a bittersweet send off: "That was a very sad goodbye, because it was the last time I saw her."

Once in L.A. and still flush with money, Susan paid cash for a sporty new black convertible sedan. She also took out a lease in a rental house in Beverly Hills, at 1527 Benedict Canyon Drive, the same home she would move back into later and be murdered in. In those days, it was a lovely, cheerful place. The owner, Dee Schiffer, maintained it well.

Susan was in good company. Among the celebrated who lived on the canyon road were Jacqueline Bisset, Elizabeth Montgomery, until her death in 1995, Mike Myers, Eddie Murphy, Martin Lawrence, Stephanie Powers, and Ann Margret.

By all appearances, Susan Berman enjoyed living in Beverly Hills. She frequented Martindale's Book Store on Santa Monica Boulevard, where her father had taken her shopping as a girl for Nancy Drew and Beverly Cleary books. She looked up her cousins, Tom Padden III and Tom Padden Jr., who were living in Los Angeles at the time. "It was a big deal for her to be in touch with any family," Tom III said. Even though Susan had a car, she often called on Tom to drive her to appointments. He'd have to drive miles out of the way to avoid any roadway that remotely resembled a bridge, because of Susan's phobia. "It was irrational at times," he said. "I really did enjoy spending time with her, but I also had to deal with that. I didn't know where it was coming from. It was part drama and part real, I think."

Back then, Tom pointed out, "Her priority was to make

it big as a writer. Everything else, she put on the periphery. It was her main focus. She aspired to reach higher levels."

Susan also gravitated toward people in the business. So it came as no surprise when Susan met an aspiring writer and became romantically involved with him. They met two months after Susan arrived in Los Angeles, standing in the script registration line at the Writers Guild office. His name was Mister Margulies. ("Yes, that was his name," Susan wrote in her memoir.) He was twenty-five and a starving poet. Susan was thirty-eight with stars in her eyes for Hollywood.

The day Susan met Mister, she wore a large gold necklace and pendant with the words "Easy Street" spelled out. Her friend Elizabeth Mehren remembered the jewelry well because the pendant stood out. "It was too big," Elizabeth commented.

That big pendant caught Mister's eye. When he and Susan began chatting, he told her, "I know you." Mister recognized her from her author's photo on the back book jacket for her memoir *Easy Street*.

Mister's father, Jay Margulies, had once worked for Susan's dad and, when Susan's books were each released, he bought them, including the novels. "My father loved your dad," Mister told Susan. In fact, he said, according to Susan's account in *Lady Las Vegas*, "My Hebrew name is David Abraham. I was named for your dad. I'm from Vegas."

Like Susan, Mister's childhood was spent in the Mojave Desert. Susan was instantly attracted. And instantly smitten. He was someone who knew where she had come from. He not only understood who her father was, but his father had known her dad. "Oh, my God, you're from *Vegas*?" Susan squealed, incredulously.

"Yeah, I'm from Vegas, and I'm a writer," Mister said.

He didn't seem to mind or notice the age difference. She

later wrote that she fell in love with Mister "for the brilliant, loving, unique person he was."

Ruthie Bartnof, who was best friends with Mister's mother, until her death in 2001, said, "Their fathers were close, but Susan and Mister had never met [as children], so it was amazing that they met by accident in the script registration line at the Writers Guild."

Mister soon moved in with Susan. Not long after, they made plans to marry.

Just before her wedding, Susan had dinner with Elizabeth Mehren, and Susan talked about her upcoming wedding as well as her writing projects.

"There was always a project she had going about Las Vegas," Elizabeth said. "I don't know if she was trying to answer the questions to her life or whether she genuinely was interested in what she was doing. I remember thinking, *This is a woman who made a career out of being the orphaned daughter of the Jewish mobster from Las Vegas.*" "It was so pathetic," Elizabeth continued. "She was stuck there. She never could shirk that part of her life. She basically exploited it. And it's all just an illusion. She couldn't give any of it up, right down to the little-girl hairdo."

Rilo Weisner grew up in the desert with Mister and his sister Candace. "I knew Mister when he was a kid," Rilo said from her Las Vegas home. "His sister Candy and I were the same age. He was always her little brother to me. We went to Sunday school together." They graduated from high school in 1969, with Mister a year behind them.

"Mister and Susan had similar backgrounds," Rilo said. "Jay [Mister's father] ran the gift shop at the Riviera, and Mister was always going to the Strip. He was used to being treated like he was Las Vegas royalty, similar to Susan. My mother and his mother were very close friends.

"When I knew him, he didn't have a drug problem. He was an observer. There was a sense of mystery about him, like he had a secret. But he was witty and bright."

Mister became a drug user long before he met Susan. Susan, her friends say, like her father before her, never indulged in alcohol or drugs, except to drink an occasional glass of wine at Passover. Rilo didn't realize, until after Susan's death, that Mister had used drugs during his teenage years.

Las Vegas teenagers "were certainly exposed to drugs," according to Guy Rocha, who graduated from Clark High School in 1969. "I can tell you this," he said in a telephone interview from northern Nevada, "there was a great deal of drug use at Clark when I attended. I remember that even some of the star football players were strung out. Things were much different in Las Vegas {than in other cities}— rampant drug use, race riots, and overall life in the fast lane."

In the summer of 1984, Susan and Mister married. Susan paid for a lavish wedding on Stone Canyon Road at the elegant Hotel Bel-Air, a red-tiled Mediterranean villa nestled on eleven-acre park-like grounds and gardens. Susan ordered expensive ice swans, eerily reminiscent of the ones her father regularly ordered for the Flamingo Hotel.

Susan and Mister's June wedding was held outdoors, near the hotel's Swan Lake. Guests sat under a canopy of trees. Absent her father and Uncle Chickie, Susan asked Bobby Durst to do the honors of walking her down the aisle. Without hesitation, Durst agreed. After all, Bobby was family, like a brother. He had evolved from the brother she never had to a father figure she'd long ago lost. Bobby tucked Susan's arm under his and walked her down the aisle to give her away. She couldn't have been more proud. At the reception, well-known movie producer and Paramount Pictures executive Robert Evans delivered a toast to Susan, calling her "the most seductive woman I ever met." Susan could not have been prouder.

The wedding venue was the same hotel where Susan's cousin Raleigh Padveen was married some thirty years earlier when Susan was a young girl. Raleigh was Davie Berman's favorite niece, and Susan remembered how happy her father was at Raleigh's wedding. "He stood for hours talking to friends and relatives as he watched the swans swim in the outdoor pond," Susan wrote in *Easy Street*. It was as if, with her own ceremony, which cost her thousands of dollars, Susan tried to relive that moment, the day she witnessed her father so happy, by replicating her cousin's wedding.

"Susan's wedding was a child's fairytale dream," her cousin, Deni Marcus, told MSNBC. "She wanted to be the bride, to walk down the aisle, throw the bouquet, and retire forever to a house with a picket fence and kids and dogs playing in the yard."

Mister moved into Susan's rented Benedict Canyon home. "There was love in the house," Kim Lankford, Susan's friend since the 1980s and whom they each referred to as "sisters in arms," said in an interview with *New York* magazine. "They were crazy about each other."

For her wedding day, Susan tried to play Cupid by setting up Elizabeth Mehren on a date to the wedding with one of the Durst brothers.

"I was living in Santa Monica and I remember having dinner with (Susan) one night at the old restaurant on Wilshire called the Bicycle [Shop] Cafe," Elizabeth said. "At some point, she told me she was dating and she had fallen in love with this man. He was younger than she was. By a lot.

She told me his name. Mister Margulies. I asked her, 'Well, what do you call him for short?' She looked at me, mystified, and said, 'Mister.' She wanted to invite me to her wedding at the Hotel Bel-Air. She wanted to set me up with her friend and wanted me to sit at the table with one of the Dursts, either Bobby or Doug. I just dimly remember 'Bobby' as being part of the discussion. I didn't go to the wedding because I was in the process of being swept off my feet by another man."

That was the last time Elizabeth heard from Susan. Susan never forgave her for not attending her wedding.

Her cousin, Tom Padden III, however, did attend. "I met Durst," Tom said. He remembered him that day as being "quiet and offish." Shortly after the ceremony, Susan picked out a home in Brentwood, another classy neighborhood—a years-old habit of living amidst and hobnobbing with the elite. It was comprised of mostly mansions for the well-to-do. Susan bought the home in the exclusive community, located just off Sunset Boulevard, at 12030 Coyne Street, around the corner from the Bundy Drive townhouse Nicole Brown Simpson would live and die in.

Even a beautiful home, however, could not give Susan the happiness she sought nor save her marriage. Susan's cousins, Tom Padden III and Tom Padden Jr., regularly visited Susan and Mister during the time the relationship began to crumble. "When things went bad with Mister and his drug use," Tom III said, "we backed away."

Mister had fallen back into his drug habit. Their relationship, in turn, unraveled. Susan was heart-broken.

The marriage had lasted just seven months. Susan called friends, crying. "It's over. He's been doing drugs again, and he's been abusing me," she said.

Susan Berman knew when she married Mister that he'd done heroin, but she thought he'd quit. Susan wasn't a user, friends said. "Her friends were very druggy, but she wasn't," Stephen Silverman recalled. "[And] she just didn't like alcohol, although that might also have had something to do with her allergy to wheat."

On January 10, 1986, two-and-a-half years after Susan had met her future husband and after the couple divorced, Mister, at age twenty-seven, died of a self-induced drug overdose. Susan wrote in *Lady Las Vegas* that Mister was "on the brink of Hollywood success as a screenwriter" when he died. At the time, Susan and Mister were working at reconciliation. She had told friends of her hopes of one day getting back together with Mister.

Following his death, Susan had an emotional breakdown. As her cousin Tom Padden III put it, "She was in a depressed state." She began talking to a New York psychic, Barbara Stabiner, to help her through her depression. At one point, Susan threatened to jump from a Los Angeles rooftop, but Stabiner, during a phone session, talked her out of it. With the loss of Mister, Susan developed allergies and more phobias.

With yet one more loss in her life, it appeared almost too much for Susan to bear. First, she lost her father, then her mother, her Uncle Chickie, and Aunt Lil, and, now, Mister Margulies. Despite the divorce, Susan's friends described Mister as "the love of her life."

After Mister's death, Susan stayed in contact with his mother, Harriet Margulies. "Susan was very close to Harriet," said Harriet's best friend Ruthie Bartnof. "She remained in touch with her, and Harriett felt as though Susan was a part of Mister. Susan was broken up about his death. Her whole life was so tragic."

But amidst the tragedy and sorrow in her life, Ruthie noted, "It was so much fun being with her. She was *really* fun. She knew everybody. She had a way about her. She had her own groupies, people who loved being around her.

Even with the sadness, she had a great sense of humor. Her heartache was really that of an abandoned child."

To help her work through her grief in losing Mister, Susan eventually penned an unpublished biography about him.

"She wrote a manuscript about Mister," Ruthie Bartnof said. "I read it, but I don't know what Susan did with it."

In the wake of Mister's death, Susan was prophetic about her own fate, writing in *Lady Las Vegas*, "Mister didn't make it out of Vegas alive. . . . Did he meet the doom meant for me? Is there a curse on Vegas parents and their children?"

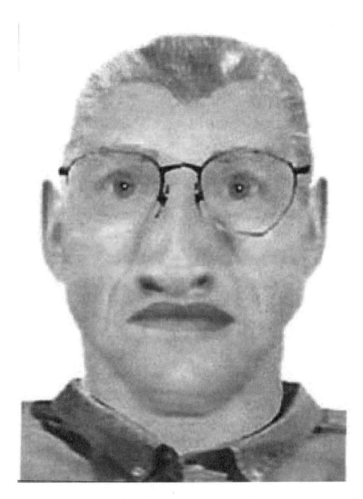

Composite police drawing of suspect, which a witness
and police say resembles Robert Durst, in the
northern California kidnap case, dubbed the
"Mr. Potato Head" sketch

Susan Berman at book launch in Venice beach, California

Susan Berman (courtesy Dial Press, *Easy Street*)

Davie, Gladys and Susie Berman at the Flamingo Hotel
during happier times (courtesy UNLV Special Collections)

Racketeer Gun Greenbaum (left), Mob boss Davie
Berman, and gangster Willie "Ice Pick" Alderman at the
Flamingo Hotel

Susan Berman's Benedict Canyon home, where she was
found dead (photo by Cathy Scott)

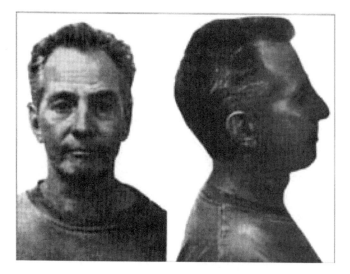

Police mugshot of Robert Durst after his arrest in
Galveston, Texas

Gladys and Davie Berman in Minnesota shortly after
their marriage (courtesy of *Dial Press, Easy Street*)

Police rap sheet for Davie Berman in Superior, Wisconsin

Inscription from Susan's Book Lady Las Vegas on display
at the Nevada State Museum in Las Vegas, Nevada

The plaque that marks Susan Berman's grave at the
Home of Peace cemetery in Los Angeles.

# CHAPTER 8

# SUSIE AND BOBBY

IN 1967, A HANDSOME, suave, and wealthy man walked into Susan Berman's life, where he would remain for more than three decades.

"I'm Susan. What's your name?" Susan quickly blurted out to a fellow student almost as soon as she sat next to him.

"Bobby."

Susan met Bobby Durst during her last year at UCLA, where she did her undergraduate work before transferring to UC Berkeley. Bobby wasn't taken aback by Susan's abrupt introduction in the quad area on campus. Susan was attracted to Bobby's quiet charm and he with her quick wit. They became fast friends and almost immediately each other's confidant. It was strictly platonic.

They had much in common. During that first conversation, Susan learned the Bobby, too, had lost his mother at a young age, which gave them an instant connection. They each were raised by wealthy fathers.

Susan looked up to Bobby and often talked about him to her friends, like a proud younger sister.

From that initial meeting on campus, Susan Berman and Bobby Durst forged a tight bond that would span more than thirty years. Susie, the daughter of a notorious Las Vegas gangster, and Bobby, heir to the billion dollar Durst real-estate fortune, were drawn to each other. Susan was intrigued with Bobby's well-to-do background; Bobby was fascinated by Susan's underworld history. While they didn't take classes together—their majors were different and they were enrolled in separate programs—they met up on campus. They slowly got to know each other. They began getting together in the library and cafeteria, then off campus at local student hang-out spots. Durst became part of Susan's inner circle of friends. Bobby, however, didn't appear to have any friends from school, other than Susan.

While Susan was drawn to Bobby from the outset, she was never attracted to him romantically. "Never," Ruthie Bartnof said. "They were like brother and sister." Bobby was simply a "guy friend." Her friends said, from the start of their relationship, it was always, "Bobby this and Bobby that." Susan referred to him as her "big brother," the older sibling she never had. She went to Bobby for advice about school work. She was thrilled to learn that Bobby was Jewish. That was always a bonus for her, her friends said, to meet someone she liked, then find out he was Jewish, just like her. Susan's friends never knew precisely what to make of Bobby Durst. All they knew was that Susan adored him. A photo was once snapped at a party of Susan holding Bobby's face in both of her hands. It was typical of her doting, sisterly nature toward him.

To friends, Susan "generally gushed about him," Stephen Silverman said. "One always had the feeling that, for whatever reason—I somehow thought it had to do with his vast wealth, though that could have been my own personal bias—it would not be wise to proffer any criticism about Bobby, as Susan wouldn't stand for it. This was, it should be noted, a rather odd circumstance with her, given how she so adored ripping people to shreds behind their backs." Throughout Silverman's friendship with Susan, and while living next door to her in New York, he noted, "Bobby Durst was around."

Kathie Durst, her friend Gilberte Najamy said, understood her husband's friendship with Susan. "Kathie wasn't jealous of Susan," Gilberte said. "They were friends. They liked each other. But Susie was clearly Bobby's friend. She turned on Kathie after she disappeared, because Susie was protecting Bobby. And I was more of an antagonist with Susan than a friend, because I kept saying, 'Bobby killed Kathie.'"

Oftentimes, wherever Susan was, Bobby would show up. Danny Goldberg agreed, saying, "Bobby was always around."

"I met Bobby Durst briefly, close to twenty years ago, sometime in the seventies," Goldberg said. "Susan's friends were the closest thing she had to family, and Bobby was in her inner circle."

Nyle Brenner also commented about Bobby. "He's always been somebody in her life," Brenner told the *Los Angeles Times*. He noted that after police announced that they were again looking closely at the Kathie Durst missing person case, Susan mentioned she was "worried about Bobby [Durst]."

It wasn't only Bobby's intellect and wit Susan was drawn to; she was also attracted to his prestigious position in life. "Susan was a woman who had a lot of friends who were famous or near famous or formerly famous," her friend Linda Smith told *New York* magazine, "and she moved in circles that were very interesting for her."

On December 19th, five days before her body was

found, Susan began commenting to friends that she had information that would "blow the top off things." Everyone assumed she was referring to blowing the lid off of a mob case. Later, after her murder, they instead believed she was talking about having damaging information in the decades' old Kathleen Durst missing person's case. Because Susan was a "drama queen," as some referred to her, they didn't press her for more information. Her friends simply listened. The truth was, nearly everything was a drama with Susan. They couldn't tell when the theatrics were based in truth and when they were dramatically blown out of proportion. In retrospect, after Susan's murder, the saga appeared to be real. It was comparable to the boy who cried wolf. No one gave it any mind, because Susan had told them tall tales so many times before.

Susan, according to Ruthie Bartnof, had a good relationship with Bobby Durst and regarded him as a brother, a sibling she was protective of him. She was never afraid of him. But was Bobby really protective toward *her*? Some say he felt sorry for Susan more than he was protective.

"She was very close to Bobby," Ruthie said, "and he was very, very generous toward her. Always. He gave her away at her wedding to Mister like he was her father."

Susan was so close to Bobby that after Kathie Durst's disappearance, Susan Berman was Bobby's unofficial spokeswoman. Susan fielded questions from family members, friends, and the media.

Some friends said Susan knew too much and that Bobby was worried she would say something to New York authorities that would land him in prison. Twelve months later, after things had settled down, Susan moved from New York City to Los Angeles.

Private eye Bobbi Bacha described Susan's departure

from New York as "fleeing," and she repeated it often to a variety of reporters. "Susan got out of town as soon as Kathie Durst disappeared," Bacha said. But that wasn't accurate. Susan didn't leave New York City until 1983, the year after Kathie Durst's disappearance, and, then, it was, at least on the surface, to pursue a screenwriting career, to expand as a writer.

Berman's friends—and some law enforcement members— strongly believed her killer to be a lifelong friend, one she trusted to her death. Could it have been her trusted friend Bobby Durst? And what would have been the motive? "It's hard for me to believe he turned on her," Ruthie Bartnof said. "He was sympathetic toward her. He felt sorry for her. I never dreamt this would happen to her."

A motive, however, seemed clear: New York state authorities were looking to re-interview Susan about the disappearance of Bobby Durst's wife, Kathleen, nineteen years earlier. That, friends said, made Bobby nervous. But did it unnerve him enough to want to cause Susan harm? The evidence against Durst was compelling, although, as of November 2013, he had not been charged in connection with Susan Berman's murder. Along with a motive, there was opportunity, with Bobby in California at the time Susan was murdered, where his attorney said he was.

Tom Padden Jr., Susan's cousin once removed, added even more insight. He strongly remembers Susan telling him in confidence that "Durst buried his wife under a house. Susan didn't say *what* house," Tom noted, just that it was a house.

For Gilberte Najamy, a Newton, Connecticut, woman who was a friend of Kathleen and Robert Durst's during their marriage and one of the last people to see Kathie alive, the link to Kathie's disappearance was obvious. "I find it hard to believe there is not a connection between Kathie's disappearance and Susan Berman's murder," Gilberte said. "For him to kill his wife and to kill Susan Berman is unbelievable. The Susie I knew was at the top of her game. Things were going well for her. I saw a woman riding high on her reputation who had gotten a huge payoff on her book *Easy Street.*

Meanwhile, Los Angeles police were still looking at Brenner as a person of interest in Susan's murder. Even so, the case appeared to be at a standstill—that is, until ten months after the death when her best friend, Robert Durst, was arrested in Galveston, Texas, and charged in another murder. That appears to be when police interest in Brenner moved over to Durst.

It looked like the break in the case police were looking for. With Durst, as they had done with Brenner, Los Angeles detectives did not arrest or file charges against Bobby. In fact, they still had not had an in-depth interview with Durst. They only spoke with him once on the phone, and it was not considered a formal interview. Rather, they appeared to be still aiming in another direction, still snooping around Susan's personal manager Nyle Brenner. Eventually, though, police interest in Brenner faded too, turning up no evidence linking him to Susan's murder.

Susan's death left one out-of-town prosecutor looking for more answers, especially when it came to Bobby Durst.

"The timing of Susan Berman's death is extremely curious," Westchester County District Attorney Jeanine Pirro said in a phone interview.

That's because, she commented, New York State police needed to ask Susan what she knew about a phone call that Kathleen Durst supposedly made to inform her medical school dean that she was sick and would not be at school.

The call was placed the day after Kathleen vanished. It was widely believed that Susan, and not Kathleen, was the caller. That, and whatever else Susan might recall, was what authorities wanted to question her about.

"I think it was Susan Berman who made that call," Kathie Durst's friend, Ellen Strauss, told "48 Hours." "I think that's why Susan Berman was killed. Once the story broke about the case re-opening, I think Bob was trying to mop up all the loose ends."

It wasn't like Susan to keep secrets from her friends, they said. She mostly spilled her guts during her regular marathon telephone conversations to a sundry of people.

One secret, however, that Susan Berman *was* able to keep under wraps for nearly two decades was what she eventually confided to at least one friend.

According to a report in *New York* magazine, Susan revealed the bombshell news that Bobby Durst had confessed to her that he had killed his wife. Susan's friends, after her death, wished that they had pressed her further to ferret out more details. Maybe they could have helped her, or, at the least, advised her, they said.

After police reopened the Kathie Durst missing person's case, investigators were eager to question Susan. Durst learned that the investigation into his missing wife's disappearance had reopened.

It wasn't easy to miss.

The news broke prominently in the *New York Times* on November 11, 2000, a Saturday, that police had searched, using a cadaver dog to detect human remains, Kathie and Robert Durst's former Westchester house, which Robert had sold years earlier.

The *New York Daily News* contacted Durst about the revelation. He told them, "I know nothing about it, but I would not have any comment." Then, Bobby Durst's brother, Douglas, issued a statement: "Robert Durst continues to maintain his innocence."

Susan Berman was part of the breaking news. It was reported that New York State and NYPD investigators, working together, were seeking to speak with Susan, because Susan served as Robert Durst's representative in the aftermath of Kathie's disappearance. Police wanted to know what Susan knew.

With the Kathleen Durst investigation reopened after being dormant nearly two decades, Kathie's family and friends were hopeful the investigation would be reclassified from a missing person's case to a homicide. As the new inquiry took off, Bobby Durst fled New York and hid out in Galveston, Texas, living incognito and in disguise as a mute woman.

Durst was wanted for questioning as the Number One suspect in his wife's disappearance, but he was nowhere to be found.

In the meantime, investigators left Susan Berman several phone messages, seeking to speak with her, but Susan did not return the calls. Did Susan tell Bobby Durst the police had contacted her? Did Bobby feel pressured?

Forty-nine days later, Susan Berman was found dead before detectives were able to interview her. The coincidence of Susan's death as police sought to interview her was not lost on investigators, nor on Kathie Durst's friend, Gilberte Najamy.

She blamed New York state authorities, in part, as well as the media, for tipping off Durst about the re-investigation into Kathie's case.

"There was a leak that New York state police wanted to interview Susie Berman," Najamy said. "They got her killed because Bobby found out they wanted to re-interview her."

Once word was out that the case was reopened, "Susan Berman was at risk," Najamy said. "New York state police should have protected her, or interviewed her immediately. I even gave them a map leading them straight to Susan's house. But they didn't go."

Gilberte Najamy also blamed Robert Durst's family for not warning both Susan Berman and Kathie Durst of Bobby's dark side. "They should have said something," Gilberte said.

About the same time police were arriving at Susan's Benedict Canyon house the afternoon before Christmas 2000, Robert Durst was on a plane from northern California to New York City, his attorney Dick DeGuerin—a mild-mannered Texas rancher who carries a Stetson and wears leather cowboy boots into court—said in a surprising admission. Durst owned a three-unit building at 52 Telegraph Place in San Francisco, a mere five-and-a-half hour drive to Susan's Benedict Canyon home. He owned the home in downtown San Francisco, which he had purchased just before his marriage to Kathleen and sold just after Susan's murder.

Furthermore, in an exclusive interview from his Houston law office, Durst's attorney offered up an alibi for his client. "He was on an airplane when Susan's killing occurred," said DeGuerin, well known for his successful defense style and named by the State Bar of Texas as "Outstanding Criminal Defense Lawyer of the Year" in 1994. "Mr. Durst was on his way to New York from northern California. He has an alibi."

But that alibi was not completely accurate, and certainly not air tight. That particular day, the Sunday before Christmas, marked the afternoon Susan's body was found, not the day she was murdered. The fact was that Susan Berman's door had been left open sometime between the late hours of Friday or the early hours of Saturday, which was indicated by neighbors who saw her dogs loose outside her home. The dogs were loose until officers arrived Sunday afternoon. That put the time of death at a day and a half before Susan's body was discovered. Which put Durst in California at the time of his friend's murder.

As for the reason the killer left Susan's back door open, LAPD Detective Paul Coulter told Dateline NBC, "I don't care who you are. I mean, when you've done something bad, your heart starts pounding and your adrenaline is running. And you don't care about the door being open. You don't need to re-secure the place. Your thought is, 'Get away.'"

And get away, the gunman did.

Was it Durst, as police have suspected for a dozen years? Durst's airplane alibi did not help him. Instead of making him appear innocent, it pointed toward circumstantial evidence that Durst was in close proximity to Susan's house, placing him squarely in California before and after Susan's murder.

Authorities checked out defense attorney DeGuerin's statement that his client was in northern California at the time of Susan's murder. They did it using Durst's own receipts and bank activity during that time span.

It is this latest evidence that debunks Durst's alibi and instead shows that he would have had enough time to have been able to pull it off, according to police sources. Detectives in Los Angeles and San Francisco have documents that place Robert Durst in Los Angeles on the day of Susan's murder.

LAPD Lieutenant Tom Thompson, who in 2012 oversaw the Berman investigation, told me, in a phone interview, that San Francisco police had reached out to LAPD's Homicide-Robbery bureau to assist in the investigation.

The news that San Francisco police shared with the LAPD was stunning. "San Francisco police contacted us when Durst resurfaced there," Thompson told me. "They said they could put Durst in Los Angeles at the time of the murder." That information, coupled with DeGuerin's statement as to his client's California whereabouts and LAPD's documentation—plane ticket and use of credit card—could be given either to a grand jury or the Los Angeles County District Attorney's office as the evidence needed to hand down an indictment for murder against Robert Durst. The details point to a classic scenario for murder: motive, opportunity, no alibi, and the last person to see the victim alive. The question is, why have Los Angeles authorities not charged Durst?

It's certainly not without trying on the LAPD's part. A source inside the police department told me that former Detective Paul Coulter, who led the Berman investigation for several years, approached the Los Angeles County District Attorney's office on several occasions, presenting what he had against Durst and asking that the case be prosecuted. But, I was told, the district attorney declined.

The district attorney's office did not return my calls for comment. A source inside the LAPD, however, confirmed to me that the FBI, in conjunction with the LAPD, has been investigating Durst in connection with several missing person cases across the U.S., most notably the case of Karen Mitchell, a sixteen year old from Eureka, California who disappeared in 1997. Durst, police say, was in and out of San Francisco on a regular basis between 1995 and 2001. He had a house in Trinidad, about 300 miles north of San Francisco and just 20 miles from Eureka. Durst had frequented a homeless shelter where the girl worked as a volunteer. Durst also, police said, visited Karen Mitchell at her part-time job as a shoe-store clerk.

Witnesses told police that Karen Mitchell was last seen getting into a car with an older man. A woman working as a prostitute in the area witnessed the abduction and gave police enough information for a composite sketch of the suspect. Among police, the sketch became known as the "Mr. Potato Head composite," and it strongly resembled Robert Durst. Eureka Police Detective Davis Parris announced to reporters at the time that Durst was one of several people under investigation in connection with Karen Mitchell's disappearance.

In another case, police investigated the disappearance of Kristen Modafferi, a young woman who lived in the San Francisco Bay Area. She'd turned eighteen just before her disappearance. Modafferi has not been declared dead and, according to inspector Sgt. Kyra Delaney with the San Francisco Police Department's homicide unit, Modafferi's case was never classified a homicide. Modafferi disappeared five months before Mitchell. Modafferi left her server job at a San Francisco restaurant and headed for Land's End Beach on San Francisco Bay.

Detective John Bradley, originally with Eureka police who went on to become an investigator with the San Francisco District Attorney's Office, investigated Durst's connection to northern California through a search warrant that Eureka police obtained to get Durst's financial records and credit cards. The records, Bradley said, placed Durst in northern California on the weekend before Kristen Modafferi's disappearance and on the day of Karen Mitchell's disappearance. Durst has not been named a suspect or person of interest in those cases.

Another vital piece of information emerged from tracking Durst's movement across the state. Durst's financial records placed him in Los Angeles at the time of Susan Berman's murder.

It was such a big enough finding that then-Eureka police

Detective Bradley contacted the LAPD's Robbery-Homicide Unit to share the information. Lieutenant Tommy Thompson then brought it up to me when I contacted his office shortly before Thompson's retirement from the force. Armed with documentation that Durst was in L.A. when Susan Berman was killed, the case, nevertheless, was still not presented to the D.A.'s office for possible prosecution. Now, though, with the FBI's involvement in the case, specifically Special Agent Eric Perry who, according to a source, is heading the investigation, Susan's murder case has a good chance of moving forward toward an indictment.

The latest LAPD detective to lead the Susan Berman homicide investigation at the LAPD is Detective George Shamlyn, who was brought in during the summer of 2012. When reached at his office in downtown Los Angeles, Shamlyn said, "The lead detective, Paul Coulter, retired. He was in charge and he passed it on to me. I can't comment." Shamlyn did not mention that the FBI was working in concert with the LAPD on its own probe.

According to the timeline laid out by law enforcement, it shows that Durst would have had enough time to drive the 375 miles south on Interstate 5, to Los Angeles, turning around and returning on Saturday to the San Francisco Bay Area in ample time to catch his plane to New York the following day, on Sunday morning just before noon, which was when Susan's body was discovered. That's the same day Durst's attorney, Dick DeGuerin, confirmed that Durst had left on his flight to New York.

As for all California crimes now under scrutiny by the FBI—the disappearance of teenagers Karen Mitchell and Kristen Modafferi and the murder of Susan Berman—now-retired Eureka Detective John Bradley commented, "We have a hunch that all of these cases are interrelated."

In the final four years of Susan's life, she'd connected with a new group of friends, all from Nevada. The group included Deke Castleman, Hal Rothman, and Guy Rocha. She regularly phoned them. What was noteworthy is that she never mentioned Bobby Durst to them. In the 1970s and 1980s, Susan constantly spoke of Bobby to her friends, even though many had never met him.

That was not the case in the late 1990s. Her relationship with Bobby had changed. He drifted away from Susan, isolating himself. She no longer had easy access to him.

What Susan did not know was that Robert Durst had been living several different lives, including as a woman. Wearing dresses and teetering on high heels, he lived as "Diane Winn" in New Orleans. Then, he popped up in Galveston as a mute cross-dressing man donning fake dark eyebrows and a white mustache who frequented gay bars.

In Galveston, he sometimes referred to himself—in a small notepad he carried to jot notes to people—as "Roberta" instead of Robert.

It was bizarre, and Susan, had she known, no doubt would not have been amused.

He went back and forth to New York City's Manhattan, where he lived as a man. Susan was unaware of Bobby's bizarre behavior and odd dress, and she was unaware that he was living in a rundown weekly apartment near Galveston Bay and that his erratic and bizarre behavior was escalating.

It was that very strangeness about Bobby Durst, Susan's friends later said, that put her in harm's way. Because Susan was so defensive and protective of her lifelong friend, she may have disregarded his odd behavior, accepting him no matter what. Durst knew that about Susan. Did Durst use Susan's undying loyalty as an opportunity to catch her off guard?

# CHAPTER 9

# ROBERT DURST: "MR. POTATO HEAD"

FOUR PEOPLE WHO are believed to have crossed paths with Robert Durst are either dead or missing. First, his wife disappeared and Durst told police he was the last one to see her alive. Second, Susan Berman, his good friend, was murdered. Third, Morris Black, a neighbor of Durst, was murdered and chopped up and Durst admitted to killing him, but in self-defense. And fourth, Kristen Modafferi in Eureka, California, was last seen getting into a car with an older man who police said matched the description of Robert Durst.

The seemingly domino effect of deaths and disappearances crossing Durst's path began in 1981 when Robert's wife Kathie went missing. Did Durst have anything to do with their demises, cutting down those he thought could tie him to Kathie's disappearance, most prominently Morris Black and Susan Berman? On the surface, it appears plausible. His life-time confidant Susan Berman knew him better than anyone, and she too was gone. Any information about Kathleen's disappearance and secrets Durst may have shared with Susan went to the grave with Susan Berman.

Though they don't say it publicly—but do utter it privately—many in law enforcement, including those in the Los Angeles Police Department, believe Robert Durst murdered Susan Berman, including Detective Paul Coulter, who took the case to the D.A.'s office only to be turned away.

Durst's criminal attorney, in his client's defense, adamantly denies that Robert Durst had anything to do with Susan Berman's slaying.

From his jail-house cell, Bobby Durst also denied it. Durst told this to Sareb Kaufman, while in jail for the murder of Black in Texas.

Morris Black, described by those who knew him as cranky, cantankerous, paranoid and eccentric, lived at 2213 Avenue K, across the hall from Dorothy Ciner, who was really Bobby Durst and who rented apartment No. 2. The building where Durst lived was a nondescript thirties-era bungalow that had been converted into a fourplex. It was typical of a Galveston neighborhood on a palm tree and cottonwood-lined street with homes that had hurricane shutters and gingerbread trim. But this particular bungalow was rundown.

Durst, fifty-eight at the time of his arrest, initially told Texas State District Judge Susan Criss that he was innocent of murdering and bail-jumping.

Durst was originally arrested October 9, 2001, in Galveston but was inadvertently released on bond. He was living as a cross dresser when he was caught on November 30th, this time in Pennsylvania, where law enforcement formally charged him with murdering Morris Black.

Events leading up to that arrest began in November

2000 when Westchester County District Attorney Jeanine Pirro announced that the long dormant Kathleen Durst missing person's case had been reopened. A flurry of national headlines followed. A month later, Susan Berman was dead.

"We were interested in talking to her and we wanted to make that happen," Pirro said after Berman's death. "We were extremely disappointed when we heard what had happened."

Acting on several tips that Berman might have critical information that could help the case, New York investigators sought to find her.

They got there too late.

Susan's death prompted authorities to dig even deeper into Kathie's disappearance. "We really didn't get involved in the case until after Susan Berman was shot in Los Angeles," Pirro noted.

Authorities were hopeful that the Texas murder charge against Bobby Durst would be the break they were looking for in the disappearance of Kathie Durst and the murder of Susan Berman. They were looking for a possible link to the cases. Those hopes were temporarily dashed when Durst failed to appear for a Texas bond hearing scheduled for October 16, 2001. Durst had officially become a fugitive on the lam for two-and-a-half months. He eluded police by cross dressing.

The Durst manhunt was featured on FOX TV's "America's Most Wanted" show. And Robert Durst was the subject of several television shows in early 2002, including ABCs "Vanished" and "Prime Time Live."

His double life ended when he was arrested for shoplifting less than $10 worth of merchandise from a Wegmans Food Market in Hanover Township, Pennsylvania. Police found $37,000 in $100 bills in the car rented by Bobby. Prior to his arrest, Durst was seen at an area diner wearing a woman's brown wig and donning a fake white mustache. Another report of bizarre behavior had Bobby arguing with himself over a beer at an area bar.

When they finally arrested Durst, the intentions of the Westchester County district attorney was clear. "It's good news," said Anne Marie Corbalis, spokeswoman for the office, "because we have what we believe to be a dangerous person out of people's way, and they're now out of harm's way. We'd like to bring closure for the Kathleen Durst family. We have a missing person's case we'd like to solve."

Suddenly, a possible Durst connection to the Berman case piqued the interest of the national media. By early February, the press had invaded Susan's former Benedict Canyon neighborhood. The questions being asked by the national media were this: Was Susan killed because she'd been harboring a secret about Bobby? Had he given her cash out of kindness or as hush money to buy Susan's silence?

The LAPD was not as optimistic as New York State authorities at what might come out in probing the two cases to find possible links. Just days into Susan's murder investigation, LAPD detectives expressed skepticism at a connection between the Kathie Durst missing person's case and Susan's murder. A month later, with all the media scrutiny, the LAPD began working with New York detectives, looking for clues that would lead them to a connection between the cases.

But that phase of the investigation—looking at Robert Durst as a suspect—cooled after the LAPD and the Los Angeles District Attorney's office received letters from Durst's New York lawyers requesting that investigators not contact Durst. It was a strategic move on the part of Durst's camp. With the veiled threat of litigation, the LAPD pulled back.

Through a Plexiglas barrier inside the Galveston city jail in early March 2002, Sareb Kaufman, Susan's surrogate son, spoke with Bobby Durst. Bobby wore powder-blue jail-house garb. His hair was growing out on his once-clean-shaven head. When Durst was arrested a month earlier, he was bald, including his eyebrows.

Sareb went to the jail to hear Bobby's side of the story. "I went not knowing what to think," Sareb told *New York* magazine about his two-hour visit with Durst. "How could I not go? This was a person my mother trusted more than anyone. I came out feeling that this was one of Susan's dearest friends, and I want to give him the benefit of the doubt."

Eighteen months after Susan Berman's death, the LAPD had not filed a case with the Los Angeles County District Attorneys office for prosecution of Robert Durst for Susan Berman's murder, according to Joseph Scott, a spokesman for the D.A.'s office. Durst remained an unofficial person of interest in the murder of Susan Berman.

During Sareb's jailhouse visit, Bobby Durst asked how Sareb thought Susan might have reacted to the admission he'd officially made in court that he killed Morris Black in self defense.

Sareb told him, "She'd be standing by you, like she always did." It was a testament to Susan's unwavering loyalty to Bobby, no matter what. Many say Susan subscribed to the *omerta*, or code of silence, which bound her to the Mafia credo to never snitch on friends to authorities, to be a stand-up person, no matter what.

To the screenwriter and author whose book Susan had been editing, she expressed her devastation at the news of

Durst's arrest, telling him that "my best friend got charged with murder for something that happened eighteen years ago." Susan was referring to the disappearance of Robert Durst's wife. She assumed he'd been arrested for his wife Kathie's murder. She was wrong. Instead, his arrest was for the murder of Morris Black in Galveston, Texas. Susan made call after call to her friends, expressing her distress over the shocking news.

The screenwriter, whose name police did not release, described Susan as "brilliant but crazy." He told police that he rescheduled the editing session with Susan because he "needed a break." He also told detectives that someone had been stalking Susan.

Back in Galveston, poor Morris Black's body had been dismembered before being discarded in Galveston Bay in trash bags on or around September 10th, 2001. Bobby used the dead man's driver's license to rent a beat up Corsica from Rent-a-Wreck. Then Durst checked into a Marriott Hotel in Alabama, in Room 327, where he also had used Black's identity. Durst evaded capture for a few weeks until October 20th.

After his arrest, one New York law-enforcement detective, in a telephone interview, described Durst like this: "He's crazy as a fox. He looks bizarre."

It hadn't always been that way.

Robert Alan Durst, nicknamed Bobby, was the oldest of three boys and the son of New York real-estate developer Seymour B. Durst, patriarch of a family real estate empire worth billions. As a young man, Bobby appeared to have it all—a moneyed family, good grades, handsome looks, and charisma. He was raised in the well-to-do Westchester suburb of Scarsdale, New York.

Something, however, went terribly wrong with Bobby.

Bobby Durst's seemingly comfortable early years were forever marred by tragedy when, on a rainy autumn night in 1950 when Bobby was seven, his mother, Bernice, dressed in a nightgown, climbed out of a second-story bedroom window and onto the slippery roof of their suburban Westchester picturesque stone mansion.

Bobby discovered his mother, through an upstairs bedroom window at the back of the house, standing on the roof. Bobby screamed, "Mommy, Mommy," and then ran downstairs to tell his father. An emergency call was made and firefighters arrived in a fire truck and observed Bernice Durst standing on the peak of the roof, looking up at the star-lit, 35-degree night with her toes half dangling precariously over the edge of the roof. Bobby stood below, looking up at his mother.

Then, in a shocking act, she either fell or jumped from the rain-slick roof of the mansion, landing on the driveway. Bobby was the only one of her children who watched their mother fall to her death.

Newspaper accounts at the time stated that Bernice, just thirty-two years old, had become disoriented after an overdose of asthma medication. Privately, family members acknowledged that Bernice had committed suicide. Bobby was stoic about his mother's death, at least on the surface. He underwent counseling for bouts of depression and angry rivalry battles with his younger brother Douglas that increased after his mother's death.

As time passed, Bobby appeared to develop emotionally into a typical teenager and looked as if he had recovered from the tragedy. The children young Bobby grew up with were all sons and daughters of some of the wealthiest and most influential families in the country. Their fathers were either corporate big-wigs, heavy-duty lawyers, or prominent Wall

Street bankers. Their mothers were socialites. Their children led comfortable and sheltered existences.

That well-do-do background didn't alter who young Durst was becoming. By the time he was ten, he grew angry. As a teenager, Bobby grew relatively calm by nature and was an undistinguished student. His family and friends described him as quiet, shy, and a loner—that is, unless you got to know him. That's when his loud and often crude comments and dry sense of humor kicked in.

As a young man, he was handsome and a charmer who hobnobbed about town with celebrities like Jackie Onassis and Mia Farrow. He had a high-profile affair with Mia's sister, Prudence Farrow, whose beauty was the inspiration for the Beatles song "Dear Prudence."

As time went on, Durst unraveled and appeared to have gone mad. Longtime friend Julie Baumgold said Durst fought demons his entire life. "I don't think he really knows who he is," Baumgold, a novelist, told the *Guardian*. "He has spent his whole life trying to work that out."

That madness led Robert Durst to become a fugitive of justice and go on the lam for more than two months, only to be caught because of shoplifting, dumbfounding those who knew him. At the time, his family owned ten Manhattan skyscrapers and a billion-dollar real estate holding company.

The senior Durst, Robert's father, was once one of New York City's richest and most powerful real estate developers who built a half dozen office buildings on Third Avenue in Manhattan after World War II. He died in 1995. The name Seymour Durst often can be found alongside other notable New York developers such as Stanley Stahl, Sol Goldman, and Harry Helmsley. The elder Durst was also noted for his frequent ads on the front page of the *New York Times* bemoaning the national debt and expressing his views on other political matters. Seymour Durst, described by those who knew him as "intelligent, soft-spoken and cultured," paid for the widely recognized National Debt Clock on New York's Avenue of the Americas. City University of New York dedicated a library to him. The library, in the school's graduate center, contains Seymour's extensive collection of New York historical books and memorabilia. The collection once filled every inch of Seymour's palatial East Side town house, including books stuffed in his refrigerator.

Seymour was the son of Joseph Durst, a Jewish immigrant from Poland. After thirteen years working in the garment district, Joseph had saved enough money to buy a Midtown Manhattan office building. The purchase became the cornerstone of the Durst family's real estate empire. Joseph's elder son Seymour eventually took over the helm of the Durst Organization. Seymour and his wife Bernice had four children. Robert was their eldest son, with brothers Douglas and Thomas, and sister Wendy.

As his business prospered, Seymour moved his family to Scarsdale, a tony suburb with architecture reminiscent of its English roots.

A bustling ritzy village of mostly single-family estate homes worth millions, Scarsdale offered Robert Durst an enviable quality of life in one of New York's wealthiest real-estate families. Born in 1943, Bobby grew up on Hampton Road and attended Scarsdale High, from which he graduated in 1961. Like Susan Berman's background, it was a childhood of privilege. But also a childhood filled with sadness.

One high school classmate, Richard Guggenheimer, knew Bobby's brother Doug and his cousin Peter but could barely recall the reserved Bobby, just a year ahead of him. And Dorothy Ciner, whose name and identity Bobby later used, was in the same class but didn't know him. He left little in the way of lasting impressions. Bobby's charisma developed later, during his university years. The 1961 Scarsdale High yearbook showed a single photo of Robert and no mention of extracurricular school activities.

After graduation, he went on to college at Lehigh University, a private institution, in Bethlehem, Pennsylvania, in a tree-lined city of 45,000. His college education began in fall 1961 and lasted through to spring 1965—a hundred miles from the hubbub of New York City, where the family business was based. The registrar's office showed that Bobby Durst graduated on Monday, June 14th, 1965, with a bachelor of science degree in business administration and a declared major in economics. In the summer and after college, Bobby worked on and off for his father at the Durst Organization in Manhattan, which eventually built the Bank of America Tower in New York City and co-developed, with the Port Authority of New York and New Jersey, One World Trade Center.

In September 1967, Robert Durst enrolled in graduate school at the University of California at Los Angeles, where he met Susan Berman. From day one, she was his friend and confidant. Bobby's scholastic emphasis was again on economics. He left UCLA in March 1968 without earning a graduate degree, according to the registrar's records. The next year, Durst went to work full-time for his father, in New York City.

Two years later he met his future wife, Kathleen McCormack.

Kathleen, a dental hygienist, had recently moved to the city from her home in New Hyde Park, New York, renting an apartment in a building owned by Durst's family. That's when Bobby and Kathie met and started dating. It was a whirlwind romance; they moved in together almost immediately after just two dates. They soon relocated to rural Vermont where they opened a natural health-food store called All Good Things. *To hell with business and economics,* Bobby is said to have remarked.

They were a striking couple, he with his good looks, athletic body, and charm, and she with her pretty face, caring disposition, and pleasant personality. He had a dry sense of humor and was sometimes aloof; she was outgoing, smart, and funny. Seymour Durst was disappointed that his son, with his economics background, chose to run a health-food store instead of joining the Durst Organization. Eventually, at pressure from the senior Durst, Bobby and Kathie returned to New York in 1973, where they married. They appeared, on the outside, to be a charmed couple and very much in love.

Although Bobby joined his father and brother Douglas in the family business, he resisted the trappings of the upper class, preferring, instead, to drive an old Volkswagen Beetle, wear casual hippie-like attire, and sport a goatee. It was that off-beat nature that first attracted Kathie to him.

Conversely, his wife Kathie loved the bright lights of the city and the good life afforded by Bobby's family's fortune.

"It was as though Cinderella had married Prince Charming," Kathie's older brother, Jim McCormack, told *New York* magazine. "He had the resources to do the things she had dreamed of doing. Robert was shy—not exactly antisocial but reluctant to enter into conversations. Kathie was the exact opposite—vivacious, witty, ready to enjoy life. She brought out the best in him."

Still, their life together was far from perfect. Robert didn't want kids and, at one point in their marriage, Kathie had an abortion.

She told friends she was unhappy with what she

termed "living below our means." In spite of their wealth, Kathie drove an older Mercedes sedan and complained that Bobby was too cheap to buy her a new one. She was also disappointed that Bobby did not want children. In perhaps the most telling statement Kathie confided to friends was that Bobby was still deeply disturbed by his mother's death when he was a boy. It was an explanation, in large part, as to why Bobby appeared to have gone mad as an adult.

By 1980, their marriage was unraveling. Kathie wanted a career of her own and decided to pursue becoming a doctor, first gaining a nursing degree from Western Connecticut State University in Danbury. During the school week, Bobby stayed at their country waterfront stone cottage on Truesdale in the tiny Westchester County village of South Salem, while Kathie remained in Manhattan at their penthouse on the Upper West Side at Seventy-sixth Street and Riverside Drive. To escape New York City's annual wave of summer heat and high humidity, Bobby and Kathie were among the elite with the means to find refuge in their rural retreat. On weekends, the couple went to their South Salem property. They often invited their friends to visit them at their lakefront estate.

"Kathie was very much in love with Bobby when I met her," said Gilberte Najamy, today a women's counselor who became Kathie's friend after meeting her in 1976 while they were undergraduate classmates at Western Connecticut. "From Monday until Friday she would wait by the phone for Bobby to call."

Later, after Kathie was admitted to the Albert Einstein School of Medicine in the Bronx, Najamy and other friends visited the city on weekends, when Kathy was there, to party with her.

Using Bobby's connections, the group got reservations at expensive restaurants and trendy nightclubs like Studio

54 and Xenon. Sometimes Bobby accompanied them, but he seldom seemed to enjoy it.

"Bobby was not thrilled with her circle of friends," Najamy said. "I think he suspected that we were telling her that she didn't need him or his money, which we were." Bobby became "possessive and abusive," Najamy recalled, sometimes taking his anger out on bystanders. At the Durst's penthouse after a night of clubbing, Bobby assaulted one of Najamy's friends, a photographer named Peter Schwartz, because Schwartz was too slow to move when Durst ordered everyone out of the apartment.

Kathie's brother Jim McCormack told friends he once saw Bobby grab his sister by the hair and jerk her off a sofa at their mother's home in New Hyde Park.

Then, on January 6, 1982, three weeks before her disappearance, Kathie was admitted to Jacobi Hospital in The Bronx with bruises on her face and head. The injuries, Kathie told hospital attendants, happened during an argument with her husband. Kathie told friends she was afraid for her life.

She had valid reasons to be fearful. According to statistics, partner violence escalates with time. Susan Murphy Milano, an expert in the field of intimate partner violence and homicide before her own death after an illness in 2012, dedicated three books to the subject. In her book *Time's Up*, she wrote, "The system doesn't work. These men will stop at nothing."

It has yet to be determined if that's what happened to Kathie Durst when she disappeared in the winter of 1982 after eleven years of marriage to Bobby Durst.

With Kathie's disappearance, Bobby Durst simply stopped talking about his wife. He immersed himself in the family business. He managed Durst properties, buying and selling new ones and drumming up additional business.

Then, at a Christmas party in 1988 at the Rainbow Room, seven years after his wife went missing, Robert Durst met real estate agent Debrah Lee Charatan. He dated her off and on for twelve years.

In 1990, Durst dissolved his marriage by publishing paid notices of his pending divorce to Kathie in a Westchester County weekly newspaper. It was part of a legal requirement that he attempt to notify his missing spouse. He didn't tell anyone about the divorce. Durst was moving on. Kathie's family, however, wouldn't learn about the divorce for another decade.

Bobby continued to work hard for the Durst Organization. But in a huge blow to Bobby's future—and ego—the aging Seymour Durst decided on a successor: Bobby's brother Douglas. When Bobby heard the news that his younger brother was taking over the family business, he walked out of his office, never to return. He never spoke to his family again, only speaking with his sister Wendy and a bevy of family attorneys.

Today, the Durst empire owns eleven prominent skyscrapers, including buildings that house the headquarters of Pfizer and AOL Time Warner. The family business, now run by Douglas, is reportedly worth $2 billion.

In 1998, New York investigators reopened Kathie Durst's file after receiving new tips and fresh information on the case. The reopening of the case sent Bobby's world spiraling. He had become a prime suspect and he knew it. The investigation was moving from a missing persons case to a murder probe. Witnesses were being re-interviewed. Susan Berman was at the top of the list of people to talk to. The darker side of Bobby began to surface. He started cross dressing, moving about and living sporadically in California, New York, Louisiana, and Texas.

On December 11, 2000, less than two weeks before Susan was killed, Bobby married Debrah Charatan. Durst told no one about the quiet ceremony, not even his best friend Susan. Susan never liked Charatan, Gilberte Najamy said, because she had replaced Susan. "Susan was always Bobby's confidant," she said. "He stopped telling her things. Debrah replaced her in that respect." As a result, Durst did not tell Susan—or anyone else—about his new bride. The marriage came to light when Charatan, forty-four years old at the time of Durst's arrest, arranged for Bobby's bail on the Galveston murder charge. She had to provide a marriage certificate to prove her relationship to him, because it was his money she used to post bond.

Kathie Durst's family long suspected Bobby of foul play. In 1983, the family argued in Kathie's estate proceeding that Durst's behavior "strongly suggests that [Kathie] may have been murdered and that Robert Durst is either directly responsible for her death or privy to information concerning her disappearance."

In early 2002, a death certificate was issued for Kathleen Durst, allowing her $130,000 estate to be settled. Kathleen's mother, Catherine McCormack, shared the proceeds from the estate with Bobby Durst. By agreement, approved in Manhattan Surrogate's Court, Bobby's share was to remain in escrow until the investigation of Kathleen's disappearance was concluded. After Bobby's arrest for the murder of Morris Black, Catherine McCormack went back to court and successfully had her daughter's estate closed to keep Bobby's half out of his reach.

# CHAPTER 10

# MISSING PERSON'S CASE

*If anything ever happens to me, don't let Bobby get away with it.*
—Kathleen Durst, to a friend

IN 1998, NEW YORK State Police Investigator Joe Becerra unknowingly embarked on the case of a lifetime. The arrest of a flasher by the name of Timothy Martin started it all. Martin was looking to make a deal.

"He wanted to have a sit-down with me and said he had information regarding this woman Kathie Durst from Lake Truesdale," Becerra told reporters.

At the time, Becerra had never heard of Kathleen Durst. When she disappeared in 1982, Becerra was still in high school.

He pulled the police file and educated himself by reading as much about the case as he could. He learned that Kathie Durst had vanished in January 1982, seemingly from the lakeside cottage in South Salem she shared with her husband.

Timothy Martin, looking to trade favors with authorities,

told state police he knew what had happened to Robert Durst's wife, Kathie. "The information that he provided did not pan out, but it did get us to look into this case some more," Becerra said.

If Kathleen Durst were alive today in 2013—which marked the forty-first year of her disappearance—she would be fifty-nine years old. The last night Kathie was seen, she had been at her fellow nursing-school friend Gilberte Najamy's Connecticut home attending a party. Bobby had called the house several times, ordering Kathie to return home.

Kathie did as she was told, but not before telling Gilberte, "If anything happens to me, Bobby did it." It would be the same words Kathie would utter to three other friends before her disappearance. Kathie had been drinking that night, but left for home anyway, alone, at about 7:30 p.m. Drugs and liquor were reportedly free-flowing among the reveling crowd, and there were reports that Kathie also took drugs that night.

Eleanor Schwank, one of Kathie's best friends, told "ABC News" that Kathie said something similar to her about being afraid of her husband. Schwank quoted her as saying, "If anything ever happens to me, don't let Bobby get away with it."

Bobby first said Kathie went home to their South Salem cottage, then changed his story and said she went directly to their Manhattan penthouse because she had to attend classes, at Albert Einstein School of Medicine the next day, on Monday. Bobby admitted to police that the couple had fought, but he said it was an argument over the phone.

Five days after his wife's disappearance, on Friday, February 5, 1982, Robert Durst, with his Norwegian elkhound at his heels, walked from his apartment at Riverside Drive and Seventy-seventh Street into the New

York Police Department's Twentieth Precinct. The busy office at 120 West Eighty-second Street on Manhattan's Upper West Side covers 1.1 dense square miles and includes in its jurisdiction the American Museum of National History, American Museum of Folk Art, Manhattan Children's Museum, Julliard School of Performing Arts, and New York Historical Society.

There to handle the missing person's case was NYPD Detective Mike Struk. Bobby officially filed the report, telling Struk he did not know where his wife was and that he had nothing to do with her disappearance. He also matter-of-factly told him he had contacted Kathie's friends and none of them had seen her. Bobby's demeanor, whether it was sad, subdued, worried, angry, stoic, or unemotional, was not noted in the police report.

Bobby said he had dropped off Kathie at the Katonah train station on January 31st, 1982, after she came home from her friend's party. She and Bobby had an argument about her staying out late, he told Detective Struk. He also told the detective that forty-five minutes after his wife arrived, she left with a suitcase for Manhattan, to Kathie's rented apartment on East Eighty-sixth Street. He said he put his wife on the 9:17 train in Katonah, Westchester County, near the couple's South Salem home, bound for their Upper West Side apartment. He said he had spoken with Kathie on the phone from home just after 11 o'clock that night after she arrived at their penthouse. Detective Mike Struk with the 20th Precinct was assigned the case. He would later become a technical advisor for the TV show "Law & Order."

Three witnesses backed up Bobby's account of that evening. The dean of the medical college said he received a call—albeit unusual from a college student—from Kathie the following morning saying she would not be in class. An elevator operator at her Seventy-seventh Street apartment, where she stayed during the week in a sixteenth-floor penthouse, said he had seen someone who appeared to be Kathie in the Manhattan apartment building. And the building super said he saw her on the street the next morning leaving the building.

New York state police questioned Durst in South Salem. But they did not search his home.

Investigators soon learned that Bobby had made several phone calls from Ship Bottom, New Jersey, to the Durst Corporation in the days following Kathie's disappearance. The area has long been storied to be the grisly dumping site for bodies left there by members of the Mafia.

Bobby made headlines a week after he reported his wife missing when the New York *Daily News* ran a front-page story with Bobby's offer of $100,000 for information about Kathie's disappearance. Police said that no real leads had come in as a result of the reward money.

Then, Durst's story changed when Susan Berman became his unofficial spokeswoman. Through Susan as his spokesperson, Bobby told police and reporters that instead of calling Kathie from the South Salem house, he had made the call from a pay phone while out walking his dog, Igor.

The problem with that version, however, was that the nearest public telephone was miles away, and it was a cold night, with slushy snow on the ground, making it improbable that he had walked his dog that far.

That's why some family members and friends began believing that Kathleen Durst had not made it out of Westchester alive that night.

After Bobby Durst told police his wife was missing,

he walked out of the police station a free man. It was the first and last time Durst would cooperate with police about his missing wife. To address the media, Durst called on his best buddy Susan Berman, herself a member of the working press. On behalf of Bobby, she told the media that Durst was heartbroken and unable to cope with the disappearance of his wife. He's completely distraught and is clinging to the hope that Kathie is alive," Susan told the *New York Post*. "He loves her very much and he's terribly worried."

The New York Police Department issued a missing person's bulletin about Kathie Durst. Years later, with the advent of the Internet, the bulletin appeared on NYPD's website, stating that it was from the Long Term Cases, and a photo ran with it. (NYPD misspelled Kathie Durst's first name, spelling it "Kathy"). The release stated:

MISSING PERSON: Kathy Durst
DESCRIPTION
At Time of Disappearance: Sex: Female
Race: White Age: 29

Last seen: On January 31, 1982, in Manhattan, New York, within the confines of the 20th Precinct.

If you know the whereabouts or can add to the circumstances of a person classified as missing, please notify the Missing Persons Squad at 1-646-610-6914. Favor de notificar a Missing Persons Squad 1-646-610-6914.

On the evening of March 19th, a Friday, Kathie Durst's friends wanted answers. They went together to Detective Mike Struk's office at NYPD's Twentieth precinct station house in downtown Manhattan. Eleanor Schwank, Ellen Strauss, and Gilberte Najamy told him they believed Kathie was murdered by Bobby and wanted to know why Bobby had not yet been arrested.

At best, all Struk had was circumstantial evidence, not enough to convince the district attorney to charge him, he told them. To arrest Robert Durst and make it stick, they needed a body. What Struk did not say was that the district attorney had refused to prosecute the case, saying they needed more evidence, otherwise the powerful Durst Organization and their team of seasoned attorneys would fight the charge on behalf of Durst.

Based on eyewitness accounts, investigators initially believed Kathie Durst arrived safely in Manhattan and focused their search there. Later, however, they came to believe that the witnesses who reported seeing or hearing from Kathie Durst were either mistaken or deceived.

Either way, the Kathie Durst case was at a standstill. Following Detective Becerra's reopening of the Kathie Durst case eighteen years after her husband first reported her missing, investigators dragged the bottom of nearby Lake Truesdale. A body, however, was not located.

"The lake, the house, and the property was [sic] all searched at various time, but I can't go into particulars at this point on what was and was not found," Becerra told Westchester News 12.

Weather records showed that the lake was frozen over with twelve inches of ice when Kathie disappeared, so disposing of her body would have been impossible. Disputed by a neighbor was Durst's story that he had spent the night at the couple's lake cottage the night of Kathie's disappearance. A neighbor told police that no one was there that night, because no lights had gone on and no cars were in the driveway.

Westchester District Attorney Jeanine Pirro, who

spearheaded the once-dormant investigation, said with confidence that "Sooner or later we're going to find out what happened to Kathleen Durst."

Still, officials were slowed down when Bobby Durst refused to cooperate with or even talk to investigators. "Robert Durst has the right to remain silent, and he has refused to cooperate with us," Pirro told News 12.

At that point, Bobby was put on a hefty monthly allowance from his family. In exchange, he agreed to remove himself from any connection to the family business. Bobby did as asked and kept his distance. For the next ten years, he kept a low profile—that is, until he surfaced in Galveston.

After Galveston Judge Susan Criss issued a gag order in the Morris Black murder case, specifically naming Pirro and others, Pirro said, "There is no legal precedent to gag a D.A. in another jurisdiction." Still, Pirro's office stopped talking to reporters.

Gilberte Najamy traveled to the Easton, Pennsylvania, courthouse to directly confront Bobby Durst. During his court hearing to extradite him from Pennsylvania to Texas for the Morris Black murder case, Durst's face was devoid of emotion.

After the court proceeding, Najamy tearfully pleaded with Durst. She said beforehand that she wanted to confront him face to face. Outside the courtroom, tears streamed down her cheeks as she stared at Durst, the man she believed had killed and then disposed of her best friend's body.

"I was ninety-five-percent sure Bobby did it," Gilberte told me in an interview from her Newton, Connecticut, home. "I told myself I needed to be sure. So I thought, *Here's a good opportunity.* As Bobby was escorted out of the courtroom by deputies, I asked him, 'Tell me what you did to Kathie.' He looked me in the eye for a moment, looked down, and walked away. I knew then that he had done it. I knew I needed to make eye contact with him to make sure I was right, that he had done it. And I was right. I know he did it."

Gilberte Najamy had been extremely vocal about Kathie Durst's 1982 disappearance beginning the day it happened, pushing detectives to reopen the investigation.

"The only hero in this case is Joe Becerra," Gilberte said. For more than two decades, she said she tried to find answers. "Detective Becerra has been at the helm, continuing the investigation."

Najamy was adamant that New York City and state police in the 1980s allowed Bobby Durst to get away with murdering his wife because of who he was: the son of one of the most powerful real estate developers in Manhattan, a man with clout. Durst initially had been questioned in his wife's disappearance but was never charged or formally named a suspect.

"When I said that Bobby had murdered Kathie, no one believed me," she said. "Now they do."

Initially, Kathie's disappearance gripped New York City for months. Eventually, though, it faded from the headlines. But all those years later, the pieces of the cold missing persons case started coming together, like a puzzle, near the stone cottage in northern Westchester when detectives dragged Lake Truesdale, combing the lake bottom for a body. The lake borders the Durst couple's former country summer home. Investigators also searched the house. They removed a piece of a wall from the cottage. Later, to insiders, Detective Michael Struk said there was blood evidence taken from the house. Still, Bobby Durst was not arrested.

Kathleen Durst had vanished days after she told her husband she wanted a divorce. Police, after reopening the case years later, strongly suspected Kathie was murdered and were following up on new leads, including talking to Susan about what she may have known. Then Susan was killed.

Upon hearing of Susan Berman's death, state police expressed extreme disappointment. Susan was not the only person authorities were looking to interview. They were re-interviewing and questioning everyone connected to the case. But Susan was considered a key person who investigators were looking forward to re-interviewing, hoping she'd shed light on the case.

Westchester County District Attorney Jeanine Pirro had this to say about Susan's death: "Miss Berman was a friend and spokesperson for the Durst family. When our office reopened the missing persons case about two years ago, the entire case was reviewed and there were re-interviews in the case. Susan Berman was one of the individuals that this office was very interested in. Definitely, she was a person we were interested in speaking to."

"She's dead, so anything she had to offer is dead with her, which is real convenient for (Bobby Durst)," said Detective Michael Struk upon hearing of Susan's murder.

As for Gilberte Najamy, the last conversation she had with her good friend was when Kathie told her she was afraid of what her husband might do to her.

That was January 31, 1982. Kathie Durst has not been seen or heard from since.

# CHAPTER 11

# MORRIS 'JACK' BLACK

ON SUNDAY AFTERNOON, September 30th, 2001, a thirteen-year-old boy, looking for minnows while his stepfather, David Avina, fished in a shallow area of Galveston Bay off Channel View Drive, made a grisly discovery. It was a dead body. The boy noticed it floating and bobbing in the water. At first, he thought it was a pig.

But it was no pig. It was a headless, armless, and legless human torso.

In a search of the area, police later found the dead man's arms and legs, in separate black plastic trash bags, in the water 80 feet from the torso. The body was identified as that of Morris "Jack" Black. Black had lived across the hall from Bobby Durst. Police never found the head.

Law enforcement started building a case against Bobby Durst, who had fled his tiny apartment. Durst was wanted again, but this time it was for fatally shooting and then carving up a senior neighbor.

Six months later came the bombshell: On Wednesday, March 27th, 2002, Bobby Durst confessed to killing Black, but he said in court, through his attorney, that it was an "accident" that he did in self defense. It was a bold move and a tough case to defend.

The jury heard how and why Morris Black died.

It came straight from Durst. On September 28th, 2001, Bobby Durst took the stand and told the court that he had returned home to find Black in his apartment watching television. A scuffle ensued with his senior neighbor—who's been described as an odd, wiry, scrawny man with a peach-pitted face—Durst's pistol went off accidentally, and Black died of head trauma. Attorney Dick DeGuerin declined to elaborate after the hearing about why Bobby chopped up Morris's remains, saying he was under Judge Susan Cress's gag order.

Before the gag order went into effect, DeGuerin told *TIME* that Durst "was just then coming off a forty-year high of smoking marijuana every day and getting drunk every night, self-medicating the emotional problems he had."

To the court, DeGuerin said his client's admission would eliminate the need for DNA evidence. The attorney requested a three-month trial delay because he had not received the autopsy report on Black. The request was granted. The trial of Robert Durst for the murder of Morris Black, originally scheduled for June 2002, was reset for September 9, 2002, then postponed again until February 2003.

Gilberte Najamy contended that Morris Black knew where Durst had disposed of Kathie's body. Plus, Najamy believed, Black knew what happened between Durst and Susan Berman that later caused Susan to be killed.

"Morris Black knew too much," Najamy said. "That's why he was killed." No evidence brought forward, however, has shown this to be true.

Hang around the port city of Galveston, a wind-blown town, long enough, and you learn about the ebb of tides and currents, and exactly when and where *to* and *not* to toss a body into the water. That's what Bobbi Bacha, a private eye who grew up in the area, said.

"The water's deep," Bacha said, "but the current washes everything to shore, including bodies."

A newspaper asked for Bache's help in finding Black's relatives. After the search, in which she successfully located Black's estranged family, Bacha continued working on the case, she said, for herself.

Bacha and a dive team went on two searches hoping to find Morris's missing head. They didn't, but they found women's clothing and wigs. They also found make-up, including unused lipstick still in packages, eye liner, and mascara. After Bacha was quoted by several newspapers, Judge Susan Criss, who coincidentally happens to be Bacha's distant cousin, issued a gag order in the case.

"She [the judge] needs to recuse herself," Bacha said, "because we have the same great-grandfather. We're second or third cousins. We're not close, but we're blood cousins." The judge, however, did not remove herself from the case.

Reached for a second time at her Houston office, Bacha said, "My cousin is mad at me. She doesn't want me talking about the case. There's a gag order on me."

She, like attorney DeGuerin, was bound by the judge's gag order. But before the order, which was placed on everyone connected to the case, Bacha said in a telephone interview that police were led to Durst's building after they found a copy of the *Galveston County Daily News* with an address label on it in one of the garbage bags containing Morris's limbs, leading them straight to Bobby Durst's run-down apartment complex. Blood in the hallway, leading to Durst's apartment, prompted a search warrant. Police searched Bobby's apartment and found traces of blood throughout the apartment as well as a bloody knife and boots. They obtained a search warrant to thoroughly search the premises. Bobby Durst, who was still in the area, was arrested October 9th, 2001, while in his rental car. Located in the car, among other things, was a 9-millimeter handgun.

Bobbi Bacha said Black's missing head was crucial evidence in the murder case against Robert Durst. It would show the cause of death. Most important, it would show the trajectory of the bullet. Was Morris Black's head discarded because it would have shown that Morris, like Susan Berman, was shot in the back of the head?

Galveston Police also were anxious to find the head. Bacha's search was done in an area where Black's limbs and torso were found. Six private investigators waded through waist-deep water while two divers searched farther off shore. A Galveston police officer was on hand. By the end of the search, the divers came up empty.

Attorney DeGuerin said neither he nor his client knew the whereabouts of Black's head.

Even after Bacha's work for both the Galveston paper and the Black family was finished, she continued digging into the backgrounds of people connected to Bobby Durst.

"I'm not doing research for anyone," she said. "I like to finish what I start. I looked for Morris Black's head, did what I could, and, in the process, started looking at more things."

The question that begged to be answered was why Durst killed Morris Black in the first place.

The autopsy of Black suggested that Bobby Durst had severely beaten him before he killed him. The report, released by a judge, also showed that Black fought back. Black's body had multiple bruises in an area 6 by 2-1/2 inches in the center of his chest. A triangle of bruises was on the right side of his chest. There were bruises on his shoulders, upper, mid, and lower back, left leg, and elbows. And a bone in his upper right arm was broken in four places. The most shocking aspect of the murder was that Black was beheaded and dismembered. The autopsy report said cuts in the muscle were sharp and "without significant fragmentation," meaning Durst knew what he was doing when he carved up Black's body.

The autopsy also revealed a series of parallel cuts on Black's right and left index fingers, suggesting Durst tried to cut them off, which would have made identification of the water-logged and decomposing body difficult and near impossible.

For more than twenty days, Morris's dismembered remains were at the Galveston County Medical Examiner's Office before members of his family knew he was dead. Then Bobbi Bacha, vice president and investigator for Blue Moon Investigations in Webster, Texas, was asked by a Galveston newspaper reporter to help locate Morris's family. The police, she said, weren't looking for them, so, as a favor, Bacha started to search. She found Morris's sister Gladys Black first, through the ex-wife of Morris's brother Harry, and then the others. Another brother, Melvin Black, she learned, had died four years earlier in a psychiatric facility in Norfolk County, Massachusetts.

Bacha said Morris was a loner who could be cantankerous. He had drifted from state to state, living in sparse surroundings without a telephone. He lost touch with his family.

At the time of Durst's arrest, Galveston police thought they'd arrested a destitute transient. Standard bail was set. There was a $250,000 bond for the murder charge and a

$50,000 bond for possession of marijuana. Durst posted the bonds, then took off.

In the meantime, LAPD detectives flew to Galveston to interview Durst about Susan Berman's murder. When they arrived, to their surprise and everybody else's, Durst had already made bail. It was one more setback in Susan's investigation.

After Durst posted bail and fled the area, Galveston police learned that Westchester County, New York, law-enforcement officials had re-opened its investigation into the disappearance of Durst's wife, Kathie, and that he was a wanted for questioning. Authorities launched a nationwide manhunt.

"We had no idea who he was," Galveston Police Lieutenant Michael Putnal said afterward. "Here was a man living in a $300-a-month apartment, who didn't have a telephone, and who wouldn't have looked out of place standing on the corner outside the Salvation Army." They didn't realize the man they believed to be a transient was a multi-millionaire who easily posted $300,000, and then disappeared among the drifters and homeless wanderers in Galveston, only to resurface in his college town of Bethlehem, Pennsylvania.

Assistant District Attorney Kurt Sistrunk echoed Putnal's statement, saying, "We were not aware of any criminal record. All this New York stuff came to our attention *after* we made our [bail] recommendation. He said $20,000 was the usual bond for first-degree murder. We went out of our way to set a very high bond," Sistrunk said.

Later, Putnal told reporters, "Clearly, he was acting like a fugitive long before Morris Black was killed. He seemed like a strange character to begin with. He was acting like he was running from the police long before Galveston had reason to take an interest in him. To me, that just adds to the level of suspicion in his involvement in the other crimes."

Galveston PD's "Wanted" poster on Durst stated that police believed him to be "armed and dangerous" and that "he may be dressed as a woman to avoid detection." In addition to the Black murder charge, Durst had other legal problems: On October 29, 2001, Morris Black's sister filed a notice of intent to sue Durst in civil court over her brother's killing.

Jim McCormack, Kathie's brother, was surprised Durst was allowed to go free in Galveston.

"I'm flabbergasted," McCormack told the New York Post when he learned Durst was free on bail. "It's an amazing circumstance. Here you have a man who is arrested and charged with an obviously heinous crime—based on being tied to the crime by physical evidence and a tipster—and he's allowed to walk free on bail. How could you allow this man to get back in society?"

Morris Black never married and had no children. Private investigator Bacha said Morris befriended Galveston resident Trudy Black, a sister-in-law to Morris, who told Bacha that Black had several bank accounts and asked her to collect the money if anything should happen to him.

While Morris had no visible means of support, police discovered nine separate bank accounts in his name in South Dakota totaling more than $137,000. Detectives speculated that his neighbor Bobby Durst had been giving Morris money. Morris had been a merchant seaman decades earlier and, for a brief period, a watch repairman. He'd also worked in building maintenance. But he'd never made that kind of money.

In January 2001, Morris Black rented an apartment in a four-unit building in a low-rent section of Galveston.

Bobby Durst, estranged from his wealthy family for a decade, moved in early summer, across the hall from Morris. Durst paid $300 a month for the sparse unit while simultaneously leasing a luxury condominium in Dallas and owning two homes in San Francisco, California—one on Nob Hill and the other on Telegraph Hill—a home in Trinidad, California, one in Colorado, and two in New York City's expensive Manhattan borough. Diane Bueche, the woman from whom Durst purchased the Trinidad home, which was 300 miles north of San Francisco, lived next door and became a friend, and Durst periodically visited her.

Police didn't know why Durst moved into the Galveston Bay fourplex nor had they uncovered whether Durst and Morris had known each before Durst moved to Texas.

Galveston Police recovered a 9 millimeter handgun from Durst's car. Los Angeles Police traveled to Galveston after Durst's arrest. Ballistic tests were done on the gun by Galveston police, and the results were given to Los Angeles police, LAPD Lieutenant Clay Farrell said. The results, however, were not made public. Galveston police also found another handgun, a 22 caliber, in a garbage can behind the K Street fourplex that Durst and Black lived in.

Durst was first arrested October 9, 2001, while driving a silver Honda CRV in Galveston. A police search of the car turned up a bag of marijuana, a 9mm handgun, and a bow saw. He was released the next day after his second wife, New York real estate broker Debrah Lee Charatan posted the $300,000 in bonds. Bobby was free.

Police later discovered that the man living in the cheap Galveston apartment was, in fact, the Robert Durst of the billion-dollar Durst Organization, a real estate empire, from New York, and not the poor, simple man police thought he was. Authorities immediately froze $1.8 million from one of Durst's accounts and suspected he might have had at his disposal other accounts with similarly large sums of cash.

After Durst failed to show up for his October 16th arraignment, basically jumping bail and skipping town, Galveston Police released the following press advisory to the media:

On September 30th, 2001, a thirteen-year-old boy discovered a human torso floating in the water of Galveston Bay off Channel View Drive. The body's legs, arms, and head were deliberately severed. The arms and legs were recovered in the water approximately 80 feet from the torso. The arms and legs were in separate plastic trash bags.

The follow-up investigation led to the identification of Morris Black M/W/10/21/1929 as the victim. He was identified through fingerprints provided by North Charleston, SC Police.

It was learned that Morris Black resided at 2213 Avenue K #1. It is believed that Robert Durst visited and/or lived at 2213 Avenue K #2.

A search warrant conducted at 2213 Avenue K #1 and 2213 Avenue K #2 lead to the recovery of physical evidence that established sufficient probable cause to request a warrant for the arrest of Robert Durst for murder. On October 9, 2001, an arrest warrant was issued with a bond of $250,000.

On October 9, 2001, Robert Durst was arrested in the 1300 block of Broadway. A small quantity of marijuana and a 9 mm handgun were recovered from Durst's 1998 Honda CRV at the time of his arrest.

Durst was also charged with Possession of Marijuana [sic] 2 oz with an additional bond of $50,000. Durst was released on the $300,000 bonds the same day.

This morning, Durst was scheduled to appear at Justice of the Peace, Precinct 2 for a bond hearing.

Durst failed to appear in court. His bonds were revoked. The case was also presented before a Galveston County Grand Jury on October 16, 2001.

The Grand Jury indicted Durst for Murder and Bond Jumping. His bond on the murder indictment has been set at $1,000,000. His bond on the Bond Jumping indictment has been denied. The FBI has also charged Robert Durst with Unlawful Flight to Avoid Prosecution.

Durst has homes in California, New York and Connecticut. He previously resided in the Dallas area and is known to have been in New Orleans, LA since his arrest. Durst is known to use several aliases and is believed to sometime dress as a woman to avoid detection. Durst should be considered armed and dangerous.

Anyone knowing of Durst's whereabouts should contact their local police department immediately.

Galveston Police Department
Criminal Investigation Division
(409) 797-3760
(409) 797-3702

A couple months later, on January 9, 2002, Durst was arrested in Bethlehem, Pennsylvania, where he'd attended college as an undergraduate student. He was caught by Colonial Regional Police after stealing a sandwich and a Band-Aid for a cut above his lip. A sign in the grocery where Bobby Durst was arrested read, "Shoplifters will be prosecuted to the full extent of the law."

Indeed, authorities picked up Durst after security officers at the Wegmans grocery caught him red-handed on their surveillance cameras stealing a Band-Aid from a box and a chicken salad sandwich on pumpernickel from a deli case.

Durst's identification and capture happened just hours before he was scheduled to be profiled on Fox TV's "America's Most Wanted: America Fights Back."

Robert Durst left a string of aliases in his wake. Police tracked his footsteps and came up with a timeline.

Investigators found a receipt from a New Orleans dry cleaner in Bobby's possession when he was arrested. Police also learned that Durst on October 12th gave a New Orleans' telephone number while trying to lease a Dallas apartment by phone. Then, a private investigator working for the Durst trust fund told police that Bobby had made a telephone call from a New Orleans pay phone on October 17th.

A few days later, Durst was spotted at a northern California campground where he'd spent the night in a pup tent in the midst of a group of retired police officers. The Lazy Devil B campground is about fifty miles north of Eureka, California, near the coast. Diane Bueche owned the campground and had known Durst since 1994 when she sold him a house in Trinidad, California, about 300 miles north of San Francisco. Bueche was his next-door neighbor until Durst sold the house in 2000.

A campground manager recognized Durst from a magazine photo published on Halloween 2001 as the man who had pitched a pup tent at his campground ten days earlier, which was during the time Durst went on the lam for two-and-a-half months.

After his arrest in Pennsylvania, Bobby fought extradition to Texas, but lost. He was extradited and delivered back to Galveston, fifty miles southeast of Houston. His January 21st, 2002, appearance was his first time in a Texas courtroom. This time, he was held on a $1 billion bond. His hearing came twenty years after his wife Kathleen's disappearance in New York state.

A stoic Robert Durst, dressed in a gray sport coat, gray slacks, and black-and-white sneakers, stood before Judge Susan Criss. After the murder indictment was read, Durst told the judge, "I am not guilty, your honor."

The judge later rescheduled his murder trial for February 2003 to give both sides more time to prepare. In the meantime, Bobby Durst was being held in the Galveston jail in solitary confinement and allowed to take a walk around the exercise area daily and use the facility's library.

As for Diane Bueche, Durst's former next-door neighbor who sold him his Trinidad home in Northern California and helped police with details of his whereabouts after he hid out in a campground, she passed away at age sixty-four, in her home east of Eureka in November 2002. She died from what authorities called a self-inflicted gunshot wound after purchasing a firearm and obtaining a concealed weapons permit. Durst, at the time, was in jail awaiting trial in Galveston, Texas.

The blood trail that ran across the hall from Black's apartment led to Durst's first arrest. But it was the theft of a Band-Aid and a sandwich that ultimately brought Bobby down. Security cameras at Wegmans were focused on a man in the health and beauty aids section of the store. Cameras zoomed in on the suspect as he pocketed Band-Aids, went in to the store bathroom, exited with a Band-Aid on his face, under his nose, grabbed a newspaper, and concealed a sandwich. Once the man left the store, security moved in on him in the parking lot. The man, who had about $500 cash in his pockets, was arrested for shoplifting $9.18 in merchandise. The suspect volunteered his real name and birth date, that of "Robert Durst," but gave two different social security numbers to store security and police.

"I can't believe how stupid I am," Bobby repeated over and over to Officer Dean Benner.

The officer thought he was being melodramatic. "It's just a misdemeanor," Officer Benner told Durst.

But when the officer ran both Social Security numbers through national law enforcement databases, he learned that Robert Durst was a wanted fugitive on murder charges out of Texas.

"When were you last in Texas?" Officer Benner asked Durst.

Bobby's eyes got wide, then he said, "I want to talk to an attorney."

# CHAPTER 12

# DATELINE LAS VEGAS

*I think it will always be a small town to me,*
*for how can we separate our childhood's from*
*our hometowns?*

—Susan Berman from *Lady Las Vegas*

"I WAS BORN to write," Susan Berman once said in an interview. "I handicapped the Academy Awards for my block when I was nine."

Susan seemed to always fall back on her Las Vegas background. Whether it was part nostalgia, part searching for her roots, part cashing in on her town, or all of the above, Las Vegas held an allure for her, held her at bay. People have always been curious about the desert oasis and its past, so throughout her writing career, Susan wrote about the town she felt she knew best and had grown up in.

Included in the February 1998 issue of *Las Vegas Life*, a glossy magazine started a year earlier by the owners of the *Las Vegas Sun*, Susan had allowed an excerpt of *Easy Street* to be published in the magazine as an article titled

"Growing Up On Easy Street." Then, in July of the same year, the magazine published another article by Susan, titled "The Heat: Memoirs of an Earlier Vegas." The pieces were excerpted from her original memoir from seventeen years earlier.

It wasn't Susan's proudest moment. She told friends that "it's beneath me" to write for a smaller publication. To be sure, the local magazine didn't pay the $2 to $4-per-word rate national magazine writers were getting at the time (Susan was lucky if she was paid even $150 for each piece). But at that point she was broke and needed the money. So when Susan was invited to write something for *Las Vegas Life*, she acquiesced. The article also provided publicity for her books.

Mister Margulies' best friend, Kevin Bartnof, who grew up with Mister in Las Vegas, also wrote a piece for *Las Vegas Life*, published in its July 1998 issue. After Mister's death, Susan and Kevin became good friends. "She and Kevin were so close," said Kevin's mother Ruthie. "They weren't romantically inclined at all. They were like brother and sister. She would help him with his writing. He was upset about her death, then six months later Kevin died." Before his death, Susan helped Kevin with his *Las Vegas Life* piece. He wrote about his search in Las Vegas, as a teenager, for his idol Elvis Presley. "So much time has passed," wrote Kevin, then a Foley artist in Hollywood. "My friend Mister died eleven years ago in January. Every day something reminds me of him. . . . I wound up in Los Angeles, doing sound effects for the movies—honest work, a heck of a paper route.

"But on an unseasonably cool night, I realize that the collection of Elvis paraphernalia atop my fireplace is not merely a shrine to the King of Rock 'n' Roll, but an acknowledgment of youth and friendship, a memorial to our adolescent journey, a time that's forever lost, but not forgotten."

Susan, like Kevin, was a big Elvis fan, and they had that in common. When Susan was a young girl, Elvis was in town. "Of course, I was crazy about Elvis Presley," Susan said in her A&E network documentary *The Real Las Vegas.* "I was somewhere with my dad and I knew that Elvis Presley was playing the hotel, and I said, 'You know, if you're so important, have Elvis Presley sing "Happy Birthday" to me,' and he did. That was something." Elvis signed a photograph and gave it to Susan. It read, "To Susan, Best wishes, Elvis." It was dated 1957, for Susan's twelfth birthday.

Six months after Susan was killed, Kevin Bartnof, on June 30th, 2001, suffered a massive heart attack and died.

Susan had wanted to be as successful as Shana Alexander, a veteran journalist and literary author living in New York, whom she greatly admired. Unfortunately, Susan's successes with her early writings were short-lived.

"She so wanted to make it big," said Stephen M. Silverman, a fellow writer who has penned nine books. "But she was not big. She would have liked to have been Shana Alexander, but she never came close. Her writing was too uneven. Besides *New York* [magazine], she also wrote for the *Times*, though she was ticked off that all they asked her to do was a story on picnic baskets for their recently launched food section. She thought picnic baskets were beneath her."

Not making it big was Susan's greatest disappointment. "She wanted recognition," Ruthie Bartnof said. "Hers was a pursuit of recognition for her writing, for her talents. I think she wanted that success so badly."

Susan's biggest successes came when she parlayed her Las Vegas background into writing projects. But she turned away work when she felt it didn't pay enough, causing lengthy gaps between assignments and projects—and paychecks.

Still, in December 1982, Bantam Books released a paperback edition of *Easy Street*. To celebrate, Bobby Durst threw Susan a party at Elaine's, an Upper East Side Manhattan nightspot. Susan and Bobby posed for photos. Susan beamed. Book sales initially were swift once again. It was an important book for her, especially on the heels of the failed movie deal of the same title. Life couldn't be better for Susan.

In 1987, Susan met the man her friends have said was her last real boyfriend. He was a financial adviser with Hollywood aspirations and a single father with two teenaged children. Kaufman and his kids moved into Susan Berman's Brentwood home, just around the corner from the townhouse where Nicole Brown Simpson and Ron Goldman were killed. And, for a while, he made her happy. Susan adored Kaufman's children, Mella and Sareb, who were twenty-four and twenty-six, respectively, at the time of Susan's death. They considered Susan their mother. "She held my hand through everything difficult in life," Sareb, who works in the recording business, told *New York* magazine. "She was the only person who was always on my side and never judged me."

Her relationship with Paul, who was described by his son Sareb as an "ex-hippie," ended in 1992 about the time Susan ran out of money. Susan and Paul had begun working on a Broadway musical based on the Dreyfus affair, about an anti-Semitic case set in Nineteenth Century France. Susan put money from the last of her assets into the new project. It failed and, with it, their relationship. The bank foreclosed on Susan's Brentwood home and she was forced to file bankruptcy. The financial difficulties and the failure of the musical undid her relationship with Paul Kaufman and they separated. Mella stayed with Susan, while Sareb moved in with his father.

Susan was broke. A friend generously offered her temporary use of a condo near the Sunset Strip, at 2121 Avenue of the Stars, also a street famous for its celebrity residents, including Norman Lear, television producer, writer, and director. Susan and Mella lived there for five years, rent free.

"Being a mother to these kids was one of the proudest and most satisfying things in her life," comedy writer Rich Markey told a reporter.

Susan began writing mysteries and short stories to pay her expenses and for Mella's private-school tuition. She and Mella also co-wrote an unpublished manuscript, titled *Never a Mother, Never a Daughter.*

Susan had desperately wanted children of her own. At one point, she even discussed with her friends about asking Bobby Durst to father a child with her. After Susan met Paul and he and his children, daughter Mella and son Sareb, moved in with her, Susan no longer talked about having a child of her own. She had the children she had longed for.

After five years of living in the apartment rent-free, Susan was back on her feet again financially. She telephoned her former landlady, Dee Schiffer, and asked if she could move back into the Benedict Canyon Drive house. The rented house was about to be vacated, so Dee said yes. In 1998, Susan moved back into the house where she ultimately was murdered.

The biggest thing to come out of that period when she lived again in Benedict Canyon was Susan's return to writing about Las Vegas. She turned to what she knew best—the Las Vegas scene—as fodder for her writing.

It meant another book deal and an A&E network special called *The Real Las Vegas*. It brought her new acclaim and fresh cash (and showed, perhaps, a lack of caution, since she had once told Julie Smith that, after *Easy Street*, she'd been warned, *Don't ever mess with us again*). "My Dad was one of the Las Vegas pioneers—gangsters, mobsters, whatever you want to say," Susan said on camera in the A&E documentary. She was proud of her heritage and comfortable talking and writing about it.

The second half of the 1990s were a financial roller coaster for Susan. Although she landed another book deal, she had trouble getting contracts for her other projects. And while she lived in the Beverly Hills enclave, she struggled despite living among the rich.

Susan could have gone out and gotten a full-time job. But because of her early opulent background, she felt entitled to money without having to eke out a full-time day-to-day living. Instead, she hit up friends for loans.

Las Vegas, Susan had written, "taught me always to eat out, to stay only in the best hotels, and to appreciate a good sense of humor." She considered Las Vegas her hometown. But she didn't have anywhere to go while there. Her parents were dead. She was an only child. Her friends were her family now. She visited occasionally and stayed at inexpensive hotels. She couldn't go home permanently, though, back to her roots in Las Vegas. It wasn't the same. Susan instead wrote about her desert home.

She had "arrived with much fanfare, great talent, and then for years and years and years, nothing happened," Julie Smith told *New York* magazine. "She went through all her money from the movie sale and the book royalties."

Her childhood friend, Bob Miller, talked about her

writings. "She had good credentials," he said. "She was a small child when she left, but she certainly touched the right bases when she came back. We discussed on the phone several times who she needed to talk to, what Las Vegas had become. I read her books. I thought she had an interesting writing style. She was nostalgic. In context of her earlier book *Easy Street*, it was nostalgia. She had a rivalry with her background."

Detective Brad Roberts of the LAPD's West Los Angeles Division homicide unit said Berman had paid her rent through March and was scheduled to move out in June 2001 after the long-running dispute with her landlady. Susan joked with her friends that she was going to end up homeless.

She hit up her friends for cash, about $1,500 at a time. But it was Bobby Durst who, over the span of their friendship, would loan her larger amounts. When Susan needed private school tuition for her surrogate daughter Mella, Bobby sent her $20,000.

By summer 2000, Susan's old convertible Chrysler began to fall apart. It had a wiring problem that caused it to catch on fire. She found a 1988 Isuzu Trooper advertised for $7,000, but she didn't have the money to pay for it. Susan turned to Bobby for help. When she couldn't reach him by phone, she wrote him a letter, sending it to him through the Durst Corporation. In the letter, she asked Durst for a $7,000 loan to buy the used SUV. Because Durst had stopped confiding in Susan the way he had for so many years, she was no longer in regular contact with him. Durst had replaced Susan, his lifetime confidant, with Debra Charlatan, who was now married to Durst.

But Durst did respond to Susan a couple weeks after she wrote to him. Susan received a check for $25,000, accompanied with a note in the envelope postmarked from the northern California. "It's not a loan. It's a gift. You can always call on me for help," Durst wrote.

Susan was relieved. She bought the car and finally junked the twenty-year-old black convertible Chrysler she'd purchased after leaving New York City during her financially stable years.

Two weeks after the first check from Bobby arrived, she received a second check from him for the same amount: $25,000. It arrived just before her death. Bobby included another note. This one said, simply, "This is a gift."

Susan sent Durst a note back telling him what a good friend he'd been to her over the years, "Like the brother I never had," and said that their relationship "was never about money." She explained that she was "strong and I work every day trying to turn this around." She also noted that she was "thin and on Prozac from the lack of security and no feeling of well-being about the future."

The final $25,000 check allowed Susan to settle up with her landlady and buy her some breathing room. Lee Schiffer regularly showed up at Susan's house unannounced to argue about overdue rent, the dogs, and repairs. The standoff escalated into a three-year eviction battle. Susan told friends she was afraid of Dee and feared she would harm her dogs. In the weeks before she died, however, Susan, with Bobby's check, paid her rent through March, and a lawyer worked out an agreement for Susan to leave the property by June. She told friends—at least those she admitted her situation to—that she was relieved it was all finally over. She bought the SUV and caught up on her bills.

Her cousin Deni Marcus said Susan was not proud of having to ask for money. "Bobby wasn't trying to buy her silence. He was simply helping a friend. She said to him, 'I don't know what I'm going to do,' and he gave her some money. She was devastated to have to take it. She was embarrassed. But she needed it to live."

Her longtime friend Stephen Silverman agreed. "Susan was humiliated by her financial situation," he said, "but she made jokes about it as best she could, calling herself homeless and the like, as if listeners were supposed to laugh. Mostly we would gasp." Susan would often joke and end a telephone conversation with, "I'm going to get into the bathtub with my hair dryer now."

She was able to get freelance work, just not enough to pay all her expenses and her back rent. Susan didn't look for full-time work. Instead, she went to friends. At one point, she even sold her mother's jewelry.

Ruthie Bartnof said she once suggested to Susan that she find permanent work. Susan was offended.

"It was the only time we had words," Ruthie said. "I told her, 'You know, I think it's time to find a way out of this.' She was left a great deal of money. I don't know what happened to it. For some reason, she just felt that it wasn't her heritage to work. She was really trying to grab what she'd lost when her parents died."

Detective Paul Coulter had his own perspective on Susan's financial situation. "Susan Berman had been in dire straights for a while," he said. "It was only after the *People* magazine article that the money from Durst started coming in. Was it a gift? I don't know. Was it to keep her loyalty? I don't know."

The article Coulter referred to was a piece in the December 4, 2000 issue of *People* magazine by Bill Hewitt titled "Resuming the Search: Police Reopen the Case of Kathie Durst, Who Vanished 18 Years Ago." Berman was killed days after New York police had arranged to question her about Kathleen Durst. Police had made their quest to interview Susan public. In doing so, did the publicity spook Durst into killing Susan so she wouldn't have a chance to tell police what she knew?

In August 1995, an excerpt from *Easy Street* was included in *Literary Las Vegas: The Best Writing About America's Most Fabulous City*, a 358-page paperback published by MacMillan, edited by Mike Tronnes, with an introduction by author and poet Nick Tosches. Excerpted were Susan's recollections of her father teaching her math by giving her a slot machine to play with and the Sabbath meals that her Grandmother Florence prepared for her father's Jewish gangster associates.

Being included was a break for Susan in that it validated her as an expert on 1950s Las Vegas. Moreover, it expanded her body of work. It also gave her a royalty check, which she desperately needed at the time.

Susan was in good company. The book was touted by the publisher as offering views "through the eyes of some of America's best writers." A 1964 article that Tom Wolf originally wrote for *Esquire* was included, as well as an excerpt from Hunter S. Thompson's classic *Fear and Loathing in Las Vegas*, plus a diary of Noel Coward's Las Vegas experiences, and a 1952 article from the *New Yorker* about atomic bomb testing when rooftop parties welcomed the flashes of light in the desert.

The anthology was well received. *Booklist* gave it a glowing review, writing, "The essays and short stories in this collection reveal the glitz and history of a city that has gone from 'mobster and starlet hideaway, to haven of sin and vice, to its present incarnation as low-roller heaven' and still remains the marriage capital of the U.S. As the editor notes, 'Who else but Las Vegas would make the A-bomb a picnic?' An honest-to-God picnic.' Believe it or not, tourists would travel to a local hilltop, with lunches provided by the casinos, to view the test blasting of the atomic bombs. There is plenty of more fascinating reading for those who love, hate, or never even thought much about this city. There are tales of lounge lizards, millionaires, showgirls, gangsters, gamblers, and businessmen from writers such as Joan Didion, Noel Coward, Hunter S. Thompson . . . ." Ingram Books called it "a humorous, anecdotal history of Las Vegas" that "chronicles the days of glitter gulch to the building of modern resorts."

Another break came for Susan in 1996 when Morrow/ Avon publishers released her novel *Fly Away Home*, a paperback edition about a young woman's search for her missing sister. The culprit, it turned out, was in the heroine's midst: the boyfriend of her character's missing sister.

The last lines of Susan's book, although fiction, read: "If I can't take anything positive from the lives of my parents, maybe I can find something positive in the way I've handled the revelations. They say life is a gift. I may soon be ready to open it."

In her dedication, Susan included a group of friends. Bobby's name topped the list. "This book is dedicated with love and gratitude," Susan wrote, "to my treasured friends with whom I have been fortunate to share life's journey: Bobby Durst, Nina Feinberg, Danny Goldberg, Judith Sherwood Hafeman, Susie [Amateau] Harmon, Sheila Jaffe Krimshtein, Florean Mader, Laraine Newman, Ainslie Pryor, Bede Roberts, Julie Smith."

On the cover of the book was a short review by friend Smith, author of the acclaimed *House of Blues*. She wrote, "A fast, sexy read. . . . Susan Berman is a terrific new writer on the suspense scene." The book, however, did not stay in print more than a couple of years. It was another huge disappointment for Susan. Still, Susan persevered. She continued pitching projects, hoping that one would bring her the wealth she was seeking.

Things continued looking up for Susan in 1996 when she was offered a chance to co-produce *The Las Vegas Story*, a documentary for A&E. In the documentary, for which Susan received a Writers Guild of America nomination, she delved into the shady beginnings of Sin City. It brought her even more recognition from her colleagues.

While in Las Vegas doing research for the A&E documentary, Susan attended the Golden Nugget's 50th anniversary party. "Steve Wynn knows how to throw a party," Susan later wrote. Wynn publicly announced Susan's presence and introduced her as "Davie Berman's daughter." Old-timers approached Susan and told her that her dad was "a great guy."

Then, at the A&E premier, held Thursday, November 14th, 1996, at Planet Hollywood in Beverly Hills, Susan signed a copy of *Lady Las Vegas* for the state of Nevada's archives. Guy Rocha, archivist and historian for the state and a consultant on *The Real Las Vegas* series, handed Susan the copy. Susan wrote, "To my hometown Lady Las Vegas. I have the utmost respect for you. You're the greatest hometown in the world. I'm 51 & you're 91. We face the millennium together. Love, Susan Berman."

The blurb for the A&E series went like this: "It's a city that's larger than life. A city without limits. A glittering Mecca of excess and forbidden desires. Discover the fascinating story of this fabled destination and the people who created it. From the mobsters who made Vegas into their version of the American Dream to the tycoons of today's family mega-resorts, this is the ultimate insider's tour of America's neon oasis. Illuminating interviews with luminaries like Alan

King, Wayne Newton and Debbie Reynolds, writer Nick Pileggi, entrepreneur Steve Wynn and Howard Hughes front man Robert Maheu offer a unique, unvarnished look at the fabled city, while never-before-seen footage opens a window to its tumultuous past. Tour the incredible casinos of the world-famous strip and even get tips on how to beat the odds! Bonus: With any order of *The Real Las Vegas*, receive the companion hardcover book by author and series writer Susan Berman, daughter of Bugsy Siegel's partner Davie Berman."

*Lady Las Vegas's* publisher, TV Books, included on the book's jacket, "Berman takes her memories, her candor, and pain and revisits the town where the American dream is chased, found and lost a thousand times a day. Las Vegas is Susan Berman's hometown. . . . Berman grew up alongside Las Vegas, maturing with the city."

As the daughter of Davie Berman and because she had carved out a niche for herself, more and more, Susan was being called upon as an expert on Vegas's early mob days.

On January 27, 1997, she appeared on National Public Radio's "Fresh Air" show, to discuss her book *Lady Las Vegas*.

In another high-profile opportunity for Susan, "This American Life," from WBEC Chicago's Public Radio International, aired a piece on September 19, 1997 titled "The Mob," which featured Susan Berman in Act II. The station titled it "Mob Daughter."

The commentator, Alec Wilkinson, explained Susan's role like this: "So let's say your father is a big-time gangster. And, like the man in the *Godfather* movies, actually *does* try to protect you from ever knowing what exactly he does for a living. What happens when you find out? Well, Susan Berman's father died of natural causes when she was twelve. Her mother died a year later, and the first time anyone directly told Susan about her father's underworld ties was when she was in college. Another student told her about this new book that talked about what her father really did for a living."

Others interviewed were Danny Toro, a member of a Chicago street gang, Teresa Dalessio, daughter of a New York Mafia family, New York underworld reporter Jerry Capesi, and Wilkinson of *The New Yorker*.

Wilkinson described Susan's seven-minute reading and thirteen-minute comments as "Susan Berman's memories of Jewish gangsters and their gangster-style Jewish mothers." Then, he said, after a break, "Act Two. Mobster Daughter. Susan Berman, author of the memoir *Easy Street*, reads from her book about her father Davie Berman, a Jewish gangster and one of the men—with Meyer Lansky and Bugsy Siegel—who created modern Las Vegas. Act Two continues after the break. More from Susan Berman on her father, who was a cold-hearted mobster by day and a devoted family man at night, just like gangsters in movies like *The Godfather*."

Susan explained, on the air, how she reacted when she learned that her father was a big shot in—a boss—in the Jewish mob: "I rushed to Martindale's book store in Beverly Hills (no longer existent). And, you know, quickly found this book the *Green Felt Jungle*. There was a huge display of them and I quickly looked at the index, "Davie Berman."

"It dedicated an entire chapter on the Flamingo Hotel and Ben Siegel's death, and it said that after Ben Siegel was dead, that Davie Berman, and in parentheses, 'who could kill a man with one hand behind his back,' and a little later in the chapter it said that he had been wounded in a shootout with an FBI man in Central Park and done eleven years in Sing Sing, and then it went on to talk about his other partners. Well, I started to throw up in the book store, I was so shocked. Literally. How gross, right? It was just a visceral reaction, you know? I couldn't believe it. And, of course, I didn't think it was true."

The commentator continued. "She worked so hard at believing this wasn't true, he said, "that eventually she forgot this ever happened. Years later, she was a reporter for the *San Francisco Examiner* and interviewed Jimmy Hoffa just a month before he vanished. He and his men all knew her dad. One of them said, 'He was much smarter than the guys running the Outfit now.' And, *still*, she didn't want to believe her dad was with the mob. Finally, when someone showed her father's files, finally then, reluctantly, she believed."

Authors Ed Reid and Ovid Demaris, in *Green Felt Jungle*, described Susan's father as "an ex-con who served time in Sing Sing for kidnapping and a former Siegel thug who was soon to become the muscle behind Greenbaum." Dave Berman is referenced five times in the book, which today is a classic.

She also did an interview to talk about Bugsy Siegel for "Mysteries & Scandals," hosted by A.J. Benza for E!, which first aired April 27, 1998. Susan talked about her father and how he and his partners took over the operation of the Flamingo Hotel immediately following Bugsy Siegel's murder.

Even Susan's own novels eerily resembled her life. *Spiderweb*, a paperback released in 1997 by Avon, seemed loosely based on her own experiences.

Amazon.com's description read: "Few crime novelists come to their craft with more impressive credentials than Susan Berman, who grew up in a Mafia family, became a topnotch newspaper and magazine journalist, and made her fictional debut with the well-received *Fly Away Home*. Her second novel is equally exciting and obviously drawn from the same deep well of personal experience transformed into art. Elizabeth Manganaro's mother supposedly committed suicide when Elizabeth was nine; her daughter never believed it, and twenty-six years later the recently widowed Elizabeth finds that her doubts were justified. She also finds that the truth can be very dangerous."

Ingram Books wrote a short review: "Determined to find the mother whom she is convinced is still alive, Elizabeth Manganaro travels to Los Angeles with her young daughter, unaware of the terrible price the reunion will carry."

Susan organized her book launch in Venice beach, California for both *Spiderweb* and *Fly Away Home*, an earlier novel. Her friend Ruth attended, as did her personal manager Nyle Brenner. Her cousin Dave and his wife Beth traveled down the coast from Oregon to attend.

"It was at a lovely book store in Venice Beach," Ruth said. "It was crowded. Susan had such interesting friends. I met Nyle at the bookstore."

1998 started out as an exceptionally good year for Susan. On Monday January 12th, Susan was rewarded for her hard work on the A&E project when The Writers Guild of America, East and West announced its nominations for outstanding achievement in television and radio writing during the 1997 season. Susan's name was on the list. It marked the 50th Anniversary of the Writers Guild Awards and was celebrated in gala ceremonies on both coasts. Susan's nomination was for her co-writing work, along with Jim Milio and Melissa Jo Peltier, on "*Las Vegas: Gamble in the Desert.*

Susan could not have been more happy or proud. She attended the awards dinner with Nyle Brenner.

Kevin McPherson, a producer on the A&E project, worked closely with Susan for months. He said Susan worked tirelessly on the documentary and landed hard-to-get interviews because of her Las Vegas contacts. But working with her wasn't always easy, McPherson noted. "On the daily stuff, it was difficult," he said. "She was always worried. I felt sorry for her. It seemed her whole identity was derived from being the daughter of a mobster." The last time McPherson saw Susan was at the Writers Guild awards banquet.

Part 1 of the four-hour series first aired on the evening of Sunday, December 1, 1996. Part II aired the following night, on Monday, December 2, on cable's Arts & Entertainment channel.

Susan received glowing reviews for her work on the documentary. In one, headlined "The Voice of Reality," writer Melissa Jo Peltier glowingly wrote, for an article in the September 1999 issue of *Written By*, about Susan's role. Peltier, who worked beside Susan on the project, wrote:

"In writing the A&E special *Las Vegas: Gamble in the Desert* with my partner, Jim Milio, and our co-writer, Susan Berman, it was Susan's voice that determined the voice of the piece. Susan had grown up in Vegas and pondered the absurdity of its existence and significance for years. Although Susan, primarily a print journalist and novelist, had the most passion and the most clearly defined point of view about the subject, Jim and I contributed our craftsmanship in the genre. As her co-writers, it was our job to help shape and define Susan's voice, while keeping it intact. I believe it was the combination of our craft plus Susan's vision and passion that made this project worthy of the Writers Guild nomination for nonfiction in 1997. The experience helped me realize something simple: The documentary writer's voice comes as much from passion as it does from craft."

Likewise, in the November 28, 1997, issue of *Critic Pick*, a column titled "The Las Vegas Story" raved about the series.

Writer A.D. Amorosi wrote in the *Philadelphia City Paper's* November 28 to December 5, 1997, edition:

"Frank, Dino, Sammy and Debbie Reynolds? The A&E network's award-winning 'Biography' series and author/mob daughter Susan Berman have collaborated on what can be considered the ultimate Las Vegas home companion. Their two-part product, *The Las Vegas Story*, is four hours' worth of garish gaudy fun, guns, gambling and politics and the insider's scoop on what it means to be in the ultimate city of lights. The daughter of Nevada mob honcho Davie Berman (partner to Las Vegas creator Bugsy Siegel), Berman takes an intimate look at Vegas history that's valuable, accurate and loads of twisted fun. Based on her books *Easy Street* and *Lady Las Vegas* (Penguin), the two-part series—*Gamble in the Desert* and *House of Cards*—features performers Alan King, Shecky Greene, Wayne Newton, casino owner Steve Wynn, journalist Nicholas Pileggi and a baker's dozen worth of local sheriffs, strippers, administrators and hangers-on. They mull over archival footage of Las Vegas from when it was a dusty prairie gambling stop for war veterans and Hollywood's elite up to its present-day cardboard family outlook. Along with two Rhino label CDs (Jackpot! and Soundtracks With a Twist) full of raucous, swinging Vegas types like Tom Jones, Vic Damone, Liberace, Anka and even Tony Scotti's "Come Live With Me" (from *Valley of the Dolls*), this glittering book, CD and TV package hits 21 every time."

Helping Susan Berman land interviews for the documentary were several people in Las Vegas. One was Deke Castleman, an author and book editor who once lived in Las Vegas. He explained how he came to help Susan with the documentary and her accompanying book.

Susan Berman had a "long aversion" to Las Vegas, Deke told me. "It's my understanding," he said, "that she wanted nothing to do with the place for a couple of decades at least. But finally, in the mid-'90s, she decided to come to terms with her hometown—part nostalgia, part expiation, part paycheck.

"My details on the first deal are a bit fuzzy, but I think she pitched the idea of a long Las Vegas retrospective to a friend who owned a video production company. The friend then sold the package to A&E. And then, all of a sudden, Susan was face to face with the reality of doing four hours of TV on a city with which she had all kinds of history—mostly bad. And the fact was, she knew very little about Las Vegas post 1965 or so.

"So she went to Brentano's in L.A., she told me in an E-mail, and stood staring at the Las Vegas guidebook shelf for awhile. She decided to buy one book, pretty much at random, and picked *Compass Las Vegas*, which I wrote."

"Well, she got home," Deke continued, "opened to page one, and saw that I'd dedicated the book to 'all the Jewish gamblers who helped build Las Vegas,' including Siegel and Greenbaum and Dalitz and her father, Davie Berman. I'd loved *Easy Street* when I read it years earlier. I was utterly moved by it; those could have been my own relatives. What can I say? It's a Jewish thing. And I was so inspired by *Easy Street* that I dedicated my book to these guys."

After eight editions of *Compass Las Vegas*, Deke Castleman had not changed the original dedication, "though the more I learn about Bugsy," he said, "the less I'm inclined to thank him. But what the fuck."

"Anyway," Deke continued, "Susan told me she nearly *plotzed* (Yiddish for fainted) when she saw the dedication, and she immediately got on the phone to try to track me down. She called Mike Tronnes, a very cool character from Minneapolis, who'd just come out with a book called *Literary*

*Las Vegas*, a collection of excerpts of pieces on the town by creative writers, of whom Susan was one. I'd helped Mike a little with the book—even though he didn't excerpt me, the fucker—so he knew where to find me when Susan called asking."

What happened next, Deke said, was a pleasant surprise that launched his friendship with Susan.

"So there I am," he said, "sitting at the dinner table with my family in Las Vegas, when the phone rings. My wife answers and says, 'Yes, he is. Can I ask who's calling?' And then she turns to me and says, 'It's Susan Berman.' And I say, 'Susan Berman? *The* Susan Berman? *Easy Street* Susan Berman?' And I grab the phone and, well, you had to know her. She starts screaming.

"She'd get so excited that her voice would rise three octaves and fifty decibels, somewhere between hysterical and ecstatic, and she'd launch into a stream-of-consciousness narration . . . I always felt I was coming in the middle of a conversation with Susan. I never did find out the beginning or the end of what she was talking about. And the most amazing thing was, I wouldn't hear from her for three months, say, and when I'd pick up the phone and it was Susan, she'd just continue the conversation at the exact same place where we'd left off our conversation of three months ago.

"This time she's squealing into the phone, 'Omigod! Omigod! I started crying! I mean, when I saw my father's name in your book! I'm so touched that someone remembered him. And I'm coming to Las Vegas and I'm doing this shoot, and we must meet! It was the only book I bought! Out of all the travel guides at Brentano's! It was fate! It was destiny! You're Jewish, of course! Do you have a big nose like the rest of us? We'll put you on camera! I'm staying at Alexis Park.

What's it like? Is it the typical Las Vegas dive? And where's a good place to meet for dinner? You'll bring your wife—she sounds so sweet! And your kids! Do you have kids?'

"Obviously, after two minutes on the phone, I was totally smitten with Susan Berman," Deke said.

"So she showed up and I met her at her suite at Alexis Park—a statuesque, handsome, intense, and fiercely intelligent woman. Half the time demure and subdued, the other half manic and neurotic. I hooked her up with a few people who wound up on camera—I never did. Little did she need my help, though. She had access like I'd never seen—her Las Vegas roots went very deep."

With Susan in Las Vegas in August 1996 was photographer Gerardo Somoza. He spent a day and a half taking promo photos for the documentary and accompanying book. "The photos I took were taken at the Flamingo [hotel], near the pool, in the casino, and around Las Vegas with her," he said in a telephone interview.

Gerardo got to know Susan in a short time, because they spent nearly two days working on the A&E project.

"We had lunch and dinner together," he said. "We talked a great deal, about her childhood and what she thought about the whole Mafia connection. She was definitely sweet, nice. She did whatever I wanted [her] to do, in terms of photos. She was a very nice person, but she was a little weird. You just had that feeling. It was just the way she was as a person.

"First of all, her look was completely odd. Her shoulders were down, droopy. She didn't have this great stature. She wore very loose clothing—a T-shirt and vest with black pants. She changed into a red dress. She was tan."

He noted that she didn't exude a lot of confidence. "She was not completely sure of herself," Gerardo said. "She was definitely awkward with herself, insecure with her looks. But she was flirtatious with me.

"A couple of producers were with us. When we got to the hotel, the Flamingo, Susan told us, 'Oh, my God, the pool is almost the same.' She said there was a black curtain in front of the casino and she never crossed through it. She said the counting room scene in the movie *Casino* was incredibly familiar to her because it was exactly the same as the actual counting room in the Flamingo. I remember her talking about her dogs. She loved those little dogs. She said, 'They're my kids.'"

Somoza stayed at the MGM Hotel while others involved in the making of the documentary stayed at the Hard Rock Hotel. Susan stayed at Alexis Park, a smaller less expensive executive hotel located parallel to the Strip on Paradise Road.

"We were in town for four or five days," Somoza noted. Las Vegans interviewed for the film waited inside the state building on Las Vegas Boulevard, lining up for their time sitting in front of the camera to be interviewed.

While in Las Vegas researching and setting up interviews, Susan went to the Nevada State Museum, on Twin Lakes Drive in historic Lorenzi Park near downtown. As a child, she'd played at the park. Dave Millman, a historian and curator of the museum, met with Susan for three hours in the museum's library at a conference table. Later, she described him in *Lady Las Vegas* as "a little craggy-looking with a scruffy beard." His wife, Millman said, "didn't like the description very much."

In *Lady Las Vegas*, Susan wrote that as she left the state museum, David "asks me if I would consider leaving my family pictures to the museum in my will. I am touched. My family is history; my dad will be remembered."

"She said she had photos of her family she'd give us for our archives," Millman said. "She never did."

He described her as "funny" and "a little nutty."

"She talked nonstop," Millman said. "She was very pleasant to talk to, and I enjoyed it, but she went a mile a minute. I could see how you could give up on her as a friend." He said he'd looked forward to reading *Lady Las Vegas*. But after it came out, he said, "I was so disappointed. The book itself is not a good history book. Overall, it had a lot of mistakes. It repeats a lot of the myths. It appeared to be a money-maker, thrown in to go with the A&E series. It had a lot of inaccuracies." Conversely, he said, the earlier *Easy Street* "was excellent and accurate." "And the A&E four-part series Susan co-wrote and produced that went with the book was the best by far made about Las Vegas," Millman said. "That was certainly a high moment for Susan. It's the best ever done."

Susan also met with Rob Powers, public relations director for the Las Vegas Convention & Visitors Authority, Sheriff Jerry Keller, Nevada historian Hal Rothman, *Las Vegas Sun* publisher Barbara Greenspun, whose family Susan described as "politically active," Harrah's CEO Claudine Williams, Elaine Wynn, wife of casino mogul Steve Wynn, historian Guy Rocha, and a handful of old-time Las Vegans.

She also met with Deke Castleman, who became a close friend during the final four years of Susan's life.

Deke said Susan arranged for some heavy-hitter interviews used in the A&E documentary, getting those on camera who often don't want to go on, as well as helping a few others gain notoriety.

"She pretty much discovered [the late historian] Hal Rothman, who's a minor celebrity these days," Deke said. "She gave [publisher] Anthony Curtis some major exposure.

She got the notoriously camera-shy [author] Michael Ventura. She even got Steve Wynn, who rarely does those kinds of interviews. When I asked her how she got him, she sort of dismissed the question with a wave of her hand and said, 'Oh, I just called his mother, Zelma.' She once regaled me with stories about Bugsy's two daughters, whom she knew."

Zelma Wynn was good friends with Susan's friend Ruthie Bartnof, who met the Wynns when the Bartnofs lived in Las Vegas.

Susan wrote about Deke Castleman with affection. Deke had found a phonebook with Davie Berman's name listed. "Deke has gone to the incredible trouble of finding a Las Vegas phone book from 1956," Susan wrote in *Lady Las Vegas*. "So thin. So few of us then! 'Look, your dad was the only hotel owner who listed his phone number. There you are at 721 S. Sixth Street,' he says, kindly. I clutch the pages, thrown back for just a moment into the middle of my loving family, feeling the excitement of a floor-show opening."

Deke remembered well when he gave Susan a copy of the listing.

"When I was writing the first edition of my Las Vegas guidebook in 1989," he said, "I went to UNLV Special Collections [office] and pored through every Las Vegas phone book; they have them all, from the very first one, 1923, I believe. I was looking, mostly, for the oldest restaurants in Las Vegas.

"Jewish gamblers I'd decided to dedicate the book to. I didn't expect to actually find any of them, of course. But there were the Bermans, in the '55 and '56 phone books, if I recall correctly, with their street address—the bungalow on Sixth Street—and phone number.

"I remembered from *Easy Street* Susan's description of how hard Davie tried to legitimize himself in Las Vegas;

his name and address in the friggin' phone book were proof positive, as far as I was concerned.

"So one time when Susan was coming to town and I knew I was going to see her, I went back to Special Collections, requested the '50s phone books, found the Berman listing, and made a copy of the page. When I gave it to her, she was stunned—only time I ever saw her sincerely speechless."

Susan couldn't contain herself.

"Her eyes welled up and I could tell she was remembering those carefree days when she was nine or ten or eleven, living in the house on Sixth Street, running around her daddy's casino—the Riviera, teasing Uncle Gus (Greenbaum, who's been described by people who knew him as one of the scariest men they'd ever met, and later had his throat slashed while he was sleeping in his house in Phoenix—they slashed his wife's throat too, for good measure) and Uncle Moe (Sedway, who did a lot of Bugsy's dirty work for him) . . . a time after which there were never any more carefree days.

"Of course, her reaction made me wonder whether I'd done the right thing by reminding her of her past. But she made me feel like that nickel Xerox was the most thoughtful and important gift anyone had ever given her. That's the way she was."

While Susan was in Las Vegas, Deke said, "she did take my family to dinner at the Rio buffet. She instantly fell in love with my older son Adam, who was four at the time. Every time she called me after that, I'd pick up the phone, say 'Hello?' and I'd hear, 'How's my Adam?'

"So she shot the A&E show and went home, and then had to write the companion book. I spoke to her several times during that process, when she was totally stressed by the deadline, and helped her a little."

They stayed in touch.

"After that, she'd call every so often to tell me about one cable TV deal or another she had brewing in Las Vegas," Deke Castleman said. "She told me that she was also working on a book proposal about the women who helped shape Las Vegas, and I gave her a few names of old-timers I knew."

She worked hard to bring a TV plot to cable TV. "Toward the end," Deke said, "she was trying to sell a series to Showtime, as I recall, sort of 'Friends' meets casino gambling, and she'd pick my brain about plot, and character, and inside stuff."

Among the most feasible of the TV projects Susan proposed was a documentary about Vegas that focused on women, a pitch to ABC television for a movie titled "Diaries," based on a fictionalized account of the mob as told through the eyes of women married to or children of former and current organized crime families. She was also still trying to get "Sin City" picked up by Showtime.

The last time Deke spoke with Susan, she was "three octaves high again. It seems she was just about to close a big deal on the Las Vegas series and she promised me that I'd write one of the episodes."

Then, he said, "A couple weeks later I heard that she'd taken a bullet through the back of her head."

Deke described Susan as "my soul sister. I loved her."

Shortly after her murder, Hal Rothman, a history professor at the University of Nevada-Las Vegas, wrote a piece for *Las Vegas Magazine*. In it, he remembered the woman who had become his friend.

Susan's death, Rothman wrote, "robs Las Vegas of one of its best sources of oral history."

"The hyper kinetic Berman," he continued, "was the one scion of early Las Vegas to tell the story of growing up here, and she told it with honesty and clarity.

"Her 1981 memoir *Easy Street* offers the best look at Las Vegas in the 1940s and 1950s and from a child's point of view. Her later work, primarily A&E's two-part 1996 documentary *Las Vegas: Gamble in the Desert* and *House of Cards* and the accompanying book, *Lady Las Vegas: Inside Story Behind America's Neon Oasis*, did what outside journalists never could. Susie Berman succeeded in simultaneously humanizing Las Vegas and keeping its edge. She laughed at the local obsession with trying to evade the city's mob past. She also embraced the city and its idiosyncrasies, showing how and why Las Vegas, at least when she knew it, really was different than the rest of America.

"I worked with Susie on the A&E special and the book that accompanied it. She created that project and carried it forward with her will, both for the city and as an extension of who she was. No one else alive could claim Las Vegas as an older sister, a competitor for affection, but with Susie it seemed natural. She loved this town the way it once was, when guys such as Gus Greenbaum and Willie Alderman were everywhere, and she came to understand the new Las Vegas with its corporate leadership and thousands of tourists walking in the heat.

"Before it was fashionable, Susie Berman held her head up and was proud to be from Las Vegas. Those of us who study the town will miss her."

In a telephone interview after Susan's death, said Rothman, who died from Lou Gehrig's disease in 2007, "She had become a good friend. She was an all-around good person who wanted to get the story right. I feel a great loss." Deke Castleman said, besides helping Susan with the A&E documentary, he also assisted her with her final project.

"Susan was working on a book," Castleman said. "It

was on outstanding women in the gaming industry and the importance of women in the development of legalized gambling. She was still researching. I don't know that she had started interviewing. She said she had a publisher. She was so well set that way.

"We talked about so many people. She was looking for guidance. The first thing I told her to check was with the state because I know the very first gaming permit that was issued in 1932 was to a woman. I can't remember her name. I had sicked her on to Claudine Williams, Jeannie Hood, (and) Wilbur Clark's widow. We must have gone through a dozen or more (names)."

It was as if Susan had never left Las Vegas. Even though as she entered her teens she had moved to California and then to Idaho, her roots were firmly planted in the desert. Her life's work was invariably about the Las Vegas mob and her father's role in it. To her friends and colleagues, she seemed pleased at the acceptance of her work.

Susan arose the morning of her death just like any other day. She made a cup of coffee and sat down to read the *Los Angeles Times*. She made a few phone calls to friends, wishing them a happy holiday. She looked at her calendar and what the next week's business appointments were. She spent her days, Sareb Kaufman told police, in meetings about her latest projects.

She was still a member of the Writers Guild of America, which has stringent rules for membership. It listed Susan's writing credits as: an A&E "Movie of the Week"; an A&E four-part series on Las Vegas (*Gamble in the Desert* and *House of Cards*); and as a writer in 1978 for "People TV" on eight episodes.

"She was doing signatory work," an employee at the Writers Guild office said. "She was doing work under a recognized production company. She needed to do that in order to be a member of the Guild."

Susan was always working on a project, "the next big deal," her friends said. The last weeks of her life were spent, along with a new agent, pitching projects to book editors and TV and movie directors. Her friends and family said she was at the peak of her career. Mostly positive things were in the works. As Deke Castleman put it, she was "three octaves high" again about the projects she had in the hopper.

Dick Odessky, an author and former Las Vegan, joined in to help Susan with her final project.

"She wanted to be a tough broad," Odessky said before his own death in 2003. "That was her wanna-be. She came across to me as almost the grown up 'poor-little-rich girl.' She had been too shielded from life to appreciate what she was about. That was the impression I got. She was protected in every way. I found when I would talk to her, I would have to lead her along the path because some of it was beyond her knowledge, beyond her recognition."

Soon after Susan's murder became known publicly, one website, www.organizedcrime.about.com, received so many queries about her case that the site started a poll. It asked readers, "Did mob figures order a hit on Susan Berman?"

The Clark County Public Library in Las Vegas had a waiting list of three hundred people for her books, a list that, a library clerk said, had "grown threefold since her death."

Also following Susan Berman's murder, Amazon.com contacted several Las Vegas used book stores, including the most popular shop, downtown's Gambler's Book Club, seeking copies of Susan's books to fill their out-of-print orders. Berman's three novels and two memoirs sold for between $39 and $359 on both eBay and Amazon.

Her friend Danny Goldberg wished Susan had gotten

the recognition she desired. She was in "a pretty good mood when I spoke with her not that long before she died, maybe a month or so," he said. "She was very optimistic about what was happening to her professionally. She was in good spirits."

"She was a great journalist," he continued. "Her magazine work for *New York* and others was great. The book *Easy Street* is an extremely emotionally, powerful memoir. I think it will live on as one of the best to capture what it was like to grow up in a family of gangsters."

"On a personal note," Goldberg noted, "I remember her sense of humor. She was one of the silliest, funniest people to talk to. She had a great, amusing, sardonic spin on things, a humorous perspective that she uniquely had on situations. She had a tremendous vulnerability and pain she walked around with, someone whom I felt never completely got over her childhood and the life she lived in Las Vegas. She wore her pain on her sleeve."

Then, Goldberg added, "With the articles written about her since her death, it does make me wish she would have gotten some of that attention while she was alive, in life as in death."

Susan Berman predicted her own demise. It wasn't surprising, as she had a dark side. Not long before her death, she saw a psychic who told her about her impending demise. "She knew she was going to die violently," said her friend Ruthie Bartnof. She told me, 'I'm going to die by violence, and you, Ruthie, are going to live to be ninety-four.'"

Both predictions were spot on. In 2013, Ruthie Bartnof turned ninety-two years old, still active, still going strong.

# CHAPTER 13

# FINAL MONTHS

BEGINNING IN LATE November 2000, Susan mailed Christmas and Hanukkah cards to friends and extended family members. In each person's note, she was upbeat. In return, she received cards, gifts, and cash.

"We sent her a check for Hanukkah that year," Ruth Bartnof said. "My son, Kevin, sent it that year. She was generous to people, very generous in her gifts. She gave me beautiful gifts. I have a Louis Vuitton handbag she gave me. When she had the money, she shared it with everybody. She had very lavish parties."

Susan enjoyed having friends in high places, especially in the entertainment and publishing business, so she overlooked what she felt were their shortcomings and continued the relationships.

Her former neighbor, attorney Kevin Norte, was in touch with Susan shortly before her death. "She left me a 'Merry Christmas' message that morning, or the morning before she was killed," Kevin said. Before that, they discussed

Susan's possible contract with the Showtime network for her "Sin City" series.

Kevin and his partner, Don, were out of the country when Susan's body was found. "We got into LAX (airport) and saw her photo on the front page. We were shocked."

Susan wrote a holiday letter to her former dean Ed Bayley. He too described it as "an upbeat letter."

"There were no ominous things in it," Bayley noted. "She said she was going to get a ride up to Berkeley and come and see us in Carmel on the way, and that was right before Christmas."

Was it Bobby Durst, who owned two houses in the Bay Area, who planned to drive Susan to northern California? "She didn't say," Bayley said, "and I didn't ask."

It was also during that same span of time before her death, in October 2000, that Susan landed a lunch meeting with Mickey Freiberg, a literary and talent agent. A mutual friend had arranged for Susan to meet with Mickey.

She was able to land the appointment with Freiberg— who represented well known screenwriters and authors in both Hollywood and New York for forty years before his death in 2012, selling projects to studios, production companies, and publishing houses. At that point in time, a couple months before her death, Susan appeared desperate to find an agent, calling on friends for help. Yet she arrived unprepared for her meeting with Mickey Freiberg.

"We had lunch at Cantor's," Mickey said about his meeting with Susan at the popular kosher deli on Fairfax Avenue in Hollywood. "She was not prepared. She didn't bring a proposal with her. She couldn't articulate what her project was. It was more like a free lunch. She seemed hungry. She ordered a big meal and ate it all."

That was Susan, according to her friends. She felt entitled. She also felt that, at that juncture in her career, she shouldn't have to prove herself over and over again by preparing and writing formal proposals. Needless to say, Freiberg, at that time with the Artists Agency, did not sign Susan.

Susan also called on Stephen Silverman for help.

"We spoke a month or so before she died," Silverman said. "She left a message. She needed an agent. She was desperate to find one. Absolute desperation. She said she needed help and that she was on Prozac, but it wasn't working." He said he thought to himself, *This is a woman in trouble.*

Little did Silverman know how much trouble.

Stephen Silverman did not immediately return Susan Berman's phone call. Instead, he said, he waited a week. "I agonized over it," he said from his New York office. That's because, as he put it, "Susan was a lot of work."

"She was a difficult person to be around," he noted. "She'd wear you ragged. She was always needy, needy, needy. Boy, could she drain you of energy. I wasn't up to it."

When he did speak with her in November 2000, a month before her murder, she told him, "Oh, don't worry about it, I found an agent."

"The drama was over," Silverman recalled. "She said everything was going to be fine once the Showtime gig came through. She was always waiting for that big deal."

Susan had been pitching three projects around town. One had a working title of *Rich Girl Broke* and was based on her diaries. She pitched it to ABC as a made-for-TV movie.

She also was profiling female high rollers in Las Vegas and had hoped to turn it into a miniseries called *Sin City*. But Showtime Networks, which had shown an interest, even attaching *The Rat Pack* director Rob Cohen to it, turned it down.

The third project she was developing was "Diaries," a fictionalized account of the mob as told through the eyes of the women of both historical and current Las Vegas organized crime families.

So, after being turned down by Showtime, Susan went back to her original *Easy Street* agent, Owen Laster with William Morris, to see whether he could help place her projects. Laster, executive vice president of the William Morris Agency and also a well-connected agent, first met Susan in the late 1970s while she was finishing *Easy Street*.

"(*Easy Street*) was a terrific book," Laster told *Entertainment Weekly*, "and there was a tremendous amount of film interest in it. The book, I think, didn't do as well as we had hoped, and the picture never got off the ground."

Laster said he had not heard from Susan for a year until she called him six weeks before her death. "She said she'd been doing a lot of things for television and writing screenplays," he told *Entertainment Weekly*, "but she had an idea for two books and asked if I would look at the proposals."

He did.

"One of them was a continuation of her story," he said, "that went beyond the *Easy Street* autobiography. It just looked like a sad book. I didn't think I could encourage it." It was the "Rich Girl Broke" project that focused on her life as a Mafia princess, growing up in the midst of the major players of the twentieth century La Cosa Nostra.

But the second proposal, Laster said, did interest him and showed promise. "It was about women in Las Vegas. She'd interview people and get their experiences," he said.

Laster asked Susan to send him a more detailed proposal. She promised to get back to him.

He never heard from her again. He learned why when her murder became the top news story of the day.

"She was very outgoing, bright. She had a smiling, gay face," he said. "She was pretty. She was very excited about her book."

Susan also contacted Oscar Goodman, a mob-attorney-turned-mayor of Las Vegas. She called his office and mentioned a project, but she did not go into detail.

"I've been waiting for a telephone call from the Los Angeles Police Department," Goodman said from his city hall office. "I wrote a letter to Susan right before she died. It should either have been unopened in her mailbox or in her house. The LAPD never called me. I thought they'd be curious." He said Susan had contacted him and, in his letter to her, he was responding to her request for information about a project she was working on. "I didn't have any information that would be useful for her," he said, and that's what he wrote to her in his letter.

Another man from Las Vegas whom Susan telephoned during the same time period was Dick Odessky. Besides being an author, Odessky was once a public relations director at the Flamingo Hotel.

"Susan had been seeking background information for her latest project, a special report on women in the gaming industry," Odessky said before his death in 2003. "She didn't give any vibes of any problems. She was very happy with her work, and she seemed very pleased with the acceptance of her work."

Danny Goldberg also said as much. He spoke with her often on the phone during the last months of her life. Goldberg last saw Susan on Independence Day 2000, the same year Susan was killed.

"I moved back to New York," he said, "but my family and I would go to Malibu around the July Fourth holiday, and I would see Susan each July Fourth."

Nothing out of the ordinary had changed over the last weeks of Susan's life. She was still cautious. Among her worries was an acute fear of heights. She refused to go above the ground level of a building without being accompanied by someone she trusted. She was afraid of being thrown out a window—or jumping out of it herself. And, her friends said, she was deathly afraid of riding in elevators. While at *New York* magazine, she penned an article titled "Phobic in New York" that featured a high-rise area from the perspective of a person afraid of heights.

Susan was even cautious with the telephone. "She was very circumspect about giving out her phone number and address," Deke Castleman said. "And she never picked up the phone when I called her. I always had to leave a message, then she'd call me back."

That was around the time Susan was seeing a new psychic, something she had been doing for years. She told a couple of friends that the psychic said she was going to die a violent death. Her friends accepted it as just another drama Susan was experiencing. Little did they know at the time that it would turn into an eerie prophesy.

# CHAPTER 14

# INNER CIRCLE

*I run on instinct, immediately like or dislike*
*someone, make snap judgments, and never*
*change my mind. My loyalties to my friends*
*and family run deep and true, but I know I am*
*not easy to know.*

—Susan Berman, from *Lady Las Vegas*

SUSAN BERMAN MADE a point of cultivating
friendships with people who were successful in the
entertainment, music, and literary arenas. It became an art
and a lifetime pursuit. Her networking paid off in many
ways: She was surrounded by people in the business.

Susan also collected Jewish friends. Andrea Dresser,
active in the Jewish community in Las Vegas, explained it
like this: "I know from personal experience, when you meet
someone Jewish, you have this culture in common and there's
this instant camaraderie. It's not about religion. It is about
the culture you have in common. All of a sudden you have
this common bond."

While Susan had a loyal covey of friends, she was sometimes hard on people. She was famous for fallings-out with friends—acrimony that could last for years. "If you pissed her off," Sareb Kaufman told *New York* magazine, "she was like, 'Fine, you're out of the Rolodex. *You* obviously have an issue.'"

And while Susan lived nearby some old friends, because of a falling out with them, she did not stay in contact. One was Liz Rosenberg, Madonna's longtime publicist. "She was very close to (Liz)," said Susan's friend Ruth. "I met Liz. (But) something happened. Susie got angry with her and they didn't see each other anymore." And that, Ruth said, was the standard *modus operandi* for Berman: "She would get mad over things that weren't important. She was impatient with people. She had a short fuse and if someone didn't agree with her, that was it."

Susan's stepson Sareb agreed. "Anyone she had problems with she'd clear out of her life," Sareb Kaufman told police.

In fact, before her death, Susan even had a falling out with Sareb's sister, Mella. They never made up. At Susan's funeral, Mella was inconsolable.

After Susan's death, her friends were reluctant to talk about her to just anybody. They circled the wagons to protect her name. Some had never before met, but they knew of each other because Susan often mentioned each of them. In fact, one friend, Stephen M. Silverman, said Susan talked so much about her friends that he was careful about what he said to her.

"Susan was a loose cannon," Silverman said. "I know for a fact that she once blurted out some gossip that was totally made up. I was there. I was careful what I told her after that. She would talk to ingratiate herself and claim to know information. Her mouth would open and the words would come spilling out. There wasn't time to think. I loved her, but I'm not sure I liked her."

People who knew Susan well, and those who barely knew her, described her behavior with the same word: "Manic." Susan often called on her friends from UC Berkeley. Elizabeth Mehren, who went on to become a national correspondent for the *Los Angeles Times*, said Susan sometimes called her out of the blue. Elizabeth was in the same UC Berkeley graduating class as Susan and stayed in touch with her until the mid-1980s.

"Her murder," Elizabeth said many months later, "has troubled me all year."

After the her death, Susan's college friends spread the word throughout the alumni and faculty community that their former classmate had been brutally murdered. "I called Richard Zoglin when I heard she had died," said Susan's classmate Harvey Myman, who went on to become a TV executive producer. "I called Ed Bayley, who didn't know about it."

"If it was a suicide, it wouldn't have surprised me," Myman continued. "I dealt enough with her to know that she just floated through life."

The last time Harvey saw Susan was around 1993 at a UC Berkeley reunion at his Studio City home, eight miles from Susan's Benedict Canyon house. He termed her behavior as strange.

"We had a journalism school reception at my house and she came to that with her cousin," Harvey said. "I gave her directions on the phone. She asked if there were any bridges. I told her, 'No.' It came up at the party. I'm up in the low hills. There are two ways to reach Sunswept Drive. On one there is a kind of embankment with a guard rail and trestles. I never thought of it as a bridge.

"When Susan came to my house she was kind of pissed at me that I hadn't warned her about the 'bridge.' I smiled and said I was sorry. It struck me as odd, since she once lived in New York on an island. This woman lived in New York but was afraid to drive across bridges? I realized that she was genuinely upset that I had led her up a bridge. It was a mountain road. I would have sent her another route had I known. The charming part of Susan was eccentric. But that was pretty crazy."

New York writer Lisa DePaulo befriended a couple of Susan's girlfriends, including Hillary Johnson, a fellow journalist whom Susan met while they both worked for *Women's Wear Daily*. Hillary was also an undergraduate at UC Berkeley while Susan was getting her master's degree. After Susan's death, Lisa wrote two lengthy articles about Susan and quoted her friends. The articles were published eleven months apart in *New York* magazine and *Talk* magazine.

The *New York Observer* pointed out the sameness of DePaulo's two articles. Even more curious was the fact that Hillary Johnson had pitched a similar story to *Talk* magazine, only to have it accepted, then killed. The editors turned it away, they told her, because the idea was too much like Lisa DePaulo's *New York* magazine article. That didn't stop *Talk* magazine, however, from taking the piece instead from DePaulo and publishing it in its February issue (which, coincidentally was its last issue; the magazine folded), despite the fact that it too was similar to the first article.

The published *Talk* article, no doubt, came as a big surprise to Hillary. "I plan to write something about Susan, either an article or book, in the future," Hillary told me in a telephone interview. Also surprised were editors at *New York* magazine, since they had DePaulo's story first.

*Talk* magazine, instead, was given credit for breaking new information in the case even though it was regurgitated material from *New York* magazine's piece.

Here's what the *Observer's* Gabriel Snyder, in an April 21, 2002, "Off The Record" column, had to say about the second DePaulo article, which was also picked up and published by two New York tabloids:

"Editors at *New York* magazine were surprised to open the *New York Post* and the *Daily News* on Jan. 2 and read about a *Talk* magazine story on Robert Durst, the New York real-estate family scion charged with dismembering a man in Galveston, Texas, and also under investigation for the 1982 disappearance of his wife, Kathie, and the Christmas Eve 2000 murder of Susan Berman, a close friend. "Why the surprise at *New York?*" the *Observer* asked. "Both newspaper stories were very similar, reporting that *Talk* had dug up new information suggesting that Berman had told her friends that Mr. Durst had confessed to her that he killed his wife. The lead to the *News* story was, 'A former close friend of millionaire murder suspect Robert Durst said she was prepared to "blow the top off things" just days before she was found shot to death, according to a newly published report.' The paper then cited a conversation between Berman and actress Kim Lankford. The *Post* cited the conversation as a 'new report.'"

"But the report wasn't new to *New York*," the Observer's story continued. "Lisa DePaulo, who wrote the Durst article for *Talk*, had previously written a story on Berman's death for *New York's* March 12th, 2001 issue—and in her opening anecdote, she described the very same conversation between Berman and Ms. Lankford.

"Was *Talk* touting Ms. DePaulo's warmed-over reporting as a scoop?" 'I was a bit taken aback to see both papers lead with something we reported a year ago,' *New York* editor Caroline Miller told 'Off the Record.' "I don't know if it was pitched as new, or if there was some misunderstanding with the newspapers that this was new when it wasn't."

"Ms. Miller did praise Ms. DePaulo's piece, saying it had broken 'new ground' in the Durst saga. And the exchange between Berman and Ms. Lankford appeared deep in the *Talk* article, which had also dug up new anonymous quotes from Berman's friends saying that Mr. Durst had confessed to the murder of his wife."

The *Observer* contacted DePaulo for her take on the debacle. "Reached for comment, Ms. DePaulo said of the Lankford quotes, "It was newsworthy then and it's newsworthy now," the *Observer* wrote. "The fact that it wasn't picked up in March was a bummer, but P.R. isn't my territory. It would have been remiss to leave it out."

"Of course, relations between *Talk* and *New York* [magazine] remain touchy since Maer Roshan left *New York* last year to be *Talk*'s editorial director, taking several of his writers with him.

"Mr. Roshan said that the article was simply provided to newspapers in full—apparently, both the *Post* and the *News* carefully screened it and came up with the same lead piece of information—and that *Talk* didn't have control over what they picked up." Lisa DePaulo's meticulously researched article is packed with new information and insights that she spent months reporting for us," he said. "Her article for *Talk* is the most comprehensive study of the Durst case to date, and it speaks for itself."

Back when Susan befriended Bobby Durst, most of her friends were into drugs, said one of Kathie's best friends, Gilberte Najamy. It was the '70s when drugs, especially marijuana and cocaine, were prevalent.

But Susan was not into any of it. "She had a million allergies," too many, Stephen Silverman said, to add recreation drugs to the mix. "And," he added, "She never got over her phobias or her paranoia."

With her friends, Susan was blatantly honest, albeit sometimes hard on them at the same time.

Linda Smith commented about the dynamics of Susan's friendships. "She definitely made friends for life," Smith said from her New Orleans home. "She didn't forget you. She had some very, very close-knit friends for life. It wasn't a circle of friends, although her closest friends eventually became friends with each other. Those friends got to be friends through Susan. It's a network."

About Susan's death, her former classmate Lou DeCosta said a few years after Susan's murder, "It's been ten years since I saw her in Los Angeles at a Russian restaurant called Zorgi's. Her death was a huge shock. Nobody knew the Durst connection. Everybody was interested because of the mob connection and also because of the rumors about Susan. The word on her was that she was in debt up to her eyeballs. She was always trying to borrow money from people, was always dreaming bigger than what was likely to happen. It's sad. She really was a talent. She was a great and funny writer when she wanted to be."

Susan, just as her father had, used accountant Samuel Pop. Some of the money Susan received from the mob for her father's interest was invested by Pop, according to her cousin, Dave Berman. "He invested it in some bowling alley franchises in the Midwest, and in Brunswick," a bowling and billiard company.

Former UC Berkeley J-school Dean Ed Bayley said he and his wife were unaware of Susan's financial difficulties, or that she had received money from her father's estate.

"She never asked us for money," Bayley said. "We got a letter from her just before her death. She had just sold one of her TV scripts. She said this time it might get produced. She was very happy about that. She sold lots of scripts and they paid her up front for them but they didn't get produced."

Besides old friends and family, Susan befriended several new people, mostly men, in the last years of her life. A handful worked on the A&E project with her and kept in touch afterward. One new friend was Nevada State Archivist Guy Rocha, in Carson City, who consulted for A&E. In 2002, eighteen months after her death, Rocha was still grieving the loss of his friend. In *Easy Street*, Susan wrote that she chanted the *Kaddish* for her dead family. Rocha was touched by Susan's words. He, in turn, chanted for Susan.

"Susan used the first lines of *Kaddish* with the death of her father, mother, Uncle Chickie, and Aunt Lillian," Rocha said. "I was profoundly moved by this and her intent to carry on in the good name of her father.

"Early last year, and a few months after Susan's death, I visited Temple Emanu El in Reno to pay my respects to the congregation after the synagogue was fire bombed by an Aryan hate group. During the course of the services, the Rabbi asked members of the congregation to chant *Kaddish* for those who had recently died. I turned to my dear friend Dennis Myers from KOLO TV 8 who had accompanied me to the temple and told him I would stand up and chant *Kaddish* for Susie. I cried while I chanted, remembering Chapter One of her book. In my own way, I did for Susie what she had done for her family. It was the least and the best I could do for this woman who had touched my life, if only briefly."

Before Guy worked with Susan on the A&E series, he said he didn't know who she was.

"I had a passing awareness of who her father was," he said, "but not who Susie Berman was. We worked on the project. I got a sense of who her father was. She mentioned it in passing. But I don't think, from that, anybody got a sense of the damaged person I got to know, I mean, emotionally damaged. Intellectually she was a sharp, bright lady trying to make her way."

Like many who knew Susan, Rocha was fascinated by his friend and her mysterious background. "I decided, in order to know Susie better, to read the book *Easy Street*," he said. "I read it and was moved by it. It was cathartic. Not only did I come to understand Vegas through her eyes—her father, his loss, and some insight into her career—but I came to know her other than professionally. When we had a reception in Los Angeles, in Beverly Hills at Planet Hollywood, it was powerful. [Comedian] Rose Marie was there, and we had a chance to talk. Susie came in. She had a young man with her. I believe it was her son. We got a chance to talk. I told her I read *Easy Street*. I said, 'I understand.' She paused and looked at me, looked into my eyes. Then she said, 'You *do* understand.' I told her, 'You've suffered. You still suffer.' She said, 'I do the best I can. Sometimes life is hard.' Viscerally she knew I understood. She was damaged but she was a person who could pass for normal. I didn't always see a happy person."

Rocha felt what he called a "tremendous connection" with Susan. "I told her," he said, "'I came from a damaged background too. We clearly established a common ground. I sensed a need on her part to have credentials. Part of that having credentials is who she associated with. I sensed deficiencies in self esteem. She had all these pots boiling and things were cooking. At the time I was dealing with her, she was on an upswing. It was coming for her late in the game, but it was coming for her."

She talked "a mile a minute," Rocha explained. "She was really driven to talk. She didn't share everything, but when we engaged in a conversation it was hard to get a word in edgewise. She clearly had to *be* somebody. My speculation was that she didn't feel she was somebody. She overcompensated. I got to know her more intimately because of that visceral attraction of victim-to-victim. She was not self aware. What I saw was someone who was so busy in her life that she didn't want to look at herself.

"She was damaged but not dysfunctional. That damage would play in certain ways that at times she would hurt others. She couldn't see it. She's one of so many people who suffer as kids and don't quite know what makes them tick. They have to prove something.

"We grew close in a very short time. It was a mutual respect. I was looking at conversion to Judaism. My life has moved in those circles, so here comes Susie Berman into my life. She intrigued me to no end, this career of hers that took her to San Francisco and New York.

"Then I pick up the paper, the *Reno Gazette Journal*, and I read on page 2 this happening in L.A., her murder. I said, 'Fuck. I can't believe it. She took a shot.' I still mourn her."

On December 18, 2000, a week before Susan Berman was murdered, Sareb Kaufman went out to dinner with her, just before he left for a holiday trip to Europe. "She was happy," he told a reporter. "She wasn't writing about anything controversial." And even then, he told a reporter, "she was interested only in the human aspects of these [Las Vegas] people. She wasn't hitting nerves. There was a theory going around that the mob did it, but I don't think so. I don't think they would have anything to do with this."

While Susan may not have been hitting any nerves with her writing, she clearly struck a chord with someone crazed enough to do her in.

Jim Grady, a friend of Berman's and a former investigative reporter who covered organized crime for Jack Anderson's syndicated column, told the *Hollywood Reporter*, "She worked so hard to have a normal life and ended up having a real bizarre and abnormal death."

On the acknowledgment page in *Easy Street*, Susan thanked Bobby Durst, as she had in all her books, but offered a special thanks to Danny Goldberg, who helped sell the movie rights to her book, giving her the largest advance she would earn in her lifetime. The acknowledgment read, in part: ". . . and especially Danny Goldberg, who, when I considered stopping the search saying, 'It's just too sad. They all died,' he told me, 'But you didn't. That's why you must go on.'"

Then, Susan wrote, as was typical for her at the beginning of her books, *L'chayim*, which, when translated from the Hebrew, means "To life."

• • •

As Robert Durst's trial in the murder of Morris Jack Black was set to begin in Galveston, Texas in February 2003, the judge ruled that no mention of Susan Berman's murder and no mention of Durst's missing wife Kathleen could be made during the trial, so as not to prejudice jurors. The Los Angeles Police Department and New York investigators would have to take their own turns at further investigating

Bobby Durst in connection with those cases and any link to the Black murder.

The outcome of the Morris Black murder case was a shock for LAPD investigators, who earlier said they expected Durst to be convicted. It would have meant that their main person of interest in the Susan Berman murder would have been put away for good, regardless of which murder it was for; the point was, Durst would be off the streets. The burn for LAPD investigators came when Durst was acquitted and walked out of the Galveston courthouse a free man.

An unsolved murder, author and Miami crime reporter Edna Buchanan once wrote, is an unsolved story. Until the Susan Berman case is formally solved and the perpetrator is behind bars, her story is incomplete. Until then, a killer is out there, getting away with murder.

# AFTERMATH

DESPITE THE STRONG suspicions surrounding Robert Durst in the disappearance of his first wife, Kathleen Durst, and the murder of his confidante, Susan Berman, defense lawyer Dick DeGeurin continues to profess that prosecutors "don't have a case" against Durst.

After the murder trial against Durst for the death of Morris Black, jurors said Black's missing head—it was never recovered—complicated the case. They credited defense lawyers with a plausible explanation. "The defense told us a story and stuck to it," juror Chris Lovell told reporters. All the same, the jurors say Durst gives them the creeps. Juror Robbie Clavac said if she saw Durst walking down a street, "I would turn and walk the other way."

Following his acquittal, Bobby Durst's younger brother Thomas told reporters, according to *Newsweek*, "He'll kill again. Bob is a madman."

Upon his release from custody, Bobby Durst returned to New York. In October 2011, he paid $1.75 million for a three-bedroom, five-bath 19th—century corner townhouse on Lenox Avenue in East Harlem, New York. The townhouse, according to the brokerage firm's listing, has been divided into three apartments and a ground-floor beauty salon and was advertised as an investment property.

Durst, during a visit to the property, talked about turning one of the apartments into a duplex for himself, the *Wall Street Journal* reported. He also, the paper said, was considering the property for its investment value.

Neighbors protested the sale, calling Durst a threat to the area. Funeral home owner Isaiah Owens, whose business is in the building, told the *New York Post*, "If I disappear, go and check him out first." Neighbor Patricia Lizet, a nursing assistant, told the *Post*: "He's a killer. He should be on some island by himself. I don't want him living next to me. You can't trust him."

In 2006, the Durst Organization, in a formal agreement, permanently severed its ties with Durst in exchange for a $65 million payout. Robert Durst lives a free man.

Durst was charged, however, with a lesser offense, for trespassing after he showed up near his brother's midtown Manhattan home. For that accusation, Durst, seventy, was arrested In August 2013 and charged with a misdemeanor. Celebrity bail bondsman Ira Judelson posted a $5,000 bond and Durst was released.

As of summer 2013, Robert Durst had not been charged in the disappearance of his wife Kathleen nor in the murder of his friend Susan Berman.

The missing person case for Kathleen Durst, while not active, remains open. But the Susan Berman case was an active investigation, according to a source within the LAPD, in summer 2013. The feds were looking into Robert Durst and his ties to the Susan Berman case as well as the case of a missing woman in northern California. Time will tell if anything comes out of the investigation.

# SUSAN BERMAN'S CREDITS

Books:
*Spiderweb*, paperback novel, 1997.

*Fly Away Home*, paperback novel, 1996.

*Lady Las Vegas: The Inside Story Behind Americas Neon Oasis*, hardcover memoir, 1996.

*Easy Street: The True Story of a Mob Family*, hardcover memoir, 1981 (reprinted in paperback, 1983).

*Driver, Give a Soldier a Lift*, paperback novel, 1976.

*The Underground Guide To The College Of Your Choice*, reference, 1971.

Documentary:
*The Real Las Vegas*, A&E four-part series, co-writer, co-producer, 1996

TV
*People TV*, Westinghouse Evening Show, eight episodes, 1978

# BIBLIOGRAPHY

Birkbeck, Matt. *A Deadly Secret*. New York, New York: Penguin Putnam, 2002.

Berman, Susan. *Driver, Give a Soldier a Lift*. New York, New York: Putnam, 1976.

Berman, Susan. *Easy Street: The True Story of a Mob Family*. New York, New York: The Dial Press, 1981.

Berman, Susan. *Fly Away Home*. New York, New York: Avon Books, 1996.

Berman, Susan. *Lady Las Vegas: The Inside Story Behind Americas Neon Oasis*. New York, New York: TV Books, 1996.

Berman, Susan. *Spiderweb*. New York, New York: Avon Books, 1997.

Cantor, Norman F. *The Jewish Experience*. New York, New York: Book Sales, 1999.

Collins, Marion. *Without a Trace*. New York, New York: St. Martin's True Crime, 2002.

Demaris, Ovid, and Reid, Ed. *The Green Felt Jungle*. Cutchogue, New York: Buccaneer Books, 1963.

Farrell, Ronald A. *The Black Book and the Mob: The Untold Story of Control of Nevada's Casinos*. Madison, Wisconsin: University of Wisconsin Press, 1995.

Lacey, Robert. *Little Man: Meyer Lansky and the Gangster Life.* Boston, Massachusetts: Little, Brown and Co., 1991.

MacNee, Marie J. *The Crime Encyclopedia: The World's Most Notorious Outlaws, Mobsters and Crooks.* New York, New York: The Gale Group, 1999.

Rockaway, Robert. Paperback ed., *But He Was Good to His Mother: The Lives and Crimes of Jewish Gangsters.* Jerusalem, Israel and New York, New York: Gefen, 2000.

Sachar, Howard M. Paperback ed., *A History of the Jews in America.* Vintage, 1993 (reprint).

Sifakis, Carl. *The Mafia Encyclopedia, Second Edition.* Detroit, Michigan: Checkmark Books, 1999.

Turner, Wallace. *Gambler's Money.* Boston, Massachusetts: Houghton Mifflin, 1965.

# ABOUT THE AUTHOR

Cathy Scott, a Los Angeles Times bestselling author, is a veteran crime writer, award-winning investigative journalist, and blogger for *Psychology Today*, who taught journalism at the University of Nevada, Las Vegas for five years. She is the author of several true crime works, including *The Millionaire's Wife, The Killing of Tupac Shakur, Death in the Desert,* and *The Rough Guide to True Crime.* She also wrote *Pawprints of Katrina* after spending four months in the gulf embedded as a reporter with an animal welfare organization. She is based in Las Vegas, Nevada, and San Diego, California, where she lives with her three dogs."